THE POWER AND INFLUENCE OF ILLUSTRATI(

BLOOMSBURY VISUAL ARTS
Bloomsbury Publishing Plc
50 Bedford Square, London, WC1B 3DP, UK
1385 Broadway, New York, NY 10018, USA

BLOOMSBURY, BLOOMSBURY VISUAL ARTS and the Diana logo
are trademarks of Bloomsbury Publishing Plc

First published in Great Britain 2019

Cover design: Louise Dugdale
Cover image © Anna and Elena Balbusso

A catalogue record for this book is available from the British Library.

Library of Congress Cataloging-in-Publication Data
Names: Male, Alan, author.
Title: The power and influence of illustration : achieving impact and lasting significance through visual
communication / Alan Male.
Description: New York : Bloomsbury Visual Arts, Bloomsbury Publishing Plc, 2019. | Includes
bibliographical references and index.
Identifiers: LCCN 2018038269| ISBN 9781350022423 (pbk. : alk. paper) | ISBN 9781350022973 (epdf)
Subjects: LCSH: Commercial art. | Graphic arts. | Visual communication.
Classification: LCC NC997 .M247 2019 | DDC 741.6—dc23 LC record available at https://lccn.loc.
gov/2018038269

ISBN: PB: 978-1-3500-2242-3
        ePDF: 978-1-3500-2297-3
        eBook: 978-1-3500-2411-3

Typeset by Lachina Creative, Inc.
Printed and bound in India

To find out more about our authors and books visit
www.bloomsbury.com and sign up for our newsletters.

THE POWER AND INFLUENCE OF ILLUSTRATION

Achieving impact and lasting significance through visual communication

Alan Male

BLOOMSBURY VISUAL ARTS
LONDON • NEW YORK • OXFORD • NEW DELHI • SYDNEY

Contents

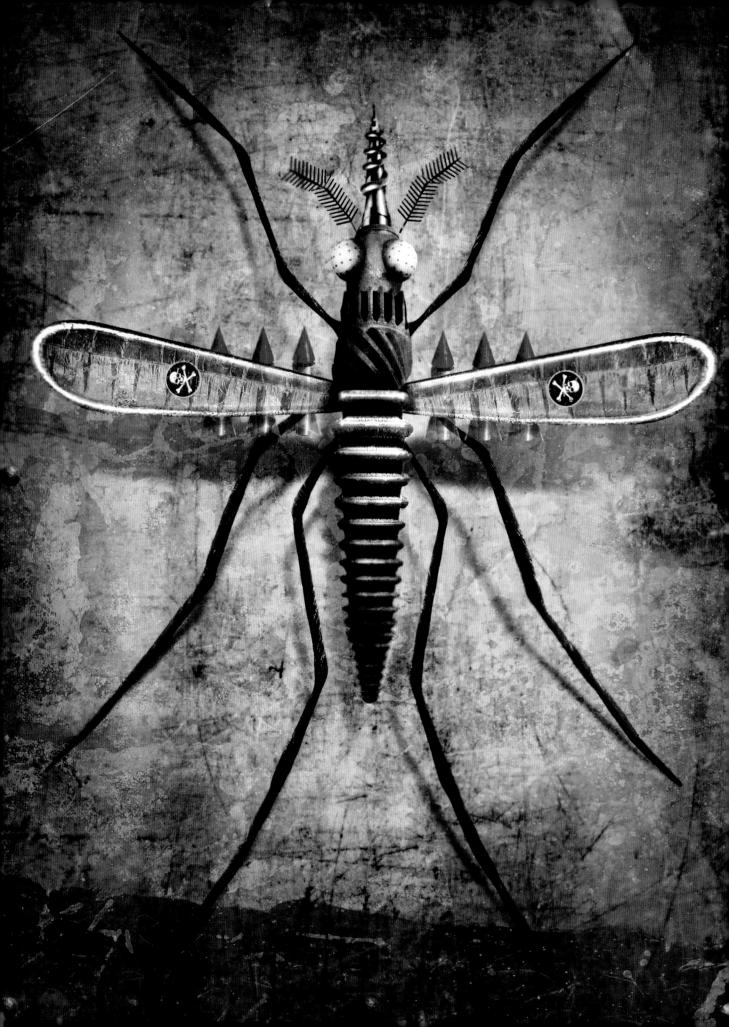

Preface

Illustration is the oldest form of contextualized visual communication; its origins can be traced back forty thousand years to the time when the earth was inhabited by peoples of the Palaeolithic era. Since then, its diversity as a visual language and its accessibility via global publishing and broadcast has enabled it to wield considerable influence on society.

By using both celebrated and dissolute case studies from the past and present, this book reveals the true essence of messages imbued in the art of illustration: ethics employed or deliberately disregarded, as well as its impact and reach regarding target audiences and its effect and sway on global communities. The book discusses how the contents of illustrative imagery can lampoon, shock, insult, threaten, subvert, ridicule, express discontentment and proclaim political or religious allegiance; stir up disagreeable reactions; worship and celebrate; be satirical and entertaining; be unashamedly persuasive and 'hard selling'; be serious and present original knowledge; and be educative or documentary material with great authority and integrity.

From a pedagogic standpoint, the book considers best approaches to application when confronted with contentious or challenging problems of visual communication. It encourages fresh and original thinking regarding a given brief or assignment, its context and the message to be conveyed. It also encourages the creation of polar tensions or friction facilitating deep learning and analysis.

Another principal remit presents the notion that illustration can and does incite considerable debate, that it is a catalyst for significant change regarding societal attitudes and that it introduces new and challenging trends and fashions in both a cultural and commercial sense. Another primary theme examines globalization and the ethical and moral dilemmas that are sometimes faced by illustrators producing imagery comprising semiotic contortion, bombast and extreme visual rhetoric. In this instance, some illustrators are unafraid to present what might be considered unpalatable truths regarding the state of the world, such as political oppression, economic upheaval and environmental disasters, not to mention basic human deprivation.

Other contextual themes might deal with controversial new knowledge regarding scientific discovery or theory, a challenge to politically correct precepts regarding the advertising or promotion of certain products or ideas, and fictional story narratives that some people might baulk at. However, there are more positive aspects; the discipline of illustration is often commended because of the way it enriches and expands the lives, imaginations and sensibilities of individuals. It is known to create and interpret cultural capital in all of its forms, notably by its contribution to education and learning, research and original knowledge. It is also known for its massive contribution to imaginative and fictionalized entertainment.

Illustrators of today and the future need to be professionally and creatively adept at delivering the most effective and felicitous of messages. They must adopt and develop the status of provocateur, author and polymath and be capable of researching and engaging with a great number of subjects and present appropriate, yet challenging viewpoints. The visual linguistics, the conceptual and pictorial power of illustration cannot be underestimated, notably by the nature and 'tone' of messages being communicated. Some of these messages are lauded and considered essential; some are damned and considered unprincipled and degenerate. This book attends to criteria that examine the broadest of contextual application for illustration and its impact and significance – criteria that assess the true *power and influence of illustration*.

Introduction

Context and Meaning

> ILLUSTRATION: APPLIED IMAGERY, A WORKING ART THAT VISUALLY COMMUNICATES CONTEXT TO AUDIENCE.

ALAN MALE, *ILLUSTRATION: A THEORETICAL AND CONTEXTUAL PERSPECTIVE*, BLOOMSBURY 2017

> ILLUSTRATION IS SEEN EVERYWHERE, ITS WORKING POSSIBILITIES ARE ENDLESS. IT INFLUENCES THE WAY WE ARE INFORMED AND SCHOOLED, WHAT WE BUY AND HOW WE ARE PERSUADED TO DO THINGS. IT GIVES US OPINION AND INTERPRETATION. IT PROVIDES US WITH ENTERTAINMENT AND TELLS US TALES. IT IS SEEN ON ADVERTISING BILLBOARDS, POSTERS, IN NEWSPAPERS, MAGAZINES, IN BOOKS OF ALL DESCRIPTION, ON PACKAGING, EVEN ON POSTAGE STAMPS. IT CAN BE ANIMATED, USED IN MOTION PICTURES AND TELEVISION, AS WELL AS ONLINE, IN E-BOOKS AND AS STATE OF THE ART INTERACTIVE IMAGERY.

ALAN MALE, *ILLUSTRATION: MEETING THE BRIEF*, BLOOMSBURY 2014

The term *illustration* is an enigma to many, in spite of its history and status as an important and influential discipline of visual communication. It is often confused with *fine art*, most likely because many illustrators use the same methods for producing imagery as fine artists; both will utilize autographic, traditional techniques such as drawing, painting, etching, photography, film and sculpting and will also employ contemporary, state-of-the-art digital media. Furthermore, the visual languages used by illustrators will often mirror genre and subject matter that have been the mainstay of fine art practice for many years – figurative and pictorial realism, abstraction and surrealism, to name but a few. But, that's where the similarity ends.

So, what is the difference between illustration and fine art? Fine art tends to be cultivated for its own sake and appeals to the minds and emotions that experience it. Its conception and production are usually driven by a subjective rationale, expressing opinions, influences or experiences of the artist, but often without recourse for any commercial drivers such as publication. Also, the work is produced to be accessed in its original crafted form, normally in galleries, but could be seen in other prescribed venues, for example, as site-specific public art. Illustration, on the other hand, is contextualized visual communication commissioned for target audiences, often reproduced in large quantities and distributed via the ever-expanding creative, media and communication industries.

What is meant by *contextualized visual communication*? *Context* means 'frame of reference' or 'the situation within which something exists or happens'. The broad parameters of illustration define its 'work', the nature and thrust of its messages, and the reach and impact on its given audience. Without context, an image cannot be classed as illustration. Context defines the reason for the image in the first place and underpins the essence of the whole brief. To successfully meet the requirements of any brief, the completed imagery should impart the required message in accordance with the context.

There are five such obligations:

Knowledge: Reference, Information, Education, Documentation, Instruction, Research, New and Original Knowledge

Persuasion: Advertising, Promotion, Publicity, Inducement and Propaganda

Identity: Branding, Logos and Corporate Identity, Packaging, Point of Sale

Fiction: Classic Literature, Contemporary Literature, Poetry, Young Audience Picture and Chapter Material, Pictorial Sequential Fiction, Scriptwriting, General Entertainment and Gaming

Commentary: Journalism, Editorial Review, Comment and Critique, Reportage

Dr Susan Hagan, teaching professor of English from Carnegie Melon University, is slightly more succinct in defining the contexts of illustration practice, yet no less profound in determining intellectual and creative accountability. Hagan's thesis proclaims *Illustrators: Collaborative Problem Solvers in Three Environments* (A Companion to Illustration, Wiley Blackwell, 2019) and expounds the following contextualized domains or *environments* based upon an analysis of the synergy and symbiosis between the illustrator and the principal essence of texts and their originators:

Argument: Journalistic Comment, Critique and Review

Description: Knowledge, Pedagogy and Information

Narrative: Storytelling, Chronicle and Report

There is an omission regarding persuasion and identity. This is undoubtedly because of the prescriptive way in which illustrators are briefed and heavily directed, particularly in advertising. However, the three environments offer significant scope for the illustrator to work with authority and intellectual curiosity, in turn facilitating the creation and determination of both content and message.

How might the meaning of illustration practice be explained? A generalized dictionary definition of *illustration* states, *'the act or process of illuminating'* and *'the act of clarifying or explaining; elucidation'*, and from the Middle English, *'the act of making vivid: illumination: spiritual or intellectual enlightenment'*. A more contemporary and specific dictionary definition affirms *'a picture illustrating a book or newspaper'*

and, a more appropriate description, *'elucidation or embellishment of a literary or scientific article or book by pictorial representations'*. Although conventional and platitudinous regarding assumptions for visual language and contextual value, there is some proffering to illustration's contemporary position.

It is from current and more informed sources that we must acquire the most felicitous of definitions. Illustration has been described as *art at the service of the people*, presumably because of the growth and popularity of certain contexts and themes. One such theme is that of sequential fiction and entertainment, the most favoured aspect being comics, graphic novels and animated films. This in turn gives illustration a cultural association with audiences of all descriptions and demographics. However, it must be noted that the term *illustrator* is still not widely used or understood; many media presenters and commentators, particularly on television and in the press, will refer to 'artists' illustrating and designing such entities as book covers, posters, children's books and computer games. Other terms frequently used and understood are *cartoonist* and perhaps the most ubiquitous and more perceptively descriptive *commercial artist*.

When 'artists' are brought into the paradigm of *commercial art*, they are the ones usually praised for contributing aesthetic appreciation, emotional expression and sensuous pleasure, qualities traditionally associated with fine art. Some consider fine art to be more illustrious than illustration. This may be attributed to the ubiquity and celebrity that is afforded fine art practitioners – and notoriety, in some instances. Generally thought of as a sister discipline to fine art, illustration has frequently endured the sobriquet *commercial art*. Testament to this can be assimilated through the provocatively regarded thesis 'The Precious High Ground Versus Unpretentious Reality: The Conflict Between the Fine and Applied Arts'. Written and presented by the author at the Fifth International Paragoné Studies Conference, September 2016, at Manchester Art Gallery, the foundation for this critique was the apparent misguided prejudice proclaimed by certain fine art acolytes that they hold the *intellectual, aesthetic and righteous* higher ground over those artists who have 'sold their souls to commerce'. It was once said anonymously, 'Fine Art is akin to a glorious symphony whilst illustration is no more than a b-movie film score'. The antithetical view suggests that illustration commands equal respect and recognition by its distinguished history of global, societal influence and efficacy.

How Illustration 'Changed the World'

The best illustration doesn't just visualize history; it shapes it. It is the potency of illustration and the strength and originality of its messages that define its true reason for being. Illustration has over the years had a significant and influential effect on society and incited a diversity of audience reactions and emotion. This can be exemplified by the impact and significance it has had by helping to devise new forms of creative expression through the vast gamut of the entertainment and literary world, such as children's books, comics, films and performance; by contributing to economic and cultural prosperity through advertising, the media, design, corporate and service industries; and by helping to preserve, conserve and present cultural heritage through education, knowledge exchange, museums and documentary broadcast.

People connect with illustration every day of their lives, and in most instances are not aware that it is illustration at all – the organizational and company corporate logos that instil recognition in our subconscious; imagery that adorns the packaging of products and services that entice and seduce; the information and identification systems that provide instruction and direction; the news media illustrations that comment, confound, infuriate and captivate. It is, however, to the past that we must look to see just how potent and influential illustration has been, often for commendable reasons but unfortunately, not always for the good.

Religion has consistently used icons and other symbolic representations, prompting its adherents to assiduously practice their faith and belief. The ancient memorials and relics that we can see today – stained-glass windows, gargoyles and icons seen in Christian churches all around the world – were commissioned to instil fear and suppression, reminding 'worshippers' that their best

afterlife option was a 'heavenly one'. However, some religious imagery was made and presented in a different way. Dating back to the early part of the first millennia through to medieval times, monks, scholars and scribes produced highly detailed and intricate illuminations and scrolls by using exquisite and superlative draughtsmanship. These 'one-off' productions often manifested as large books and presented the scriptures to the masses in a manner that ensured their sycophancy to the Almighty was upheld. Other religions, such as Islam and Judaism, were no less zealous; they used illustrative imagery to facilitate belief and worship, and ancient civilizations such as the Aztecs produced illustrations that not only identified the gods but also instructed on social class and behaviours.

Illustration has a significant role in bridging the gap between the sciences and humanities; practically every concept – every societal, scientific and cultural theory, process and morphology – has been subjected to the illustrator's research, scrutiny, analysis, description and visualization. From the polymath-driven explications and research of the Renaissance and the Age of Enlightenment to the mass of *new knowledge* being broadcast and published all over the world today, illustration provides a significant platform for audiences to be educated and informed. The power and effect of illustration on the world has been immense in terms of human understanding for disciplines and practices such as medicine and surgery, scientific research, technology, anthropology and a myriad of other groundbreaking achievements and advancements for the betterment of humankind.

The milieu having the most obvious and persuasive effect on society is that of *propaganda and politics*. Today, and in the past, the 'political cartoon' has stirred up mass hatred, incited bloody revolutions, kept discriminated sections of society oppressed and suppressed, swayed public opinion and helped to bring down governments and institutions. This context of illustration fuels intense irreverence and disrespect for almost everything held sacred or dear, from religion to culture. In the main, it is achieved by producing imagery with the sole intention of provoking either extremely disagreeable or intensely euphoric reactions in the audience. The rationale underpinning such a strategy is to present unpalatable truths or suggestions, often by introducing contentious propositions. It is sometimes 'acceptable' to observe the sanctity of certain themes and subjects bastardized, all in the course of providing deliberate shock, with most religions and faiths being lampooned and ridiculed. Consequences can be catastrophic. There are some conspicuous and disquieting examples that have shocked the world in recent years; the atrocity of the Paris attack on *Charlie Hebdo* comes immediately to mind. The revolutions and the political and militaristic upheavals of the twentieth century delivered outcomes greatly facilitated by propaganda that was dominated by illustration – posters and newspaper articles proclaiming either extreme political ideologies or, even more abhorrently, the persecution and destruction of certain peoples and races. Thankfully, illustration does redress the balance; for example, the nineteenth-century American illustrator Thomas Nast did much to sway opinion against racism and helped bring about the abolition of slavery.

Illustration has played a huge part in the history of consumerist advertising. In the days when photography was principally a black and white medium, advertisers turned to illustrators for their products and services to be visually seductive and 'irresistible'. Fashion, travel, practically every gadget available, the frivolous and the expendable, food, drink and essentials for everyday life were pictorially depicted in a sumptuous and 'must-have' manner, often in full colour and embedded in entertaining and memorable campaigns. This was an advanced form of promotion and had not been seen before. It defined a new form of capitalist culture, and illustration was at its heart, bringing vivid and ubiquitously arresting imagery to bear on society. It evoked massive changes in consumerist attitudes, first in the United States and then more latterly throughout the world.

Now and the Future

From ancient times right up until the end of the nineteenth century, the masses could not read but fully understood drawings and pictures. People were swayed and influenced by the symbolism and meaning imbued in engravings, drawings and woodcuts, and the significance of visual communication throughout the ages cannot be underestimated. But what of today?

And, how significant and influential will illustration become? It is widely regarded that there is an insatiable need in ever more responsive audiences for stimulating imagery that feeds the imagination, satisfies the thirst for new knowledge and promotes every sort of product available in the global marketplace. But there will be prolific changes to attitudes regarding many aspects of social cohesion and responsibility, and the practice of illustration will undoubtedly be affected by these altered contexts. Illustrators, like many others who commentate, record, communicate and broadcast, will have to adopt sharper moral values than were considered necessary before. Some imagery produced will have a clearly defined ethical dimension. It is also likely that visual communication will play an increased role in education, health, welfare and the environment.

The nature of illustration as a discipline will change, and not just because of precepts determined by what is fast becoming a more integrated global society, nor by the advancements in technology and digital media. The ever-expanding media and communications industry expects visual communication practice to be more generalized and not compartmentalized by discrete practices such as photography, animation, film and writing, with illustration being no exception. The new illustrator is regarded simply as a *creative* by some and as a *polymath* by others – a professional communicator able to generate ideas, solve problems and answer the most challenging of briefs. The best will also to be able to design, make and produce the most felicitous of imagery in whatever medium is suitable regarding the given assignment in hand.

To conclude, from the dawn of history, illustration has been party to significant changes in the world order: religion, culture, the economy and governance. There can be no doubt that as the succeeding years unfold, the mass of communication targeting global societies from journalism, information, promotion and entertainment will continue to be imbued and in many instances dominated by the art of illustration.

1

1

Abstract art, perhaps? It could be argued that this resembles a large, autographically produced painting, perhaps rendered in oils, acrylics or screen-print, and then displayed publically in a gallery. However, this is a digitally produced illustration by the author, commissioned to promote James Horner's musical composition *Hymn to the Sea*. ©Alan Male

2

Religious symbolism: An iconic and allegorical representation of *Death* or the 'Destroying Angel' as visually imagined from Christian Old Testament narrative descriptions. Photographed by the author inside St Peter's Basilica, Rome, this particular personification – skeletal, winged and robed, with accompanying scythe – is also recognizable as a common element in folklore, where it is popularly named the 'Grim Reaper'. There can be no doubt that this sculptural icon was originally conceived to alarm and subjugate, reminding religious adherents of their mortality and duty to the Almighty: *'The Angel of Death' administers punishments that God has ordained for the commission of sin; burning, throttling and beheading!*

The whole edifice is full of semiotic referencing, provided by both figurative representation and the symbolic icons of identity and suggestion. As well as the ubiquitous presence of the grimacing and menacing skull, there is also the attendant symbol, aloft and dominant behind, almost providing a 'Nazi-style' backdrop for a 'Hitler-like' address to be delivered.

Many would question this three-dimensional 'artwork' and 'logotype' as being illustration as it does not conform to the traditional concept of drawing, engraving or 'painting'. However, it is a commissioned and fully contextualized example of medieval visual communication, and the methodologies and procedures for its conception, design and production are principally the same as for any contemporary form of illustration practice. ©Alan Male

2

3

3

This is a seemingly whimsical illustration, in a style evocative of Victorian bawdy, music-hall comedy. However, closer examination will reveal a more challenging aspect to the theme. The overall image is an album cover, conceived and illustrated by **Mr Alan Clarke**. Its message could be construed as a deliberate slight at certain taboos within contemporary society, no matter how contextually effective it might be. ©Mr Alan Clarke

4

4

This powerful image represents the best in contemporary journalistic, editorial illustration. Created and produced by **Simon Pemberton**, it was *highlighted* at the World Illustration Awards, 2016. An uncompromising approach to subject portrayal and visual language, its message is forcefully unequivocal. The image accompanied an article published 15 December 2015 for the *International New York Times* entitled 'Uprooted, stateless and on the run'. Written by Okey Ndibe (Fellow at the University of Nevada) and borne from personal experience, it is an authoritative, insightful and damning commentary regarding the worldwide plight of refugees. ©Simon Pemberton

1
LESSONS FROM HISTORY

From the Birth of Culture to the Age of Enlightenment

In anthropological terms, this period spans millennia, from when early humans emerged at the beginning of the Palaeolithic Period right up until the mid-fifteenth century AD. With regards to *illustration* – or more broadly, visual communication – how prevalent was it across this epoch and what significance did it have? What was being communicated, why was it being communicated and to whom? And did common ground prevail across this vast period of time regarding a method for transmitting messages?

THE DAWN OF ILLUSTRATION

All forms of 'artistic' creation from the primitive symbolism and hieroglyphics of ancient times, the sculptures and murals of the classical period right up to sophisticated medieval manuscripts of church and state could only be accessed and 'read' in their original handcrafted form. The birth of media such as printing for mass distribution and broadcast had not been invented: *audiences* would be drawn to view and digest messages imbued in the 'art' at site-specific locations. Initially these locations would be caves and natural stone monuments and more latterly galleries, public institutions and religious buildings. It is also worth considering that the vast majority could not read or decipher any textual inscriptions, but because of the unambiguity of visual language and subject matter, practically all could understand the directives, information and propaganda emanating from the imagery on display.

The earliest form of illustration so far known to humankind appeared as simple geometric shapes; the oldest is a red dot dating 40,000 years ago and found in the cave of El Castillo, Spain. As time progressed, the images produced by these Palaeolithic people became more complex and pictorially representational in nature, the most common subjects being animals. Contemporary zoologists are astounded by the accuracy of these ancient illustrators, enabling them to identify very specific creatures. Human representation was rare amongst these paintings, and when human figures did appear they were abstracted and symbolic in style rather than pictorial and realistic. However, as time progressed, imagery became more complex and metaphorical in nature, depicting defined and systematic pattern work, scenes of specific human interactions and cultural practices, scenes of childbirth and astronomical interpretations. The visual language became more symbolic and developed a semiotic code with certain images prevailing across a wide geographic range, establishing what may have been the earliest form of writing: hieroglyphics.

But, what was the rationale behind the production of all this imagery? It is estimated many 'artists' created it, perhaps over a period of tens of thousands of years. The context for these 'artworks' seemingly never changed; according to the latest research, Palaeolithic people did not live in caves, and therefore it is likely that they were specific places to go and acquire information or receive religious or cultural instruction. The caves, other natural features and more latterly, built constructions adorned with images, were akin to libraries or cultural centres. However, one thing is certain: the production of all of this imagery was driven by the need to *communicate*, and when people are being communicated to, they are susceptible to influence, reaction and endeavour. The birth of *contextualized illustration* had begun.

THE CLASSICAL PERIOD

It is clear that the advent of illustration was a contributing factor in the story of the development of human consciousness. From prehistory to the initial centuries of the first millennium, the development of society and its increasingly sophisticated command of language and communication was infused with drawings, pictures, symbols and diagrams –many produced with a clear objective to fulfil a contextualized function. But what were the key themes being communicated, and what was the impact and significance of these messages?

One such theme, particularly as societies became more organized and 'politicized', was that of command and instruction: imagery served as ways in which those who ruled or led, such as chieftains, pharaohs, kings and more latterly the emperors of Rome, could broadcast to their fellow citizens or subjects a tangible legitimacy for them to reign and govern. During the Classical period and before, the great empires of Ancient Egypt, Assyria, Babylon, Greece and Rome expanded and dominated vast areas throughout Europe, the Mediterranean and the Middle East. In order to sustain credibility, authority and in some instances, approval from the people, much propaganda and jingoistic pride was needed to impress and suppress, and illustration played no small part in ensuring these precepts were adhered to. Great commemorative edifices were designed and constructed, laden and imbued with sculptural reliefs, murals and cartoons, reminding all who was in charge and how grateful they might be to belong to such a society. A typical example is the oldest surviving papyrus document, dating from 1980 BC. The Ramesseum Papyrus, 7 feet long (a little over 2 metres) and 10 inches deep (26 centimetres), dramatically conveys a celebratory narrative sequence regarding the ascension and absolute authority of an early Egyptian pharaoh.

The acquisition of knowledge was seen as an important aspect of societal life in prehistoric, post-prehistoric and Classical periods. Mathematics, astronomy and cultural mores were all subjected to illustrative treatment. The Greek Socratic philosopher and polymath Euclid of Megara published *Elements* in approximately 100 BC, a work that conveys geometric and algebraic formulations and contains the oldest and most complete diagram. However, from Classical times through to the Medieval period, illustration was dominated throughout the known world by religious patronage, which sometimes had a significant effect on the thrust and nature of knowledge transmitted. Monitored by religious order, scholars and authors were subjected to the diktats of the church as new knowledge and invention could be seen as 'revolutionary' and a threat to the clergy's supremacy and authority.

THE RENAISSANCE
However, new approaches to philosophy, research and discovery, greatly facilitated by the polymaths of the time such as Leonardo da Vinci and Copernicus, meant that commissioned illustration was not just confined to religious order:

> The period from about 1400 AD onwards bore witness to a considerable revolution in cultural and social sensibilities, giving rise to original and forward thinking developments in science,

technology, architecture, literature, music, visual art and philosophy. A rebirth of traditions gone before, many of these learned disciplines spread throughout Europe with great influence, and illustration provided a visual substructure and underpinning for much new learning and knowledge acquisition. (Alan Male, *Illustration: Meeting the Brief, Bloomsbury 2014*)

This era also witnessed the advent of many well-known universities, for example Edinburgh, Oxford, Salamanca, Bologna, Paris, Perugia and Cambridge, which in part brought about the need for published learning resources and a trade in books that in Europe began outside of monasteries. Typically these were encyclopaedias, atlases and codexes, all generously imbued with illustration. The cultural and intellectual underpinning for all of this was the Renaissance and its vast yield of original scholarship, information and accomplishment. The great polymaths of the time were regarded as the leading visual arts figures of the day and as such were able to externalize and describe their propositions, inventions and research by superb drawings and paintings. This work still holds considerable resonance and influence, its power, prestige and gravitas truly groundbreaking in human anatomy, biology, the natural world, architecture, humanities, technology and astronomy – and all of this vast wealth of new knowledge and discovery facilitated by illustration.

THE START OF THE MODERN PERIOD
In 1439, a German named Johannes Gutenberg (1398–1468) brought about what is widely regarded as one of the most significant events of the second millennium: the Printing Revolution. He invented a process known as *printing with mechanical movable type*, a circumstance that historically, ushered in the start of the Modern Period. This coincided with other 'seismic' events such as the Protestant Reformation, the Age of Enlightenment and the Scientific Revolution. In England, by the late fifteenth century, the old warlord kings were swept away and replaced by the Tudors, who in turn brought about a new politics. The feudal system faded, introducing a more fluid and upwardly mobile social structure. All of this was greatly facilitated by the printing revolution: the mass

production and continent-wide distribution of books, pamphlets and posters which then laid the foundation for what was to become the modern knowledge-based economy. As in earlier times, the greater population could not read, but they were fully able to understand the messages given by woodcuts and other block-printed images. Caricatures and other wildly distorted visual scenarios spread political and religious discontentment, with hated leaders and ecclesiastical masters presented as satanic and untrustworthy. The known world – particularly Europe – was starting to change forever: the discipline of illustration was truly coming of age!

Literature was becoming well served by illustration, with books on fiction and drama, notably that of Shakespeare and works from Classical times. Also the thirst for new knowledge and enlightenment abounded, ably supported by highly detailed and accurate engravings across all areas of erudite and learned discovery, theory and research: philosophy, humanities, geography, ethnology, botany, zoology and architecture, to name but a few. Meanwhile, visual arts continued unabated in the service of propaganda. Often at the behest of state or aristocratic patronage, work would be commissioned with messages distinctly jingoistic in tone, depicting glorious military victories with defeated and subjugated foes, as well as exploits of bravery, exploration and discovery. However, illustration also provided commentators and those in political or ideological opposition an obverse outlet. Caricaturists and satirists of the day would scurrilously ridicule royalty and politicians alike, their aristocratic lifestyles and 'leadership' decision-making lambasted and derided. Also, other illustrators such as Pier Leone Ghezzi (1674–1755) in Italy and William Hogarth (1697–1764) in England presented moral and ethical concerns, particularly in relation to the poorer echelons of society. This stratum of human existence was not the polite society of aristocratic portraiture. It was squalid, raucous, unruly and chaotic and Hogarth in particular ensured that his images conveyed the particulars of everyday life that needed attention: drunkenness, fecklessness, criminality, prostitution and overcrowded and filthy living environments. Illustration work of this nature was also artfully composed and full of invention; even the most pessimistic digesting the forlorn visual messages might detect signs of hope.

1.1

1.1

Photographed by the author in the British Museum, London, this is *The Stela of Assurnasipal II*, king of the Neo-Assyrian Empire 883–859 BC: expansionist, brutal despot and greatly feared by both subjects and foes. It is claimed he once constructed a minaret using the severed heads of his defeated enemies. A sculptural relief carved out of limestone, it dates back to the ninth century BC (nearly three thousand years ago) and was found on the site of Assyria's ancient capital Nimrud, now in present-day Syria. *Stela* defines a stone slab erected for commemorative purposes. Standing at 9 feet 8 inches (2.94 metres), its presence would have been imposing. In spite of its ancient milieu and context, it is a sophisticated production and communicates powerfully,

being imbued with substantive Akkadian cuneiform inscriptions as well as being made by 'state-of-the-art' craft and design. Its symbolism and purpose are unequivocal; the inscription begins, "I am important, I am magnificent," and it goes on to define the king's 'political' ideology: military might, service to the gods, Assyrian prosperity and above all total devotion, acquiescence and submission. Note the 'snapping' fingers and mace of authority. The cuneiform writing, already in existence for several thousand years, had replaced pictogram-style hieroglyphics. However, for those who could not decipher or read the inscriptions – which were the majority – the obtruding nature of the overall image ensured its message was clear for all to understand.
©Alan Male

1.2

1.3

1.2

All empire builders have to justify what they do, to themselves, to their own people, and to those they subjugate. The Romans developed a sophisticated world view, which they projected successfully through public 'art', inscription and architecture. Photographed by the author, this is a small section from the *Column of Marcus Aurelius*, Roman emperor from AD 161 to 180. Standing in Rome at 128 feet (39 metres), the column showcases the emperor's achievements and victories in battle, particularly his successes during the Marcomannic Wars in Germanic Europe. The whole edifice is a remarkable piece of illustration; it is a highly detailed pictorial narrative sequence that visually describes the displacement and despair of conquered peoples and the vanquishing of the 'barbarian' foe by the victorious Roman legions. Totally jingoistic in tone, the emperor, whose statue once adorned the top of the column, is represented as protagonist and in complete control of his environment. As a point of interest, if the carved relief panels were unwrapped from the column and laid out flat, they would stretch 361 feet (110 metres). ©Alan Male

1.3

This is an ancient Balinese *grotesque*, photographed by the author in the Saraswati Temple of Ubud on the Indonesian island of Bali. It is dedicated to Saraswati, the Hindu goddess of learning, literature and art. Vaguely reminiscent of European gargoyles, its gnarled and anthropomorphic features suggest that one of its primary functions was to ward off evil. Its context is clear: deference and veneration to the deity and an iconic reminder of faith and servility. ©Alan Male

1.4

1.4
Hidden for centuries in a sealed-up cave in northwest China, a single copy survives of the *Diamond Sutra*. Written in Sanskrit, it is the world's earliest complete dated, printed book. It was made in AD 868. The *Diamond Sutra* is part of a larger canon of 'sutras', or sacred texts in Mahayana Buddhism, the branch of Buddhism most commonly found in China, Japan, Korea and Southeast Asia. Many Buddhist adherents believe that the Mahayana Sutras were dictated directly by the Buddha, and the *Diamond Sutra* takes the form of a conversation between the Buddha's pupil Subhati and his Master. Produced as a woodblock print, the imagery and accompanying texts form a scroll approximately 16 feet long (5 metres). It is one of the most important manuscripts in the Buddhist faith, and its significance and power of influence are immeasurable. ©British Library Board *Or.8210/P.2*

1.5

1.5
This is one of 106 striking miniatures from the *Silos Apocalypse*, a spectacular manuscript produced in the Spanish monastery of Santo Domingo de Silos, AD 1109. The illustrations depict extraordinary scenes from the Christian Bible of the Apocalypse, the story of the end of the world where cataclysmic destruction is followed by a war in Heaven, subsequently leading to a triumphant vision of Christ in Majesty. This version of the story is an embellishment of St John's New Testament original and was conceived by the Spanish monk Beatus of Liebana in AD 776. The illustration shown is by Petrus, depicting Daniel's vision of 'beasts from the sea and the ancient of days'. It is from the book of Daniel, chapter 7. The story has over the years formed the bedrock of Christian belief, and the frightening and fearsome nature of its outcome and message has ensured a total adherence to 'pure' living and a belief in God. Illustrations such as this would have had a tremendous influence and impact on its viewers. Even to this day, there are many who fervently believe in the apocalyptic predictions expounded by manuscripts and illustrations like this one.© British Library Board *Add.11695*

1.6

1.7

1.6

This is an illustration produced in AD 1407 for one of many Christian devotional books, produced throughout Europe and known individually as a *Book of Hours*. Most were unique in theme and design but all contained psalms and prayers. The illustrations were often lavish, full-colour, complex productions known simply as *illuminations*; they could only be seen in their original handcrafted state. The image shown is a conceptual interpretation of the Annunciation and was created in Paris by an illustrator with the title Master of the Brussels Initials. The early Christian church was a prime mover in commissioning some of the first inscriptions and illustrated texts, with the first known illustrated biblical manuscript dating from AD 398. ©British Library Board *Add.29433*

1.7

Medieval England was subjected to the feudal rule of 'warlord kings', most notably that of the Saxons, Normans and the Plantagenets. This is an illustration of King John (1166–1216) engaging in a typical royal pastime by showing off his prowess as a master huntsman. Part of a much larger textual manuscript entitled *The Statutes of England*, the image is a miniature and served as a reminder to all who saw it that the reigning monarch was the omnipotent head of a ruling class, his family tree laid below and designed as a taxonomic hierarchy with the king resplendently illustrated at the top. Produced sometime during the thirteenth century, the manuscript also contains the full text of Magna Carta or 'The Great Charter' signed by King John, which laid the foundation for democratic institutions and freedom of the individual – an interesting anomaly considering the tone and general message imbued in the illustration.© British Library Board *Cotton Claudius D.11, f. 116*

1.8

1.9

1.8
A round map of the world, set in a square ornamental frame, this is an example of a thirteenth- to fourteenth-century map. Produced on parchment, conceived and made in England, it is part of a calendar and psalter and is accompanied by hymns and prayers. As well as providing information regarding the location of known places and regions, religion, as it nearly always has until modern times, dictated the contextual thrust. As well as a zone of winds, figures of inhabitants, Jerusalem is in the centre. Also, east is at the top and the Red Sea is upper right. ©British Library Board *Add. 28681, f.9*

1.9
Figure 1.9 is an image taken from *Lullius Raymundus*, a manuscript that contained illustrations of alchemical processes, furnaces and apparatus. The drawing, from the late fifteenth century, shows a large pot with a crowned head at the surface and a conical shaped receptacle with bleeding limbs and a furnace above.© Wellcome Library *Creative Commons Attribution Licence CC By 4.0*

EARLY MEDICAL ILLUSTRATION
The polymaths of the 14th and 15th centuries produced fresh insights into understanding human anatomy and the biological processes of life. This facilitated the new medical illustration of the Renaissance, which was prevalent in many types of medieval manuscripts. They were used to illustrate theological and moral concerns as well as medical theories and practices. The period also determined significant advances in understanding medicine, particularly with regard to the human condition such as the healing process and the psychological effects of illness. However, some primitive and superstitious practices still prevailed, alchemy being one: the purification of the human soul and the elixir of immortality.

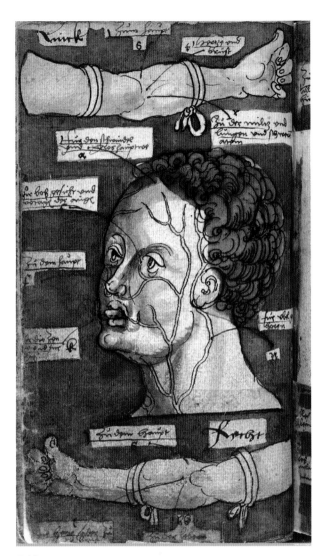

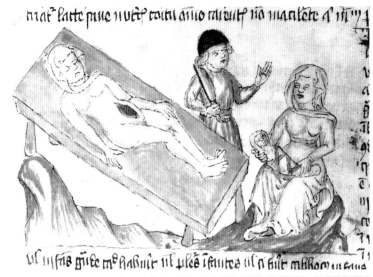

1.10

1.11–1.12

1.10
Figure 1.10 is from a German book entitled *Arzneibuch* (Book of Medical Receipts), 1524, a physicians' handbook of practical medicine with notes on bloodletting, amongst other themes. It uses a crude approach to representation, but it nonetheless clearly identifies the placement of veins in the head and arms. ©Wellcome Library *Creative Commons Attribution Licence CC By 4.0*

1.11
Figure 1.11 (top) is from a manuscript entitled *Gynaecological Texts* from 1420 and contains information about conception, pregnancy and childbirth. It shows a woman who has died in childbirth on an operating table with a doctor wielding a large cleaver after delivering the baby by caesarean section. A nurse holds the swaddling child. ©Wellcome Library *Creative Commons Attribution Licence CC By 4.0*

1.12
Figure 1.12 comes from an unidentified manuscript but its theme is unequivocal: a man sewing up a head wound. It is from the early fourteenth century. ©Wellcome Library *Creative Commons Attribution Licence CC By 4.0*

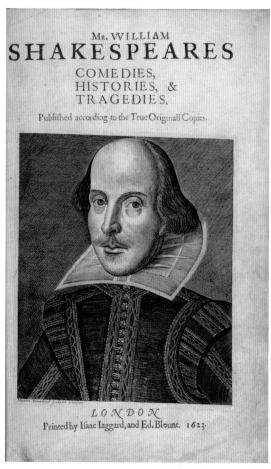

1.13

1.14

The early modern period in history, comprising most of the 16th and 17th centuries, witnessed the first known circumnavigations of the earth by the likes of European explorers such as Ferdinand Magellan (Portugal) and Sir Francis Drake (England). The Magellan expedition went some way in proving that the earth was spherical. Much earlier, during Classical times, Hellenistic astronomers started to surmise that the world was at least round, and by the time Islamic mathematicians developed spherical trigonometry, there was widespread belief by the 'educated few' that the earth was a globe and at the centre of the universe. The Renaissance astronomer Copernicus refuted much of this and concluded by way of his intense observations that the earth was indeed a sphere, but part of a 'solar system' with the sun at the centre with other planets comprising the full retinue. This led to the publication of richly illustrated atlases and other learned documents, detailing the latest theories and discoveries. One such publication

1.15
This is a celestial map and depicts the heavens according to Copernicus's system, with the earth and other planets revolving around the sun. ©British Library Board *Maps.C.6.c.2*

1.16
The Universe with a Zodiac Sphere: A comparison of Ptolemy's system to the systems of Tyco and Martianus Capella. ©British Library Board *Maps.C.6.c.2*

1.15

1.16

was the Atlas *Coelestis*, from the Latin meaning 'celestial'. Although several have been published over the years, the earliest and possibly the most influential for its time was *Atlas Coelestis Harmonia Macrocomica sen Atlas U' Amsterdam* from 1660. The dominant themes of astronomy and earth science were controversial, as the majority still believed in a 'flat earth' and the notion of biblical 'creationism'. Perhaps there was good reason for the imagery being rich in decoration and superficial details. Was lip service to the Almighty being observed by including subjects like cherubs and other religious icons, thus giving the overall illustration a 'Sistine Chapel–like' feel? Both of the images here are by the Dutch-German cartographer and illustrator Andreas Cellarius (1596–1665). A minor planet is named after him.

1.17

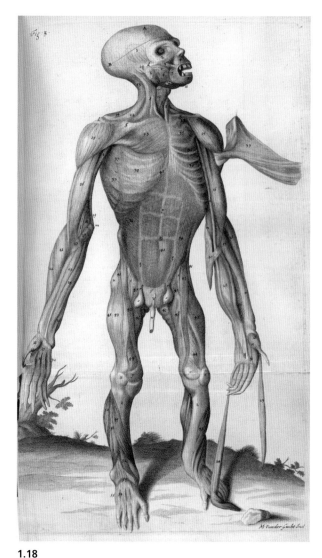

1.18

1.17

'Scientific illustration' came into existence in Classical times when scholars and illuminators observed and recorded details of the natural world. As time progressed, the Renaissance period gave rise to an intense and prolific interaction with science and art, with protagonists claiming association with both vocations. The subsequent images produced by the great polymaths of that period have become synonymous with early scientific research. The natural world held a fascination for many. New animals and plants were being discovered, their ecology, biology and morphology studied in great detail, as well as their value to humanity, such as the medicinal properties given by certain floral species. This image is entitled *Historia naturalis ranarum nosratium*, which when translated means 'pond life'. Produced in Nuremburg, Germany, in 1758, it depicts the herpetological inhabitants of a North European freshwater ecosystem. The illustrators were August Johann Roesel van Rosenhof and M. Tyroff. ©British Library Board *458.f.12*

1.18

The Modern Period that began during the fifteenth century brought about huge advancements in science and discovery, which in itself led into the Age of Enlightenment. Science, imbued with new and challenging ideas about such things as human ethnicity, race and culture, also started to raise controversial questions related to the zoology and taxonomy of animal life. For example, were some 'human beings' more animal than others? The Church decried the whole discourse as blasphemous. This is an engraving from 1699, produced in London. Whilst a highly detailed anatomical study, its remit goes well beyond pure morphology and is subtitled *Anatomie of a pygmie compared to that of a monkey, ape or a man*. The importance of this illustration, and others of its context and time, is to exemplify how even the learned and erudite were not exempt from base prejudice. ©British Library Board *548.k.13*

LORD LOVAT.
From a Drawing made by Hogarth the morning before his Lordship's execution.

1.19

1.19
William Hogarth (1697–1764) was an illustrator renowned for his pictorial satire and social criticism plus his narrative series of 'modern moral subjects', such as the highly acclaimed 'rise and fall' story entitled *A Rake's Progress*. He often featured themes that other artists and illustrators might baulk at, such as social deprivation and the excesses of immorality. Neither the upper or lower strata of society escaped his biting observations. His influence and fame – infamy perhaps, in the eyes of those he lampooned and criticized – was immense and is an inspiration to many. This is a drawing of Lord Lovatt, sketched the same day as his execution for treason. A former supporter of the House of Hanover, Lovatt changed sides and supported the Stuart claim. He was amongst the Highlanders defeated at the Battle of Culloden. He was the last person to be executed by beheading in Britain (although the practice was not formally abolished until 1973). ©British Library Board *9505.f.2*.

Victoriana to Disney

The nineteenth century saw an expansion of new and challenging genres in arts and literature, such as the Pre-Raphaelite Brotherhood with protagonists such as Burne-Jones, Rossetti and Holman Hunt, producing innovative and often controversial interpretations of classic literature by the likes of Tennyson and Mallory. These lavish illustrative and colourful treatments invited much criticism, particularly from Charles Dickens, who had already sacked his illustrator George Cruikshank for creating an unnecessary 'visual diversion' from his 'burgeoning literary genius'. Cruikshank's characterizations of infamous Dickens personalities, such as those in *Oliver Twist*, became ubiquitous and standard representations. Throughout the Victorian period, it was illustration that facilitated a connection for many people with classic and populist literature. Because of the 1880 Education Act (in Britain), schooling became compulsory for all children between the ages of five and ten, thus suggesting that vast sections of society were unable to read throughout the nineteenth century.

GOTHIC TALES, DECADENCE AND THE WILD WEST

The nature of narrative fiction became broader in terms of context, theme and message. Eroticism and 'dark' Gothic tales became popular topics, with Art Nouveau associate Aubrey Beardsley producing what was considered 'controversial imagery' for that time. Beardsley wielded great influence, not just by the nature of his graphic styling and ornate decorative designs, with their refined and graceful elegance, but also by his subject matter, the Victorian 'gentile society', describing it as 'grotesque, decadent and sexually explicit'. However, the end of the nineteenth century brought about a post-Victorian liberated fascination with sensuality. This led into the Edwardian era, a period of significant changes in attitude, aesthetic awareness and above all, a dwindling of social puritanism. Illustrators such as Beardsley, Arthur Rackham and more latterly Harry Clarke flourished in an era of new and innovative ideas and literary originality. Clarke, from Ireland, was described as illustrating 'a haunting take on one of literatures darkest minds', that of Edgar Allen Poe. His

imagery for *Tales of Mystery and Imagination* have been the mainstay for affecting gothic aficionados to this day, the film director Tim Burton a classic example. Arthur Rackham's influence is no less apparent: extremely popular in both his native Britain and in the United States, he epitomized the emergence of a new and dramatic narrative style with a compositional realism and figure characterisations that evoked great atmosphere and theatrical effect. Often dreamlike, surreal and fantastical, Rackham's influence is still immense and can be seen in the work of many contemporary fantasy and children's book illustrators and filmmakers.

The work of Dickens continued to invite illustrative interpretations, especially for children. The Brothers Grimm, Charles and Mary Lamb, J. M. Barrie, Washington Irving, Rudyard Kipling, Hans Christian Andersen and Kenneth Grahame were amongst many authors whose works were greatly imbued with illustration, providing audiences with an immediacy and identification for what were fast becoming the classics of the time. *Alice in Wonderland* by Lewis Carroll was another typical example, the characterizations developed by both Rackham and Sir John Tenniel providing the standard reference. In the United States, illustrators such as Edward Kemble gave personality and everlasting identity to the characters from Mark Twain's *Huckleberry Finn*. Other notable illustrators of influence from the United States include N. C. Wyeth, Winslow Homer, Howard Pyle and James Montgomery Flagg. The growth of the New World gave rise to stories of feats and exploitation when adventurers struck

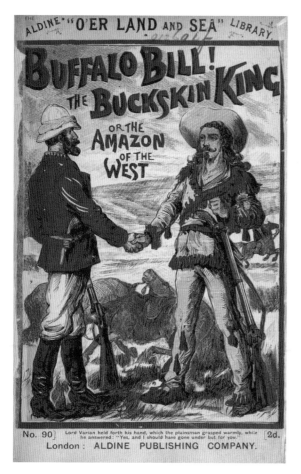

1.20

1.20
A popular fiction book cover, published in London 1890 by the Aldine *O'er Land and Sea* Library: *Buffalo Bill the Buckskin King* or *The Amazon of the West*. William Frederick 'Buffalo Bill' Cody was an American scout, frontiersman, bison hunter and showman. A legendary yet real-life figure, he epitomized the character and making of the 'Wild West'. Throughout much of his life, he toured around America, Europe and Britain with his performing show, a massive circus-like attraction that re-enacted tales of heroism and 'gunslinger sharpshooting'. This particular book was part of a series that helped bring the genre of the Western and its heroes of popular imagination to the attention of British and other audiences. The illustrations, facsimile coloured versions of slightly earlier black and white originals, provided many with their first visualization of an entertainment genre that went on to dominate throughout most of the twentieth century.
©British Library Board *012601.f*

out for new frontiers and discovery; 'the Wild West' provided numerous colourful and infamous personalities that influenced the literature of the day. In addition to stories of 'cowboys' and gun fights, the distorted and disingenuous tales told about 'bad and savage Red Indians'! This gave much for illustrators to visualize, with books recounting the 'bravery and distinction' of luminaries such as Buffalo Bill, Davy Crocket, Billy the Kid, Wyatt Earp, Annie Oakley, Calamity Jane and Colonel Custer, not to mention Sitting Bull and Geronimo. These fictional accounts, albeit based on some truth, established the foundation of a genre and culture that went on to dominate Hollywood during the twentieth century: ubiquitous characterizations, formed in the first place by illustration.

EARLY ADVERTISING

The growth of commercialization brought about a new concept for readers to connect with: advertising. Still in its infancy during the Victorian era, promotions and advertisements for all manner of products, services and entertainment were beginning to take effect. Illustration for persuasion had been around for centuries in the

1.21

These are the covers of two books that represent much that was genial, amusing and entertaining during the mid-nineteenth century.

1.21
Tommy Toddles's Comic Almanac, published by J. Heaton & Son, Leeds, England, 1862. Aimed predominately at a discerning adult audience, the content was reminiscent of the bawdy music hall double entendre that was becoming popular at that time. ©British Library Board *1077.i.11*

1.22
Funny Books for Boys and Girls, published by David Bogue in 1856, was far from being early in relation to the history of children's books. The first was *A Little Pretty Pocket Book*, which appeared in 1744, marking the beginning of a genre of publications that were imbued with innocence and charm. However, the nature of literature and other published material for children developed considerably during the hundred years or so before this example appeared. By the mid-nineteenth century, British colonial rule and Victorian jingoism were deeply embedded in the psyche of children, and books of this nature did nothing to counteract that situation. It marked the beginning of a genre of illustration that today would be considered racist, sexist and generally offensive. The book also contained games, quizzes and humour – a forerunner of light entertainment for young audiences that prevailed right up until the early 1980s. Now considered unfashionable and passé, these kinds of amusements can be exemplified by the now-defunct BBC television programme *Crackerjack*.© British Library Board *11648.f.25*

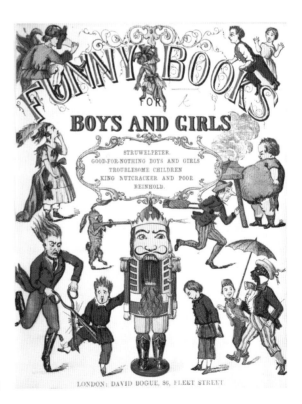

1.22

1.23

1.23

Advertising from the late nineteenth century: a nascent discipline in publications at that time, prior to this, techniques of persuasion such as selling were restricted to posters and leaflets, which relied on audiences that were largely transient and local. Now, advertisers bought space in newspapers and magazines. The advent of the railroad greatly improved means of transportation and in turn provided a circulation that could include the whole country. The soap advertisement shown here displays high quality regarding its copywriting, design and most importantly, the engraved illustration. However, many examples from that period will clearly display somewhat coarse newsprint reproduction. This meant that many illustrators relied on the age-old method of block printing for production in order to keep the image simple and to keep costs at an affordable level. *Pears Soap*, 1890. ©British Library Board *10507.e.78*

form of propaganda, but the context of advertising and promotion was a new outlet for the illustrator. During the latter part of the nineteenth century, photography was still in its infancy, and therefore engravings and block illustrations were the only form of imagery that could be printed and reproduced for the purpose.

Advertising had an immediate effect on society, and its persuasive powers to sell, influence and enhance product and company identity was immeasurable. Illustrators formally renowned for fictional work, such as the Czech illustrator Alphonse Mucha, produced drawings that advertised biscuits, cigarettes and even beer! The backdrop to the growth of commercialization was that illiteracy, particularly in the United States and Europe, was becoming a thing of the past. Education and a thirst for knowledge brought about a growing demand for reading matter. Public libraries expanded and retail outlets selling new reading material also flourished. Moreover, the means of distribution developed, with improved transportation systems such as railroad and the advent of the motor vehicle. At the turn of the twentieth century, newspapers and mass-market magazines were the dominant means of communication; the cinema and television were yet to be invented. The newly burgeoning advertising industry, particularly in New York, could buy space in mass-distribution magazines with circulations that covered the whole country. In fact, the success of magazine publishing depended on the ability to attract advertising, the revenue received from this source far exceeding subscriptions and sales.

THE ADVANCE OF SCIENCE, PHILOSOPHY AND LEARNING

This period witnessed vast changes in societal conditions, particularly in North America and Europe. The Industrial Revolution ran parallel with immense intellectual and scientific advancement, which in turn brought about significant revisions to attitudes and beliefs. No longer dominated by religion, people became knowledge conscious and were subjected to new ideas about politics, philosophy and the natural world. Exploration and discovery uncovered a vast wealth of new knowledge related to the planet: exotic places, peoples of ethnic variance and cultures, strange and outlandish animals and plants. This enrichment stimulated the need for fresh learning and platforms for research. Once again, illustration came into its own! Publishers, educational institutions and research organizations delivered a wealth of extensive new knowledge through a myriad of highly detailed and informed engravings, borne on the pages of books, encyclopaedias, pamphlets and papers. Controversy soon followed. Philosophical and scientific theories about subjects such as *evolution* or *existentialism*, propagated by the likes of Darwin and Nietzsche, gave illustration a different platform to deliver from with far-reaching consequences. For example, illustrations that depicted discoveries and ideas from the new science of *palaeontology* caused widespread disquiet amongst those adhering to the old value systems and beliefs.

POLITICS, SUBVERSION AND PROPAGANDA

Rising to prominence in the eighteenth century, the burgeoning visual language of the political 'cartoon' was firmly embedded in journalism. This was a symbiotic vocation, a counterbalance of image and word, and it incited much debate and argument throughout society. Commentaries written and illustrated by the likes of Dickens and Cruikshank presented 'stinging' satire, criticism and opposition to governance and the ruling elite. Example publications were *The New York Tribune*, *Harper's Weekly*, *The Illustrated London News*, *Bentley's Miscellany* and the first magazine to focus on and specialize in political comment, *Punch*, first published in 1841. The backdrop to all of this was industrialization. Creating greater employment opportunities, it played a huge part regarding political awareness and propaganda. In most advanced societies, education and consumerism gave rise for a demand in greater freedoms and economic rights. However, in certain countries during the nineteenth century, there were great periods of stress and turmoil, in which violent controversy about doctrine – political or otherwise – accompanied the use of force. Between 1861 and 1865, America embarked on civil war. Once again, illustration came into its own, this time in the form of imagery that decried the practice of slavery – a major reason for the war in the first place. A leading player was Thomas Nast, whose work appeared regularly in the richly illustrated *Harper's Weekly*. Followers of Nast's work tripled the circulation of *Harper's*. Political personalities that he satirized were weakened and usually dethroned, and every presidential candidate that he supported was elected, including Abraham Lincoln, who gave him full credit for his role.

Nast expressed his opinion on every important political and social issue, created the elephant and donkey symbols for the Republican and Democratic Parties and gave America its familiar portrayals of Uncle Sam and Santa Claus. Such is the power of illustration!

THE 'GOLDEN AGE' BEGINS

At the start of the twentieth century, the new and expanding communications media of publishing and advertising replaced the traditional patrons for illustration, which for centuries had been the church, the state, the wealthy individual and narrow learned institutions and societies. Advertising afforded illustrators fresh opportunities with exposure for their work reaching communities across the continent. Illustration was now mainly commercial, with hundreds of practitioners establishing successful and lucrative careers. Albeit mainly confined to the United States, this new media enterprise was beginning to enter a *golden age* – one which was to last well into the 1950s. A seminal moment occurred as a result of the growth in demand for illustration: the founding of the Society of Illustrators in New York on 1 February 1901. This is still the world's foremost professional organization for illustration and has a prestigious international membership.

POPULAR ENTERTAINMENT

Another popular medium to emerge was the comic strip. This evolved into the comic book, an iconic and innovative cultural milieu with a worldwide following. Its influence as a brand for entertainment became immeasurable, with illustration providing readers with an immediate visual reference to any story or subject. Famous superheroes appeared, representing the struggle between good and evil, eventually morphing into the live-action figures synonymous with Hollywood. However, it is the emergence of animation that transformed popular culture during the early part of the twentieth century. This new and innovative medium provided illustrators with an additional outlet for their creative endeavours. A fresh name came on the scene and changed the world of entertainment forever: Walter Elias Disney. Along with other 'cartoonists' and illustrators, Disney created a wealth of characters and films that dominate mass media to this day, with the Disney brand the most ubiquitous and well known.

1.24

1.25

1.24

The advancement of science, knowledge and ideas during the nineteenth century promoted a massive flurry of new and original illustrations, depicting much that resulted from the great discoveries and expeditions of the time, and none more so than archaeology, a discipline that yielded a tremendous amount of fresh information about past cultures and histories from all over the world. Much of the material that was discovered, analysed and written about was not in a physical state suitable for removal or transportation from their place of discovery. It was therefore incumbent on illustrators to record and embellish these discoveries with images of precise exactitude. This example was published in *The Egyptian Collections Volume XI* and shows an Egyptian tomb wall painting depicting a procession of figures with offerings. It is a facsimile part of a wall painting from the Tenth Tomb of Gourna, Thebes, and was produced on site during an archaeological expedition by illustrator **Robert Hay** sometime between 1826 and 1838. ©British Library Board *Add 29822,f.118*

1.25

The great explorations of discovery and travel wielded a myriad of illustrations that depicted exotic species of animals and plants never before seen by Europeans. Many of these illustrations caused a sensation when first seen, with many not believing such creatures existed – most notably that of the very first drawing published of an orang-utan in 1718 (from Daniel Beeckman's *A Voyage to and from the Island of Borneo*) which showed the creature to be almost human. Another such creature, less controversial but nonetheless of great interest, was the image shown entitled *The tapir sent from Bengkulu to Calcutta in 1816*. The Illustrator is unknown. ©British Library Board *Add.Or.4973*

1.26

As well as the great many books of fiction, most notably children's books, the nineteenth century saw a proliferation of publications that provided much by way of

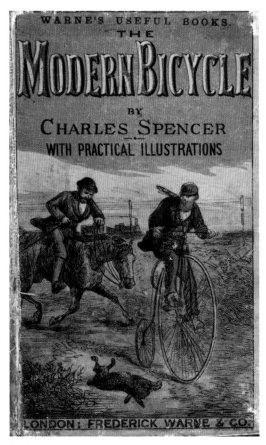

1.26

information and instruction. Rather than concentrate on subjects of deep learning and erudition (there were already numerous educational textbooks available), some publishers focussed on subjects and activities associated with lifestyle, lay interests, pastimes and leisure. One such publisher was Frederick Warne and Co., whose popular series *Warne's Useful Books* went on to form the basis of a cult collectable set entitled *The Observer's Books*. Being first published in 1937 and lasting until 2003, they covered practically every theme associated with popular interest or indulgence, from sports, music of all forms, nature and history. The book cover shown is one of Warne's original forays into this type of publishing, *Warne's Useful Books: The Modern Bicycle with Practical Illustrations*, 1877. It features a pastime that became increasingly popular at the time, exemplified by the illustration and its message: the newly invented velocipede, here represented by the 'penny farthing', which could outpace a horse! These books contained many illustrations, some being overtly diagrammatic in nature. ©British Library Board *1607/3028*

1.27

These illustrations are from *The Iconographic Encyclopaedia of Science, Literature and Art* and are based on the famed German publication *Bilderatlas*, by Friedrich Arnold Brockhaus. The section that contained these images is entitled 'History and Ethnology', with the nineteenth-century part presenting culture from every area of the world, from 'earthy' scenes of Russian peasant existence, the pomp and splendour of an oriental court to tribal life in Africa, the Pacific Islands and the Americas. The general tone of all of these illustrations was to communicate patronization and superiority, particularly towards peoples of ethnic non-white variance or to those pertaining to a 'lower social class existence'. This was an attitude that prevailed throughout the nineteenth century in Europe (and into the twentieth century). Whilst the illustrations were accurate regarding morphology and scenario, they remain largely a misrepresentation. The theme of the illustrations shown is that of the Brazilian slave trade; by the time they were published, slavery had largely been abolished in Europe and elsewhere. However, the Brazilians were the last to abolish slavery and reluctantly did so in 1888. During the Atlantic slave trade era, Brazil imported more slaves than any other country, with an estimated 4.9 million people captured and brought from Africa. These images show clearly the harsh and inhuman treatment endured by slaves, and it remains to be seen how sympathetic Victorian age society was with regards to what is being portrayed here. ©Crown Publishers, Inc

1.27

1.28 –1.29

These images were produced by Sir John Tenniel (1820–1914); he and Sir Quentin Blake (b 1932), another illustrator, both received a knighthood for their achievements. Tenniel was operational long before Blake, but there are distinct similarities: both were immensely influential, both contributed to the magazine Punch, both were renowned children's illustrators and both were known for their symbiotic working practices with notable authors, Lewis Carroll and Roald Dahl, respectively. Alice's Adventures in Wonderland, devised by Carroll reputedly when he was narcotized on opium, is one of the best-loved and surreal early stories written for children. It is imbued by ninety-two illustrations that are characterized by Tenniel's trademark style for emphasizing the grotesque and fantastical, portraying pictorial theatricalism, characterful anthropomorphism and individualized representations for humans. There have been many other illustrated adaptions over the years, including animated films and live-action motion pictures, with Tenniel's originals setting the template for characterization and ubiquitous familiarity. The Dodo *and* The Cheshire Cat ©British Library Board *Cup.g.74*

1.28

1.29

1.30

1.30

The combined genre of the Gothic and the supernatural has entertained and enthralled millions of people for many years. Since its literary origin in the eighteenth century, numerous tales of horror, monsters, ghouls, ghosts and vampires have terrorized, thrilled and fuelled people's imaginations. In a European and American context, there have been many celebrated authors and their creations:

Mary Shelley and Frankenstein, Washington Irving and *The Legend of Sleepy Hollow*, Bram Stoker and Dracula, R. L. Stevenson and *The Strange Case of Dr Jekyll and Mr Hyde*, Edgar Allan Poe and *The Fall of the House of Usher*, H. P. Lovecraft and *The Dunwich Horror* and the lesser-known William Hope Hodgson and *Carnacki the Ghost-Finder*. These are just a few of a great many, but all have given

scope for a rich backlog of films, television adaptions, stage productions, radio presentations, graphic novels and illustrated literature. Many visual interpretations of the main fictional protagonists and their settings have been used down the years as standard representations, even for state-of-the-art contemporary productions such as computer games and the cinema. The whole genre has facilitated a

massive source of material for illustrators, from the classic originals to the huge array of new literature. This figure depicts overtly less 'terror'-inflected scenes than are often seen, but nonetheless conjures the atmosphere and setting given for ghosts and haunted houses. It is from *The Haunted House* by Thomas Hood, illustrated by *H. Railton*, London 1896. ©British Library Board *11648.h.5*

1.31

1.31
This is a British entertainment poster from 1883, published in London. Little is known about the ventriloquist Miss Madeline Rosa, except that she was possibly the first female entertainer of this kind. Ventriloquism became popular and was synonymous with vaudeville in the United States and music hall in the UK. Posters such as this decorated the billboards of a great many cities throughout Europe and America, providing illustrators of the day a rich and varied outlet. Popular entertainment comprised circus performances, curio and freak shows, magic and spiritualism. © British Library Board *EVAN.2582*

1.32
This is from a calendar advertising products available at the Pharmacie Centrale de France et Maison Droguerie Menie. It is a colour lithograph of 1889 and depicts a professor teaching students in mid-sixteenth-century Paris. As well as the suggestion for superior medicines, oils and ointments, the essence of this promotion hints at the gravitas and status being afforded pharmaceutical practice at that time.
©Wellcome Library *Creative Commons Attribution Licence cc By 4.0*

1.33
For many years, 'artists' and more latterly illustrators were commissioned to produce large-scale paintings of glorious military endeavours and victories, depictions of human subjugation – a defeated foe or political enemy, the signings of treaties and surrenders, the exploits of exploration or discovery. Often at the behest of state or aristocratic patronage, the essence was propagandist, ensuring the 'right' information was being conveyed. In essence, these images bore much power and influence, making sure that the population at large remained 'on-side' regarding the vast expenditure and subsequent loss of life endured. This is *Waterloo*, illustrated by **William Heath**, from 1819, four years after the battle – a visually jingoistic reminder of Britain's strength, influence and military might, coming at a time when the British Empire was fast becoming the biggest in world history, thus making Britain a true superpower of the day. ©British Library Board *838.m.7*

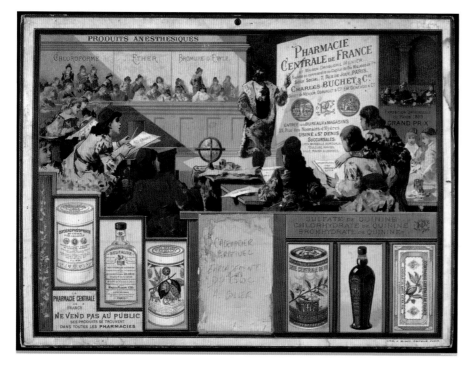

1.32

BATTLE OF WATERLOO, JUNE 18TH 1816.

1.33

1.34

This is a wood engraving by **Sir John Tenniel**, published in the satirical and current affairs magazine *Punch* from October 1885. The image had iconographic origins in Titian's *Rape of Europe*, which featured the alluring figure of Erin about to be savaged by a vulture, a metaphor for the British occupation of Ireland. In 1882, the National League was established to promote home rule and ultimately Irish independence, provoking a series of controversial and pointedly jingoistic commentaries and illustrations that fostered aggrandizement for continued British power in Ireland. Tenniel's *Irish Vampire* shows Charles Stewart Parnell, the personification of the National League, transformed into a vampire bat, about to prey on beautiful Erin, the personification of Ireland. Here, the illustrator perceived the National League as the 'face of evil from within', as it attempts to liberate Ireland from her 'English protector'. It is known that illustrations such as these wielded a great deal of influence on public opinion in England and did much to promote the anti–Irish liberation sentiment. ©British Library Board *P.P.5270*

PUNCH, OR THE LONDON CHARIVARI.—October 24, 1885.

THE IRISH "VAMPIRE."

1.34

A New World Order and the Twenty-first Century

As the twentieth century progressed, the influence of illustration across all aspects of society continued unabated. The world of advertising and promotion grew even more as consumerism expanded. This was echoed by statements like, 'You've never had it so good', coming from British prime minster Harold MacMillan in the 1950s. Attitudes towards sex, morals and exploitation were becoming relaxed and insouciant, as exemplified by illustrators such as the American Charles Dana Gibson, who created a new style of fashion illustration, perpetrated by his trademark *Gibson Girl*. No longer replicating pure figurative realism, Gibson 'invented sexy distortion' – girls who were exceptionally tall, abnormally long-legged, willowy with very narrow waists. Their physique still incites much debate and criticism today in the contemporary trend for ultra-thin female models.

MODERNISM
The early twentieth century also witnessed the birth of *Modernism*. Whilst mainly associated with art, architecture and design, it was a movement that propagated an idea that religion, politics, society and even science were outdated and not fit for purpose. This had a great influence on philosophy and thinking, and along with the destructive aftermath of the First World War led to the advent of a new world order in governance and ideology. This *new order* saw fit to lay blame for the 'disintegration' of society on everything that had a provenance of tradition and historic influence; all that went before was largely rejected. A 'dark age' emerged as fascism and Nazism dominated Europe, and Bolshevik and Maoist communism dominated Russia and China. These suppressive and super-controlling regimes needed propaganda in order to maintain any semblance of popular support. Hitler's propaganda minister Joseph Goebbels pronounced, 'If you are receiving one message all of the time you are going to believe it'. The Nazi regime spread their vile anti-Semitism and heinous ideologies by way of films, publications and posters. Jewish people were the recipients of the most virulent discrimination and treatment, and illustration had *no small part* to play: posters, printed media editorials and pamphlets were commissioned by the Nazis, with illustration at the heart of the communication. One can only guess whether or not the illustrators – of which there were many – felt any semblance of sorrow for their actions. Indeed, a large number even signed the images they created and seemingly relished the opportunity to express the views being broadcast! It poses the question, did these illustrators accept the commission out of 'fear' and command or were they genuinely enthusiastic?

SECOND WORLD WAR
Throughout the Second World War, illustration was the dominant visual language of propagandist communication for all of the military protagonists, the Allies as well as the Axis powers. Posters and various other in-print campaigns were distributed anywhere people were likely to see them and in every newspaper and magazine. With explicit, bold designs imbued with realistic-style painted illustrations, these campaigns promoted such disparate notions as 'Save the Wheat & Help the Fleet – Eat Less Bread' (UK), 'Avenge Pearl Harbor – Our Bullets Will Do It' (US) and 'American Red Cross, Our Boys Need Sox – Knit Your Bit' (US). Other ubiquitous campaigns promoted the need for spoken and social discretion, with one well-known British poster stating, 'Careless Talk Costs Lives'.

One of the most successful and celebrated illustrators of the twentieth century had his 'finest hour' during the Second World War in spite of already being immensely wealthy and incredibly well known because of five decades illustrating the covers of the *Saturday Evening Post*. With his trademark whimsical and slightly caricatured take on American society, Norman Rockwell's richly painted scenarios and character interactions represented everything sentimental and nuanced about the American dream. For an illustrator, his wartime contributions are considered immense, a classic example being a magazine cover with a character nicknamed *Rosie the Riveter*. Wearing her overalls, with bare arms and muscles flexed, eating a ham sandwich, it inspired an equally famous poster image by J. Howard Miller to boost worker morale, inspire patriotism and help the war effort. The original Rockwell artwork fetched $5 million at Sotheby's. However, Rockwell's *pièce de résistance* was his series of illustrations entitled *The Four Freedoms*.

1.35

If you see a neighbour spit
Let the warden know of it
On this matter please be firm
Handkerchiefs will stop that germ

1.36

This project propelled Rockwell's reputation even further; the four images represented the freedoms of *speech*, *worship*, *want* and *fear* and promoted President Franklin D. Roosevelt's 1941 State of the Union Address in which he declared that essential human rights should be protected. Published by the *Saturday Evening Post*, the original artworks toured as an exhibition, sponsored by the US Treasury Department, and promoted a sales drive of war bonds that raised over $132 million. Such is the power of illustration! Rockwell's idyllic and nostalgic approach, a thematic style that influenced much of the illustration seen during the golden age, created an enduring niche in the social fabric. His *Freedom from Want* is emblematic of what is now known as the 'Norman Rockwell Thanksgiving'.

1.35
The 1930s and 1940s witnessed a dark age for Europe as fascists and Nazis seized power, establishing totalitarian regimes aided and abetted by a rule of terror and genocide. Those untouched by the oppression – in other words, citizens who were considered 'worthy' and 'ethnically appropriate' by the authorities – were often in league with the state, due largely to influence by the cult of personality. This happens when an individual uses mass media, propaganda and other methods to create an idealized, heroic and at times worshipful image, often through unquestioning flattery or praise. This example, a postage stamp from Nazi-occupied Ukraine, depicts Hitler in no less of a manner, his demeanour and pose typical of his own self-inflated image of superiority. It might be interesting to ascertain the opinions of the illustrator commissioned to produce this image and whether or not his (or her) sympathies lay with the subject.
Alan Male Philatelic Collection

1.36
The 1940s and 1950s saw a proliferation of public health campaigns, from syphilis and other venereal infections (aimed at servicemen in particular), inoculations for polio, diphtheria and other such diseases and the prevention of less serious ailments such as coughs and colds. In the UK, these would be published by the Ministry of Health, often as posters and seen in doctors' surgeries and the like. Normally imbued with illustration, the message was often patronizing and trite. This example is typical of its time, illustrated by a drawing style indicative of the 'commercial art' from that period and seen in every context for illustration – from women's magazines (as accompaniment for lightweight romantic fiction), fashion, advertisements for banal household products, film posters and comic strips.
Thackray Medical Museum

THE COLD WAR PERIOD

What of communist regimes? The post-war period saw not only a consolidation of their power but an expansion of territory and influence, with both China and the Soviet Union becoming significant players on the world stage. Where did illustration feature in all of this? Illustrations commissioned by the Chinese Maoist government were produced to extol the virtues of the regime and its ideology, a credo that demanded excellence through education, unity, hard work and collectivism. The imagery and accompanying texts implied diktat rather than overt propaganda – unswerving loyalty and commitment to the regime and its leaders, with no opposition, criticism or hint of activism against the state. Any such thing, proven or not, would be classed as sedition and treason! The death penalty awaited. So, who produced these illustrations and what were the circumstances? After Chairman Mao's Cultural Revolution, all traditional art and other forms of cultural heritage were illegal and banned from sight and production. Illustrators of the time bowed to one client only – the Communist Party machine. Personal illustration styles and visual languages that did not conform to the accepted *Brutalism* or *Stalinist* pictorial representation were outlawed. Any sign of formal religious or other philosophical iconography was deemed irrelevant and banned; China was an atheist state. Anyone wishing to pursue a career in illustration would comply to one style only and do their master's bidding regarding content and message. The given brief was controlled, heavily directed and extremely prescriptive, the illustrator being no more than a 'colouring-in technician'. Today, circumstances are different in the People's Republic of China, with Chinese society seeking an engagement with Western goods and services. Indeed, there is now a creative and media industry sustaining a breadth of illustration and other forms of visual communication, albeit populist, such as Japanese *manga*. However, there is still no place for the 'political cartoon' as intolerance prevails regarding any criticism of the government.

EVOLUTION AND CONTROVERSY

Illustration contexts other than propaganda and politics also featured strongly throughout the twentieth century; knowledge-bearing illustration for science, culture and education helped facilitate significant

platforms for research and learning. The topic of *evolution* has been no exception. As a theme, it is considered an acceptable and relevant topic for young audiences to be taught, particularly in the West, where science fact and theory are respected as important and essential. However, there is still deep opposition to evolution in certain societies around the world, even though innumerable illustrations of the ubiquitous dinosaur have been in existence for over a century. For example, Charles Robert Knight's celebrated murals and publications have, for over fifty years until his death in 1953, captivated audiences and influenced scientific thinking. His work has inspired literature and numerous films from *Godzilla* to *Jurassic Park*. Many other illustrators have also been influential; Rudolph Zallinger's giant mural in the Peabody Museum of Yale University is another renowned work, detailing evolutionary development from the Triassic to the Cretaceous. However, the most vehement rejection of any scientific theory was that concerning the *Evolution of Man*. Even as late as the 1920s, Charles Darwin was still anathema to many, his proposition that humans were closely related to apes provoking outrage; his ideas were damned as blasphemous and

1.37

1.38
These are 1950s Cold War–period postage stamps from a range of 'Iron Curtain' countries: the Soviet Union, Czechoslovakia, Hungary, Yugoslavia and Poland. Postage stamps from the old communist, eastern European bloc are designed to present constant reminders of gratitude and commitment to the revolution and to celebrate the endeavours of the proletariat class in achieving strength and unity for the regime, mainly through toil and subservience. Postage stamps are also designed to extol a nation's identity and branding. In the case of the two Czechoslovakian stamps, they promote significant achievements regarding the 'space race' of the 1950s and 1960s – even though the subjects in question are Soviet.

The visual language, pictorially representational with accurate and highly detailed content, could be representative of any one individual illustrator shown here. All illustrators from communist regimes produced work in this style, as any deviation from state acceptability would be considered seditious and counter-revolutionary; 'creativity' and idiosyncratic art were seen as challenges to the machinery of state. It has to be noted that the fundamental draughtsmanship and craft of compositional drama and figure drawing is exceptional: any one of the illustrators featured here, all of whom are anonymous, would have had very successful careers producing work for the burgeoning comic strip and graphic novel industry in the Western bloc at that time. Alan Male Philatelic Collection

1.39

1.40

1.39–1.40

The post–Second World War period of the 1950s and early 1960s is considered 'light years' distant in terms of societal attitude, behaviours and ambition, particularly in the UK. Simple pleasures were the indulgence of the time. There was also an acceptance that social mobility, an expectation considered today, was not an available option. Society was administered and families defined by clear gender division and role-play; occupations, pastimes and interests were dictated by gender differentiation. This applied to both adults and children, with an expectation that boys and men favoured 'macho' games and sport such as football and motor racing and were often employed in work demanding physical exertion, a 'craft skill' or trade. Even the upper echelons or professional class of men displayed a fondness for 'tough' physical activities and interests. In contrast, women and girls were charged with 'softer' roles in play, pastime and occupation. Women did jobs that required caring, and many performed 'wifely' duties; the term *housewife* is basically redundant today. Boys played with toy guns; girls played with dolls. All of this provides a backdrop for the two illustrations shown. The full-colour image is by the illustrator **Edward Mortelmans** and was commissioned to accompany an article entitled 'A Musical is Staged' from *Girl Annual: Number Eight*, 1958. This was a general interest book, published annually for girls aged between eight and early teens. It featured stories, nature, adventure strips, hobbies, sport and real-life stories. The content focussed on themes such as ballet, nursing, equestrianism, flowers and butterflies, pets and the theatre and was lavishly illustrated throughout in the style shown. In contrast, the picture strip in black and white is from an annual exclusively for boys entitled the *Lion Book of War Adventures*, 1962. *Lion* was a weekly comic for boys and along with others of its kind – *Eagle*, *Tiger* and *Marvel Boy* – contained picture strips and features dominated by wartime escapades, science fiction and monsters from outer space, dinosaurs, detective thrillers and other stories of 'derring-do'! One such 'hero' was Paddy Payne, Warrior of the Skies, a brave, no-nonsense British spitfire pilot who systematically saw off the frightful 'enemy' single-handed. These stories represented a genre of comic strip imbued with post-war jingoism, an attitude that prevailed throughout Western society for many years. 1.39 ©Hulton Press Ltd; 1.40 ©Fleetway Publications

1.41

1.42

1.41

Illustration contributed greatly to the bourgeoning advertising industry throughout the early and mid-twentieth century. At that time, advertising was already providing many illustrators with highly lucrative careers in the United States, and it was then that the UK started to catch up. This OXO advertisement is synonymous with a campaign that started in 1908. Its essence and message are clearly couched in the fabric of English family life and represent the quasi-humour and wistful sentiments indicative of its time. Using a gender-specific narrative, distinctive by its assumption that women and girls dominate 'the kitchen' and all things culinary, the illustrator created a visual characterisation that was used many times. OXO's beef-stock ingredients ('makes you strong') also gave advertisers the scope for further gender stereotyping; a later advertisement contained the strapline, 'Katie says. . .OXO gives a meal man appeal!' ©Advertising Archives

1.42

This is a poster produced to promote the sport of motorcycle racing and a general interest in motorbikes. It was used to provide an identity (along with other similar images) for garages, motorbike clubs and sales outlets. The example shown was photographed by the author inside a restaurant that was thematically decorated by memorabilia associated with this subject. The poster's physical condition provides a clue to its provenance, which was the early twentieth century; printed on a metal plate, it is shows a certain amount of deterioration. The essence and projected message are overt and unequivocal: 'Every Boys Toys', a sentiment indicative of the poster's time and milieu. ©Alan Male

1.43

1.44

evil. These controversies brought a group of religious fundamentalists in Tennessee to perpetrate the Scopes Monkey Trial (1925), resulting in lawful insistence that state curricula teach creationism and evolution in equal measure. However, the controversy continues. A public policy poll in 2012 revealed that 60 per cent of voters across Alabama and Mississippi believe unequivocally in divine creationism, supporting rumours that illustrated educational books about science and evolution have been burnt on 'ceremonial pyres'. And what of the future – how will these developments impact on the work of the illustrator? It is widely accepted that across the world, education for the young will become more reliant on visual learning, with a growth in broadcast media and publishing to facilitate this trend. Might illustrated learning material for children be compromised for the sake of cultural acquiescence and toleration?

POSTMODERNISM

Progression through the twentieth century saw the emergence of *postmodernism*. The official Tate Gallery definition states, 'The term postmodernism is used to describe the changes that took place in Western society and culture from the 1960's onwards that arose from challenges made to established structures and belief systems. In art, postmodernism was specifically a reaction against modernism which had dominated art theory and practice since the beginning of the twentieth century'. In fact, there is no one postmodern style or theory as it embraces a totally eclectic approach to art making. Consequently, many traditional styles in art and design were rejected, leading to unhindered experimentation and expression. This had an effect on illustration, particularly in Britain, even though literal and pictorial imagery, which dominated throughout the 'golden age', remained appropriate for a few contexts and themes. However, from the 1970s onwards, illustrators began to express ideas and concepts like never before as metaphorical and conceptual illustration became the dominant visual language. There emerged a *new wave* genre that was challenging in terms of representation and interpretation. A fresh aspect to illustration practice disregarded age-old aesthetics and instead presented distortion, abstraction and surrealism, thus giving way to the avant-garde in illustration.

'RADICAL' ILLUSTRATION

A group known as the *Radical Illustrators* emerged from the Royal College of Art during the 1970s and, along with other protagonists of the same genre, pursued a style that was anathema to traditionalists. Their credo was a reactionary and overt rejection of popular mainstream illustration. However, it was not just a rejection of traditional values regarding image construction, such as aesthetic awareness and sound draughtsmanship, but a determined resolve to ensure message and content were paramount. Sue Coe has, since her early days as an illustrator, presented work that is highly politicized, often directed at the excesses of capitalism. She also campaigns vigorously through her work about social injustice, war and most notably cruelty to animals with particular regards to factory farming and meatpacking. Ian Pollock is another illustrator from that stable, immensely relevant and active today, his work the epitome of cutting edge comment and barbed narrative. His drawings are produced with a raw and irate energy, pushing the boundaries of accepted norms with portraits and scenarios representing the famous, the infamous, the fictional and the real that are wildly distorted, contentious and challenging. Notable themes include the Bible, politics and current affairs.

URBAN CULTURE AND THE DIVERSITY OF TREND AND FASHION

Today, and in a commercial frame of reference, illustration has never been broader in terms of its range of application, working practice and style. Trends in visual language come and go. As such, it cannot be denied that cultural history has considerable influence on the fluctuating trends seen in contemporary illustration. This cultural association has aided a push by clients and illustrators to link styles with projects, themes and contexts that are influenced by consumer culture, most notably the music industry, advertising and fashion. Urban culture, like punk and psychedelia before that, gave rise to a trend in illustration that is codependent with the music, fashion and graffiti associated with it. And what of journalistic comment and opinion? Can illustration continue to be a catalyst for change and new directions in politics and social attitudes? This remains to be seen as an uncertain world oscillates against the wavering thresholds of moral tolerance and ethical concerns. The tide of political populism and conflict, facilitated by global social networking and an unscrupulous media, continues unabated. However, history tells us that the arts, in all of their manifestations, have frequently given voice and affected opposition to whatever cause, idea or credo.

And so, having traversed in time through the Archaic and Feudal Ages, the Industrial Age and now into the ever-progressive Information Age, there can be no doubt that *illustration* will continue to thrive and grow as a creative and authoritative practice and that illustrators will always fight for the opportunity to exert their powers of persuasion, opinion, knowledge and influence.

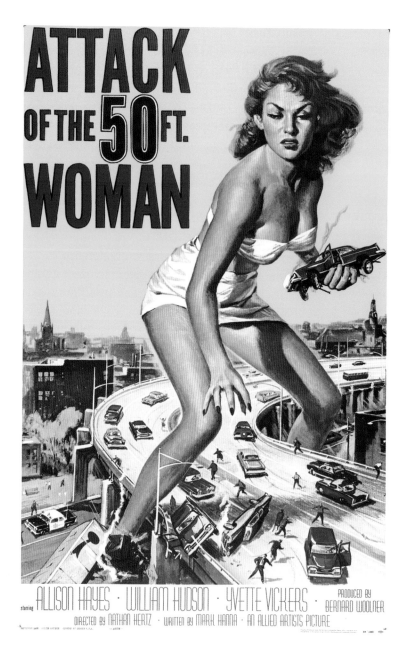

1.45

1.45–1.46

One of the most significant, lucrative and high-profile contexts for illustrators throughout the early and mid-twentieth century was that of the movie poster. This was an area of practice that enabled the illustrator to be granted much acclaim and accreditation. One such illustrator was an American called **Reynold**

Brown, who designed and illustrated a great number of posters promoting productions that are now standard fare for those who study film history and theory. The roster of film titles Brown worked on covers categories of every level of success and accord from the most critically acclaimed to the box office 'flop'. Brown's figurative and composite style,

imbued with realism, was divergent with the 'Golden Age' traditions of pictorial 'slickness' – unsurprising that he was also commissioned by the *Saturday Evening Post* and other such publications, outlets for the talents of Norman Rockwell, amongst others. With regards to the movie industry generally, the popularity and fame accorded actors and directors

was exceptional, with enormous wealth and recognition gained. Hollywood and the Oscars were synonymous with Western culture as these films influenced both fashion and attitude. The movie industry introduced and brought to life themes and storylines related to genres only touched upon by books and comic strips previously: Westerns, biblical and historical

THE ENTERTAINMENT EXPERIENCE OF A LIFETIME!

METRO-GOLDWYN-MAYER
presents

A Tale of the Christ
by GENERAL LEW WALLACE

BEN-HUR

Directed by
WILLIAM WYLER

Starring

CHARLTON HESTON · JACK HAWKINS

HAYA HARAREET · STEPHEN BOYD

HUGH GRIFFITH · MARTHA SCOTT with CATHY O'DONNELL · SAM JAFFE

Screen Play by   Produced by
TECHNICOLOR®   KARL TUNBERG · SAM ZIMBALIST   FILMED IN CAMERA 65

1.46

epics, romance, thrillers, science fiction, war and horror. These productions often screened to audiences around the world, providing entertainment and insight into subjects never before seen. One such genre, science fiction, bore a number of productions from the 1950s that ludicrously featured size-changing humans; one of the most well known was *Attack* of the 50 Foot Woman starring Alison Hayes, a low-budget black and white film from 1958. The poster that Brown produced was considered risqué, with the giant woman only scantily clad. It was also laughable to some, with one commentator observing that it 'may well be one of the worst sci-fi films of all time, but that's not to say it isn't thoroughly enjoyable'. The other film featured here held the record for winning the most number of Oscars for many years, the blockbuster, multi-million-pound production *Ben Hur* from 1959. This film grossed millions of dollars and gained a reputation for being the 'best of its kind'. Brown also established a style that was emulated in every poster for the historic and biblical epic thereafter: an illustration that is highly dramatic and action packed with greatly exaggerated foreshortening and dominated by colossal edifices. The movies may well have been the main draw, but it was the power of illustration that did so well to promote them. Public Domain

1.47

1.48

1.47–1.50
Graffiti has its origins in classical times, with examples dating back to Ancient Egypt, Ancient Greece and the Roman Empire. Today, as in ancient history, scribbling, scratching and painting on property without the owner's permission – no matter how sophisticated in terms of its appearance or the poignancy of its message – is considered defacement and vandalism. Contemporaneously associated with urban culture, graffiti has slowly established itself as a subgenre. It has not yet gained a status of recognized respectability but is considered 'public art' by some, even when blatantly illicit by presenting scurrilous or vitriolic attacks on the political establishment. Debatable if considered illustration, its stencil-style renderings, as created by the likes of British 'artist' Banksy, have had a notable influence on aspects of illustration iconography from fashion, graphic novels to editorial work. Most graffiti can be considered visual communication, whether social epigram, political disenchantment, something metaphorical or a statement of celebration. The four examples shown here were all photographed by the author: Figure 1.47 and 1.48 in the Portuguese coastal town of Cascais and Figure 1.49 and 1.50 in Brighton, England. The 'artists' are anonymous. ©Alan Male

1.49

1.50

1.51

1.52

1.51–1.52
Alcoholic drink has for many years provided advertisers with a rich source of material in order to establish some memorable campaigns. Because of alcohol's 'social' connotations and association with various cultural activities, advertisements have used these themes as platforms for promotional narratives, imbued with entertaining copy and imagery. The two examples shown encourage some form of action or engagement with the products in question. The tequila advertisement poses as a machismo myth, as there never were 'worms' either in bottles or put in glasses. It plays on enduring misinformation about enhanced virility and the hallucinations one experiences as a reward for the worm-eating bravery, the worm in question being an innocuous Mexican moth larva. The Fernet-Branca poster, which was photographed by the author, was made of metal and screwed to the wall of a bar in Cadiz, Spain. Its colourful, 'party time' message goes beyond pouring generous quantities of the liqueur into a glass; like many alcohol advertisements from this era, it relies largely on the voluptuous invitation of a glamorous female host (or barmaid) to draw in would-be male customers. These examples date from the 1970s and are typical of their time and place; the illustration styles are playful and commercial and would have been used across the vast gamut of promotions and the media. Also, illustrators at that time were considered as 'commercial artists', and all-rounders would have produced the illustrations, the design and the typography. 1.51 Courtesy Fratelli Branco Milan; 1.52 Public Domain

1.53

1.53

Gothic imagery has pervaded contemporary culture for several decades, by giving identity to the heavy-metal bands of the 1970s and subsequent rock genre by establishing a subculture of fashion, style and attitude; devising a vast range of consumer products, from interior decoration to artefacts; and recognizing its vast contribution to the world of fiction, film and art. There are Gothic influences throughout modern society, with its centuries-old literary and cultural traditions firmly embedded within the conscious and subconscious of peoples across Europe, North America and elsewhere. It is ubiquitous and encountered frequently, sometimes covertly, often overtly and not appreciated by everyone: 'it walks a narrow line between comfort and outrage, mass popularity and cult appeal, the grotesque and the incorporeal, authentic self expression and camp performance' (Caroline Spooner, *Contemporary Gothic* Reaktion Books, 2006). There are many illustrators who stylistically focus entirely on this genre and have done so for years. The *Dungeons and Dragons* stories, usually classed as fantasy yet firmly embedded in Gothic origins, are a popular choice of specialism for many illustrators. Similarly, traditional horror stories – about vampires, werewolves, zombies and other such legends – have also been favoured by illustrators since these 'death-dealing' creations first appeared in the nineteenth century. This illustration is typical of the iconography and content associated with Gothic-style illustration and was designed and produced by **Billelis**. ©Billy Bogiatzoglou

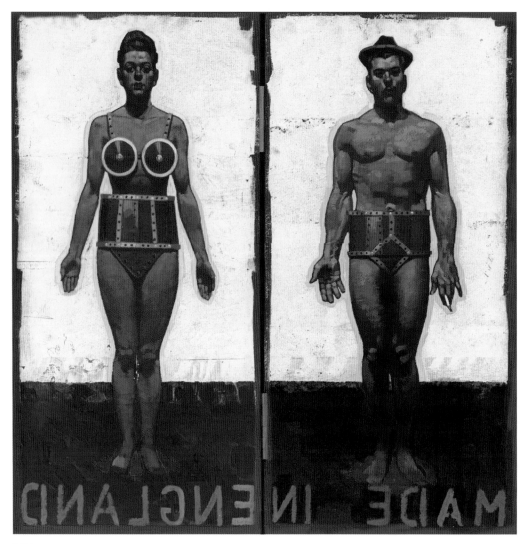

1.54

1.54
Twenty-first-century illustration continues to reflect attitudes, perceptions, culture and society in basically the same manner as times gone by. The principal differences are the issues and themes commented upon, promoted, transcribed into fiction or presented as new knowledge, and the appropriation of visual language. This illustration, entitled *This Is England*, is by **Paul Slater** and is stylistically couched in a form of 'painterly realism', a representational style that has been used by illustrators for centuries. Yet Slater uses his trademark iconography often in an unnerving and original manner to present scurrilous humour, absurd and entertaining narratives and editorial reviews. His subject matter has been described as risqué and a challenge to aspects of political correctness; some illustrations are a distinct pastiche of the 'saucy postcard' genre of the 1940s and 1950s, a deliberate slight at some of the prevailing attitudes and mores of contemporary times. ©Paul Slater

1.55

1.55
Today, the context of journalism and commentary has become enriched by reportage illustration. Produced spontaneously on location, the drawings reflect first hand the nature and circumstance of any scenario there to be reported on. The best reportage illustration will convey a narrative of some significance, either by being in a war-zone situation or other challenging environment, by detailing human conditions whatever the surrounding factors might be, or by recording and dispensing experiences related to atmosphere, sense of place and physical dynamics. The drawings go far beyond what can be achieved by photography as they apportion any unnecessary ambience or obstruction and focus on what the illustrator sees as being most poignant and meaningful.

This example is by World Illustration Award winner **Olivier Kugler**. It is part of a thirty-page journal about the plight of working elephants employed in remote logging camps in Laos, Southeast Asia. Kugler collaborated with a veterinary surgeon whilst on location in Laos, and his other work includes reporting on the plight of Syrian refugees in the war-torn Middle East. ©Olivier Kugler

1.56

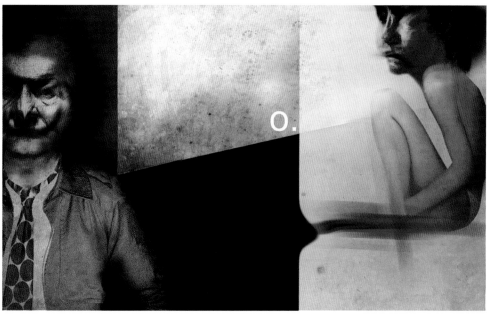

1.57

1.56–1.57
Today, illustration plays all across the world, with audiences of many creeds and cultures having access to a range of disparate and often powerful imagery. Nonetheless, there are considerable variances regarding what is acceptable to one culture and what might be to another, and none more so than the difference between traditional Western-style illustration sometimes labelled as 'Disneyesque', and the European. The Disneyesque, in spite of iconographic semblances to Gothic themes seen in contemporary graphic novels, will in the main be non-threatening and un-explicit regarding content – content that some might regard as taboo. However, the European tradition will be overtly antithetical to this approach; subjects like death, sex, dystopian societal conditions and other challenging topics will be presented without recourse. This concept is also reflected in the iconography employed, a stylization far removed from the ambient and 'soft' visual languages commissioned by Western commercialism. The images shown are part of a book, devised in a graphic novel format, conceived, designed, written and illustrated by **Valentina Brosdean**. Overtly European in style and concept, the book is entitled *Whisper of the Silent Walls*. Brosdean writes, 'Memory of the passed ones that are maybe still with us in the ephemeral form of spirits, ghosts, protectors or just in limbo'. Figure 1.56 is entitled *Leftovers* and Figure 1.57 is *Rape Me Again*. ©Valentina Brosdean

1.58

In terms of the subject and message conveyed, this illustration reflects an important juncture in history. Commenting on the outcome of the United States presidential election, November 2016, this illustration was conceived and drawn by **Benedetto Cristofani**. The context for the image is one that will continue to provide uncompromising journalistic opinion and satire. Political controversies and ideological conflict create a context that has throughout the centuries been a platform for illustration to exert its true power and influence. ©Benedetto Cristofani

1.58

2
THE LANGUAGE OF DRAWING

Identity and Iconography

Today, the term *iconography* represents an important aspect of genre throughout visual media, from illustration, photography, and graphic design to fine art, film and computer games. But what is its etymology and provenance? And, contemporaneously, what is its metier and significance in relation to the work of an individual illustrator?

ICONOGRAPHIC ORIGINS AND THE RECOGNITION OF STYLE

Iconography is sourced from the ancient Greek *eikōn* or 'likeness' and *graphia* meaning 'writing'. However, we must jump forward to the sixteenth century for the earliest known reference that cites the term *iconography*. This was a published catalogue for illustrators comprising facsimiles of paintings, symbols and emblems inspired by literature. Entitled *Iconolgia*, it was compiled by the Italian art historian Cesare Ripa. Illustrators who were commissioned by the Church would often refer to books such as this and observe the pictorial compositions, colours and character representations that the original old master artists painted because they conveyed the most significant meaning to ordinary people. These 'meaningful' images assumed an *iconic* status. Shortly after, the word *icon* became another derivation of *iconography* and was used extensively to define the visual traditions of culture; it is still associated with religious symbolism all over the world.

2.1

2.2

2.1 and 2.2

The term *icon* is often given for religious symbolism and various other forms of narrative imagery associated with faith. It is ubiquitous around the world, particularly in places of worship associated with Christianity, Islam and Judaism. The two examples, photographed by the author, are medieval in milieu and depict differing styles in representing the human form and their meaning.

Figure 2.1 is a stained-glass window detail, found in the porch entrance of St Mary's Anglican Church, Burnham Deepdale, Norfolk, England. Its iconography and message are slightly pagan; there is a deconstructed human form and the face representing the moon with the words *death is thy sting* imbued in the decorative lower section of the image. ©Alan Male

Figure 2.2 is a delineation of St Francis, and found in the Anglican Parish Church of St Andrew, Jevington, East Sussex, England. Although produced for a local family circa 1900, the iconography is distinctly early medieval. The church itself is ancient, its foundation being Saxon, with the tower dating from the ninth century. ©Alan Male

2.3

In more recent times, *iconography* is used to describe 'the science of identification, description, classification and interpretation of symbols, themes and subject matter in the visual arts'. Nevertheless, this formal definition is still some way from how it correlates with contemporary illustration practice, or any other medium of visual communication. Here, the meaning becomes focussed and more defined as 'visual language' or more commonly, *style*. Style is the feature or quality that determines what kind of illustration one is associated with; it is an illustrator's professional *identity*. It should also define the illustrator's placement within a genre, trend, cult or movement, but not necessarily a context of practice or subject matter. An illustrator's iconography determines the 'look' and not one's field of operation such as advertising, children's literature or journalistic commentary – it is to do with the language of mark making.

2.4

2.3 and 2.4

In the main, illustrators will have a distinctive style or variety of styles, prevalent throughout most of their work. It defines their professional identity and will be *known* – or become known, in the case of emergent practitioners – as their trademark. It is the essence of a personal visual language or iconography. Styles will vary considerably from one illustrator to another, facilitating considerable choice for those personnel within the creative and communication industries that commission contextualized imagery.

Figure 2.3 is by **Scott Balmer**, here utilizing his hallmark iconography to give identity and representation for the Steven King novel *It*. Containing representative features of various characterizations such as the clown and the giant spider, the overall image is a symmetrical composite, forming a humorous, yet unnerving and uncompromising visage of Gothic-style monstrosity, appropriate for the supernatural aspect of the story. ©Scott Balmer

Figure 2.4 is a fantastical and contemporaneously original representation of Batman, the fictional character best known for his appearances in numerous television adaptions, Hollywood movies and the great many comic strips that bear his name. This illustration, conceived and created by **Dexter Maurer**, is stylistically far from the heroically dramatic graphic-novel style. It goes some way to 'downgrade' Batman's hero status, his trademark sleek, futuristic super-speed car replaced by a *steampunk* velocipede. In reality, the frivolity of this image makes our superhero look rather inane and witless. The iconography is distinctive and innovative in both visual characterization and narrative content. ©Dexter Maurer

'NOISE' AND VISUAL INTELLIGENCE

An illustrator's style, whatever subject or context it is being used for, should evoke an emotive reaction in the viewer. Either by uncompromising, forthright messaging or by quiet, reflective understatement, the audience must be affected accordingly. This can be achieved by using visual literacy and image articulation to convey warmth and coldness, colour harmony or discord, cheer or discomfort, which in turn can facilitate temperament and mood. Messages are borne by a visual 'noise' charged within the image. This 'noise' is directly associated with sensory recognition and emotion, the 'look' of the image impacting directly on human subjectivity and personal preferences. The best illustration will always invoke a psychological trigger point.

The vagaries of mark making do in some part determine iconography. A style that relies on spontaneous and aggressive autography can give an image the 'fire' required to evoke audience reaction. However, a naively produced illustration may suggest a lack of *visual intelligence* shown through poor drawing and inappropriate choices made regarding colour, composition, and pictorial or conceptual elements and subjects. There also seems to be certain ambiguity when visual intelligence is recognized and associated with an image. Perhaps it can be seen as identifiable maturity. Experience, visual sophistication and contextual understanding are all important criteria to consider when making these judgements.

THE REPRESENTATIONAL AND THE CONCEPTUAL

What are the distinguishing features that differentiate one style from another? Basically there are only two forms of imagery irrespective of subject matter, message, medium, technique or means of production. All variations of visual language will be placed within one of these. *Representational* illustration tends to convey believable reality and will broadly emphasize pictorial or literal truth. Even if the image depicts narrative fiction of a dramatic or fantastical nature, the accent is on creating a scene that is credible. This might mean the portrayal of 'real space' such as a vista with plausible perspective and figures having viable interrelated dimensions. Examples of visual language can vary from hyperrealism (which can be rendered digitally or by traditional drawing methods) to painterly, impressionistic or decorative approaches. Many children's book illustrations will come into the representational category because the images will often convey scenic believability, even though they might be wildly distorted in terms of character depiction; the informal and free-rendering stylization produced by luminaries like Quentin Blake to the anthropomorphism of *Rupert Bear* are typical examples. In terms of context and message, representational illustration is often used to convey a sustainable basis for exerting power and influence: in the immediacy of character recognition, brand identity, or a sequence of 'gripping, action packed fiction'; in well-known politicians controversially 'cut down to size' in a news media 'cartoon'; in a ubiquitous household product sold internationally; or in the contents of an emotive and contentious new computer game produced strictly for an adult audience.

The second form of illustration is the *anti-literal*, which is stylistically abstruse, un-pictorial and free from representation. These are illustrations that purport to convey *concept* as opposed to the literal; they can have an allegorical or metaphorical application to a subject and depict ideas or theories. Often called *conceptual*, they are images that sometimes contain elements of *hyperrealism*, with hyperreal components free-floating within a surreal concept. A conceptual illustration can also be a diagram, an illustrated map or an information graphic. The surrealist artist and sometime illustrator Rene Magritte has been a considerable influence on those whose iconography is described as 'conceptual'. Today, we see many illustrations contained within magazines and other such publications that comment and critique themes like the economy, politics, sport, entertainment, science and discovery – for instance, ladders with little businessmen climbing up to the clouds, unnerving juxtapositions of religious symbols and artefacts composed within a warfare scenario, or a composite of biologically unrelated creatures forming one outlandish chimera designed to comment on 'unnatural' human interference. These examples relate directly to the surreal, but the anti-literal can also comprise images considered abstract or having extreme distortion.

DIVERSITY AND UTILIZATION

With regards to contemporary practice, it can be broadly agreed upon that such is the versatility of illustration regarding the breadth of visual language that it can depict anything and in any style. However, it is important to regard that stylization has to be appropriate for the subject matter, for the context of operation and to ensure a considered receptivity for the audience. Illustration practice is individualistic regarding visual language and there can be far-reaching and challenging aspects to one's style, often to the point of utilizing more than one. An important caveat to consider is that in the business and professional practice environment, many illustrators' representatives and agents will insist on promoting one style, preferring to categorize, codify and brand individuals, claiming it is easier to sell and promote an illustrator's work this way. However, this practice does little to facilitate recognition for an illustrator's wider abilities, which often includes working with a variety of styles. The specificity given for an individual's genre association goes much further than commercial order and commission. Many well-known illustration 'grandees' and acclaimed practitioners are famed for their styles: it is their distinctive iconography that gives them celebrity status. For example, *Ralph Steadman* is renowned for his wildly distorted caricatures and explicit, violent scenarios with splattered red ink as blood. *Quentin Blake* is a 'people's favourite' with his whimsical figures and 'charming' narrative interpretations. *Marshall Arisman* is known for his expressionistic, characteristically dark and menacing depictions. *Sarah Beetson*'s ultra-contemporary fashion illustrations are imbued with their trademark extravagant use of colour and flamboyant drawing style. World Illustration Award winner (2015) *Olivier Kugler*'s reportage drawings convey the personal, war-torn tragedies of inhabitants in the Middle East. *Shirley Hughes*, much decorated children's illustrator and author, has been awarded the Kate Greenaway Medal twice and has sold nearly 12 million copies of her books. *Shaun Tan* has a unique and individual style that is often dreamlike and surreal; his work has been described as 'banal and uncanny, familiar and strange, local and universal, reassuring and scary, intimate and remote. No

rhetoric, no straining for effect, never other than itself'. There are many other influential illustrators, such as *Dave McKean*, *Sara Fanelli*, *John Vernon Lord*, *Brad Holland*, *Martin Rowson*, the *Brothers Quay*, *Gerald Scarfe*, *Bernie Fuchs* and *Milton Glaser*, not to mention the late *Edward Gorey*, *Mary Blair*, *Beatrix Potter*, *Dean Cornwell*, *Tom Lovell* and *N. C. Wyeth*, all having international reputations, their work lauded for its authority, originality and visual distinctiveness.

The effect and influence on the development and professional character of many illustrators, particularly students, can be attributed to the cult of celebrity and style. This need not be a negative issue as most successful illustrators and artists will acknowledge their influences. However, it is known that in a few North American art schools and universities, studio teaching manifests as 'technical, rendering instruction', with students painstakingly copying their 'instructor's' work down to the last brushstroke. Whilst it is acceptable and often beneficial for students to be influenced by their tutors, encouragement for advanced and original approaches to problem solving through deep learning and critical study must prevail regarding one's creative and intellectual growth. It is unfortunate that some illustration tutors place importance on the superficiality of visual language and the commercial constraints placed upon it to conform to trends and fashion. In education, the student illustrator is often under pressure to 'break new ground' and push the boundaries of the discipline. This usually means the production of so-called innovative mark making that in reality does nothing to consider the real business of illustration. An illustrator's iconography should be symbiotic *with* and embedded *in* the theme and nature of the message to be communicated, whether fictional narrative, hard-sell advertising, knowledge bearing or journalistic comment.

AESTHETICS VERSUS NON-AESTHETICS

Visual language and personal iconography cannot escape the question of aesthetics or non-aesthetics. The term *aesthetics* is often used sweepingly when dealing with questions or judgements related to personal taste or 'beauty'. It must be said that if one is challenged to

2.5

2.7

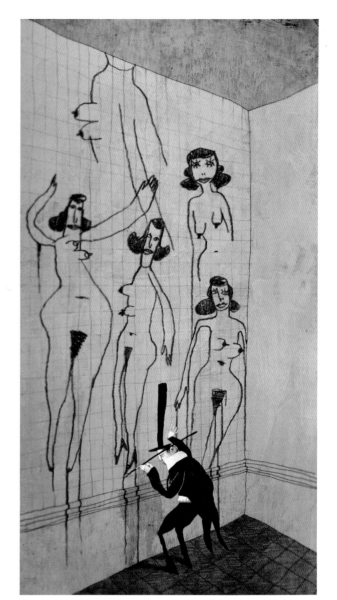

2.6

2.8

2.5
This is an image of great compositional intensity appropriating dozens of individual constituent parts to construct one giant element. Entitled *The Ever Changing Face of Bali* and produced by Balinese artist **I Gede Widyantara**, the painting, which was rendered traditionally and generically associated with the Batuan style of art, displays considerable visual intelligence. The drawings also show exquisite draughtsmanship and a defined visual characterisation for the figures interacting within its border. ©I Gede Widyantara

2.6
Representational illustration, in other words, that which conveys some sense of pictorial believability, can take many forms. It is usually associated with – and widely thought of as – *hyperrealism*, where the illustrator attempts to present an image of intense truth and visual actuality. However, perceptible credibility can take many forms, and in this instance, the illustration shown delivers a humorous exposé on how to draw, academically and objectively, by attending a life class! The narrative shown can be perceived in several ways, each in accordance with what one thinks, or would like it to be. Might the character be visually impaired, thus producing anatomically inaccurate drawings? Or might he be a perverted deviant, deliberately distorting his figures so as to display an exaggerated and inappropriate sexuality? Or might he be intentionally provocative by drawing on the walls of the studio, thus seeking mirth and collaborative amusement from his fellow 'art students'? Or might he be just 'very bad at drawing'? The illustration is by **Mr Alan Clarke**. ©Mr Alan Clarke

2.7
Believable realism or contrivance? This image is by **Maria Svarbova**, a Slovakia-based International Photography Award winner, 2016. Svarbova is critically acclaimed and has been commissioned many times by clients from all over the world. Her work evokes an ethereal stillness and a cool detachment, often representing themes and narratives that emulate some form of liminal transition. Distinctly representational, the image conveys aspects of hyperrealism, yet is decidedly surreal. A photograph (from the Greek – '*drawing* with light'), it could easily have been rendered exactly as shown by a variety of autographic (from the English – '*drawing* with the hand') techniques using opaque painting media like oils, acrylic or watercolour. ©Maria Svarbova

2.8
This country kitchen has been imagined and visually brought to life by **Briony May Smith**. It would be literally and physically impossible to 'stage manage' a live set with actual props and capture by photography the whimsy, character and quirkiness conveyed by this drawing. The spontaneity and informality, as engendered by the almost sketchbook-like approach, give the image and the iconography of the illustrator a milieu of its own – in spite of its traditional approach to pictorial representation. Compositionally, the illustration superbly conveys real space, inviting the eye to roam at random, detecting half-hidden tasty morsels, artefacts and many other rustic temptations. ©Briony May Smith

provide comment or communicate about something out of the ordinary and not considered aesthetically pleasing, then 'soft messaging' will not do; any notion of *ambient imaging* should be immediately discarded. The most felicitous of illustration delivering genuine and accountable power and influence is that which is 'noticed'. However, there is often a requirement to depict subject matter that is unchallenging and un-provocative with messages that are overtly sentimental, mawkish and trite, especially within advertising and packaging. Visually, much of what could be considered devoid of 'intelligent' aesthetics is a combination of either pictorial or composite hyperreality with distortions of an impressible or sentimentalized nature. The essence of this is more to do with content and subject matter and how it is portrayed. A list of product examples providing these subjects might comprise confectionary, pet food, younger children's toys, travel, and vacation destinations. The main aim would be to play on the desiring, pleasurable, sensory, emotive and even hedonistic senses. However, it is not the visual language that comes into question but the actual subject matter: 'doleful, wide-eyed children', 'cuddly kittens and puppies', cream-laden cookies and pies are themes that many illustrators would prefer not to undertake if wishing to transcend the level of unadulterated, commercial amorality. Much of this type of work pervades the promotional pages of illustrators' agents and representatives' books and websites, suggesting that there is a solid commercial need. However, some visual arts practitioners remain contemptuous, and even within the curriculum of the most commercially minded and vocational illustration courses, it is a style not usually encouraged. Separate the philosophies and ambitions of certain practising or would-be practising illustrators and isolate the 'chocolate box' nature of the imagery and critique objectively. As it has been said before, the most successful illustrations invoke a required response in one's prescribed audience. Therefore, if the product sells, then in some part it must be effective and 'good' illustration. Can it be assumed that in this context, illustration might be exerting a smidgen of power and influence?

WESTERNIZATION OR THE EUROPEAN TRADITION

There is also the issue of global iconographic influence. There are two streams of influence providing both a visually stylistic lead and a cultural and contextual one: the *Disneyesque* and the *European*. It could be argued that the majority of illustration both contemporaneously and historically will fall loosely into one of these categories. What is meant by this, and are there any known or unseen consequences? The Disneyesque style is remarkably ubiquitous and largely represents all that is overtly Westernized in culture and creed, with advertising, entertainment and a vast amount of illustrated literature from comics, graphic novels and children's books suitably categorized here. But the Disney brand itself has its own distinct iconography in that original 'cartoon' style of comic distortion, anthropomorphism and caricature rendered with strong, flat colour and continuous black line – think Mickey Mouse and more laterally the Lion King! Then analyse the essence and character of most other 'branded' entertainment products and observe the flavour and depictions of all the elements contained within the imagery: upbeat 'major key' representations of figures and scenarios, with an economy of detail and zero subtlety. Even in Roger Hargreaves' *Mr Men*, overtly British in substance and tone and one of the most commercially successful anthologies of books for young children ever produced, the visual language employed is distinctly Disneyesque. The power and influence of all things Disney from the 1930s right up to this day is truly remarkable.

What of the European approach? How might this manifest, and what are the distinguishing visual features? In the context of narrative fiction, this approach will present the antithesis of Disneyesque characterization, with its lightweight sentimentality, plots and scenarios and banal approaches to entertainment. The *European* embodies a much deeper and more sensitive working with subject matter and narrative, often characterized by a challenging and complex visual styling that pushes the boundaries of acceptability either regarding content or by evoking much deeper interpretation. Some illustrators associated with this style will produce work designated 'Gothic' or as *dystopian surrealism*. Sometimes pictorially representational, sometimes anti-literal, it will be charged with much visual detail depicting narratives that are thematically demanding and reminiscent of any Hieronymous Bosch interpretation of Hell. Another influence will be the work of the Polish artist Zdzislaw Bedsinski.

Many illustrators of this genre will subscribe to a more percipient and sensitive working with subject matter and narrative. Some of this is borne out of the Hans Christian Andersen tradition and will evoke emotive and exacting diagnoses. Illustrators, particularly those from Eastern Europe who work within this domain and focus on children's literature, are often unafraid to depict themes or issues related to human suffering or desire such as sex, death, family and societal problems. Approached with a sensitive and appropriate visual treatment such as an economy of explicitness, the needs of the intended audience are paramount.

When European iconography is used to depict humankind, vistas, environments and other elements, it is immediately distinguishable from its 'Western' counterpart. Whilst certain Western characters are given a strong and recognizable identity, such as those featured in *The Simpsons*, *Family Guy*, *The Flintstones* and even *Mr Men*, their personality is secured by the spoken or printed word and by the strength and immediacy of the characterful, yet intellectually undemanding and 'lightweight' narrative. Also, the traditional Western representation of a 'bad' personality is depicted as non-threatening and comedic, as shown by the animated characters Dick Dastardly or Walt Disney's Witch in *Snow White*. This would not be the case regarding European-style illustration. Messages and stories are delivered through complex visualization and highly discernable and varied characterization with an uncompromising approach for the humorous, the endearing, the frightening or the deeply disturbing. The characters shown will often invite deep analysis through a sequence of illustrations that will convey a full range of meaningful and interpretive gestures, physical postures, dramatic interactions and behaviours.

COPYRIGHT AND OWNERSHIP

There are often dilemmas confronting the illustrator: does the practitioner with a defined, recognizable style compromise in order to strengthen the impact or relevance of a message? It immediately raises the issue of a possible conflict regarding the commissioning process; a commercially generated brief would have been prescribed by a client or art director, who will have been seduced by one's style and would expect no deviation from it. Also, artworks are often based on or inspired by the work of others. It has been said that there is no such thing as an entirely original work and that all visual art owes a debt to the work that has gone before. At the same time, illustrators will often invest much time and effort into developing a distinctive style of work and will feel proprietorial about it. What protection does the law of *copyright* offer the illustrator?

There has been controversy in recent years over whether or not copyright protects an actual image, the style or treatment that produced the image or the idea expressed and embedded within the image. The question has caused consternation across the media and creative community, no less in the United States. A recent decision of the Full Federal Court reaffirmed 'the fundamental legal principle that copyright does not protect ideas and concepts but only the particular form in which they are expressed'. The effect of this principle is that you cannot copyright a style or a technique. Copyright only protects the originator of the image from someone else reproducing an illustration or painstakingly copying it down to the last detail and not from producing work in the same style.

2.9

2.10

2.11

2.9, 2.10 and 2.11
These are three illustrations, produced as traditional engravings and drawn in a figuratively representational manner by the Polish illustrator **Piotr Naszarkowski**. They are collectively known as *ex libris*, or 'from the books', and function as an inscription on a bookplate to reveal the identity of the book's owner, the content and design indicative of the 'taste' and interests of the bibliophile in question. Distinctly erotic in theme, the images are perceptibly European. Stylistically, it is an iconography strongly associated with Naszarkowski, a highly acclaimed illustrator who now lives in Sweden. In the past, he has designed and illustrated a great variety of subjects for a diverse range of clients, including stamps for Sweden's postal service. ©Piotr Naszarkowski

2.12
The design of a book cover works as product identity, the illustrator or designer mindful of marketing and retail point-of-sale functionality. However, and most importantly, the design should be evocative and consistent with the book's theme. This example uncompromisingly does just that! The image grates and tremors; it emanates a visual 'noise', charged with the discordant and uncomfortable narrative expounded between its covers. The illustration was conceived and produced by **Lola Dupre**. ©Lola Dupre

2.12

2.13

2.14

2.13
Although metaphorical in concept, this image by Milan-based illustrator **Chiara Ghigliazza** is compellingly simplistic; there is an immediacy regarding its message, the image charged with meaning and symbolic 'noise', clearly reflecting its editorial theme, *Feeding the Planet*. ©Chiara Ghigliazza

2.14
This is an illustration by **Richard Borge** and was conceived to accompany an editorial article commissioned by the *Washington Post* entitled *Fighting the Mosquito Curbs Malaria*. The style employed projects a visual 'noise' imbued with aggression, highlighting the reputation and apprehensive disquiet associated with malaria-carrying mosquitoes. The vivid colours, extreme tonal contrasts and the angry, boorish and unrestrained textures are facilitated by the 'thematically appropriate accessories' that both 'arm' and 'decorate' the insect. ©Richard Borge

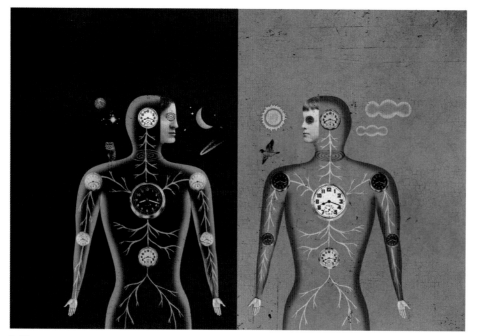

2.15

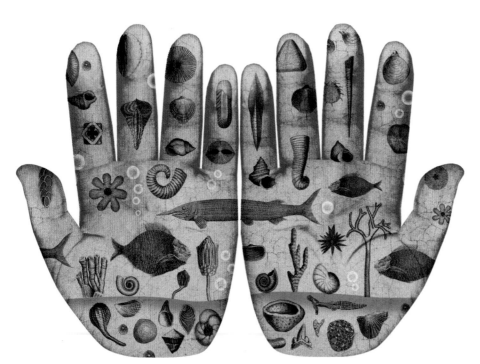

2.16

2.15 and 2.16
These images are conceptual; they have been conceived, designed and produced by illustrator **David Plunkert**, whose company, Spur Design, is based in Baltimore, Maryland, USA. Figure 2.15 is entitled *Night Person or Day Person*, and figure 2.16 is called *Have microfossils will time travel*. Both were commissioned as editorial illustrations for *Scene Magazine*. Stylistically, they represent the *anti-literal* but are not abstract: the message being communicated is immediately understood and all aspects of these composite collages are easily identifiable – the fossils could have been extracted from a textbook about palaeontology. Plunkert has won many prestigious awards. ©David Plunkert

2.17 and 2.18
Ori Tor is an illustrator based in Tel Aviv, Israel. These figures are from a series of works entitled *Gibberish Worlds*. Tor describes his work as 'abstract free style', a process that relies on total improvisation, finished artworks manifesting without any preliminary sketching or planning. Whilst abstract in visual language, certain themes and narratives can be readily detectable by the representational nature of elements within, facilitated by meticulous and tightly controlled digital rendering. ©Ori Tor

2.19 and 2.20
The versatility of Illustration is such that it will convey anything and in any visual language that is appropriate. These figures were created by Chilean illustrator **Matias Santa Maria**, whose working context comprises an eclectic mix of themes such as science fiction, fantastical landscapes and outlandish, enigmatic scenarios with unnervingly distorted characterizations and perspectives. ©Matais Santa Maria

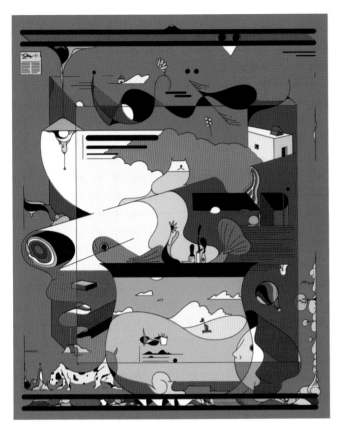

2.17

2.18

2.19

2.20

2.21

2.22

2.21

Anna and Elena Balbusso are illustrators based in Milan, Italy. They have illustrated more than forty books and won more than sixty prestigious international awards. Their style is highly contemporary, imbued with considerable meaning and symbolism, often underpinning dark and enigmatic narratives, yet evocatively compelling. This image was commissioned for Tor.com and accompanies a contemporary fairy tale by Veronica Schanoes entitled *Ballroom Blitz*. The story tells of twelve brothers, cursed to remain in a rock club for bad behaviour; their only chance of freedom would be for twelve sisters to enter the club at the same time. ©Anna+Elena Balbusso

2.22 and 2.23

Diversity and utilization is often best exemplified when the work of the same illustrator is featured. These two images are by Italian illustrator **Chiara Dattola**. Whilst both are editorials, subject matter and concept could not be more diverse. There is also a difference in visual language. Figure 2.23 accompanies an article about mosquito-borne Zika fever and was commissioned by *Internazionale* magazine. Figure 2.22 was inspired by concepts of the matriarch. Rich in meaning and visual detail, the overall illustration does well to convey a sense of matriarchal authority and responsibility, along with a sense of humility, grace and altruism. ©Chiara Dattola

2.24

This illustration is entitled *The Planets of Unfailure* and was conceived and produced by London-based illustrator and artist **Paul Davis**. First published in the *Drawbridge* and latterly for sale as a limited edition print, the image is a poignant commentary regarding humankind's woeful custodianship of planet Earth. The inference is 'how wonderful and successful other planets might be compared with what the **** has become of our beloved Earth due to humans' failure to protect it'. ©Paul Davis

2.23

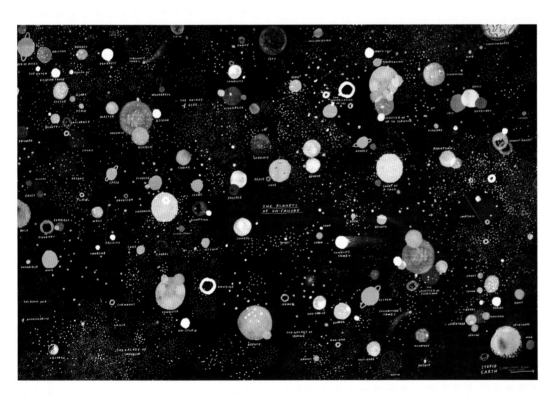

2.24

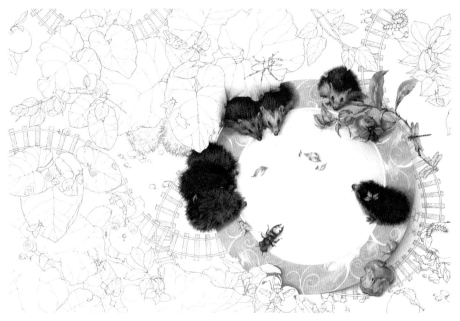

2.25

2.26

2.25
The question of aesthetics is one that not only challenges illustrators and artists, but also perplexes people across the cultural and demographic divide. What actually constitutes good taste, and how appropriate is it for illustrators to abandon the notion of using it when representing something considered distasteful? However, the contents of this illustration would *not* be considered distasteful. Designed and produced by Ukrainian illustrator and artist **Slava Shults**, it is from her children's book entitled *Tashenka and Cactus*, originally published by Astra Publishing, Kharkiv. The book is interactive and invites its young audience to colour in the blank linear sections and thus complete the story. The original artwork was rendered in graphite and coloured pencil. Whilst not to everyone's taste, a more intellectually discerning viewer might consider the visual language somewhat 'chocolate box'. However, there is no denying that in the broad spectrum of contextualized imagery, this illustration would be thought of as being 'orthodox aesthetic'. ©Slava Shults

2.26
This image is from China. Attributed to **Suen Jie**, it was first published in 2005. Upon first viewing, one could be forgiven thinking it might have originated from Europe or the UK. Whilst the drawing style is delicate, with a sensitive line and brush appropriation – as was typical in Chinese art prior to the Cultural Revolution – the aesthetic does *not* evoke any real sense of the Orient, either artistically or in subject matter: the figure looks distinctly Western. However, in recent years China has opened its borders to the world, engaged in international trade and allowed Western goods and culture to be evident within its society. Could it be that what might be considered aesthetic and having 'good taste' in the West could now be likewise in China? ©Suen Jie

2.27

In contrast to the preceding figure, this image could be considered the antithesis of good drawing. **Paul Davis** deliberately abandons any notion of 'good taste' and 'academic' drawing ability in order to decry fashion house Giorgio Armani. The crudely drawn, grimacing face is the antonym of accepted 'beauty'! ©Paul Davis

2.28

Many people would describe this image as decidedly un-aesthetic. However, its production is founded on exceptional drawing skill and the highest level of finish; the hyperrealism imbued in its textures, colours and form give the subject an animate life. But, the nature of the subject matter will incite feelings of repulsion in many people, and some will say 'that is the general idea, after all, it is meant to be a hideous, misshapen monster'. It was created by **Simon Dubuc**, a concept artist who is based in Pasadena, California, USA. Entitled *Mother Mallory and Her Ascended Form*, this is a character created for a role-playing game (RPG) called *Rise*. ©Simon Dubuc

GIORGIO ARMANI

2.27

2.28

2.29

2.30

2.29 and 2.30
These two illustrations by American illustrator **Jaime Anderson** are stylistically representative of what can be broadly described as the Western tradition for visual language: uncompromisingly straightforward in composition and characterization and produced using the ubiquitous and humorous comic book style. This is an extremely versatile iconography, seen across children's books, editorials and advertising. In this instance, the illustrations are expressing opinion about the American Constitution. Commissioned by MinnPost.com, they accompany an article entitled 'Imperfect Union: Constitutional Roots of the Mess We're In'. Figure 2.29 relates to the Electoral College and figure 2.30 to the two-party system. Incidentally, it was nineteenth-century American illustrator Thomas Nast who devised the donkey and elephant 'mascots' for the Democratic and Republican Parties. ©Jaime Anderson

2.31

2.32

2.31 and 2.32

As a visual language and literary arts genre, the European tradition is an embodiment of the uncanny. It uses dark Gothic and dystopian tales, often conveying messages of hopelessness and negativity – the antithesis of Western lightweight entertainment. These illustrations are from a story called *The Golem* and were written by Gustav Meyrink in 1913. This version was published in 2010 by the Folio Society, with linocut illustrations by Los Angeles–based illustrator **Vladimir Zimakov**. In the ghetto of Prague, artists, students and pawnbrokers eke out a living among the gloomy tenements and mildewed courtyards. Lurking in the inhabitants' subconscious is the Golem, a creature of rabbinical myth. It is a haunting Gothic tale of stolen identity and persecution set in a strange underworld peopled by fantastical creatures. ©Vladimir Zimakov

2.33

2.33 and 2.34
These are from a conceptual project entitled *Whisper of the Silent Walls*, conceived and produced by **Valentina Brosdean**, a Serbian-born multidisciplinary visual artist and illustrator based in Turin, Italy. Brosdean's heritage is clearly evident by the inherent style of these images, far removed from the whimsical and Disneyesque themes imbued in most Western iconography. Figure 2.33 is entitled *Wish you were here* and 2.34 is *Faces of Society*. These illustrations are overtly European in concept and narrative – deeply emotive, sensitive and personal. 'Walls are hiding their stories, invisible walls are between them and us . . . It's all one circle, circle of death and all that you can imagine and put inside while the stone is rolling . . .'
©Valentina Brostean

2.34

Semiotics, Symbolism and Association

Illustration is seen everywhere, yet much of it yields far more than just the signification of something verbatim or unadulterated. To put it simply, many images have a double meaning. Societies have become sophisticated readers of illustration, being able to decode the imagery subconsciously. It is this decoding that reveals how messages being communicated are interpreted in terms of the signs and patterns of symbolism imbued within the illustrations. There is a considerable differentiation between individuals, societies and subgroups regarding how one interprets and understands the essence of an image; it is built on an individual's experience, ideology, culture and expectation. People will often react differently from one another regarding the same visual communication, even within families or circles of common interest such as friendship or vocation. So, how important is this regarding our understanding of the power and influence of illustration?

SIGNS

Semiotics is the study of signs and sign-using behaviour. It can provide insight into the source and meaning of an image and also an analysis of communicative behaviour. The term *sign* conjures up many interpretations as to what it actually is; to many it is a graphic symbol providing information or instruction, or a company logotype or identifier. To others it can mean something much broader: a gesture, intimation or suggestion, evidence, an individual's attitude through body language, kinesics, sounds, even an event. These are generalizations but when applied to illustration practice, the implications are far-reaching and fundamental in achieving the prescribed affect on one's designated audience.

With regards to signs communicated by or through illustration, there are two principal components to consider:

- A sign designated as *signifier*: quite literally, the actual image as seen in its context.
- A sign designated as *signified*: the concept or meaning the signifier represents. The message or thoughts that the sign expresses thus enable the audience to interpret whatever connotations they might imagine or envisage.

The French philosopher and linguist Roland Barthes (1915–1980) once said: 'All images are *polysemous*', and underlying their signifiers is a *'floating chain'* of the *signified*, with the reader able to choose some and ignore others'. He went on to say that 'polysemy [see the glossary] poses a question of meaning and this meaning always comes through as a dysfunction'.

Contemporaneously, Barthes's hypothesis can be interpreted thus: an image can be unfettered by its prescribed context and will allow the imagination to create and conjure up whatever fantasy shock, pleasure or displeasure is suggested. It is this presupposition that enables an illustration to 'fly in the face' of non-arbitrary convention such as literal realism and connive any double entendre, subversion or subtle provocation that one might desire. However, the illustrator might unwittingly and unintentionally produce something that is capricious. A specific example is where a practitioner was commissioned to design and produce a seascape with a contemporary fishing vessel in the foreground. In order to achieve depth of field and to make the scene more interesting, a lighthouse was included in the distance. However, a discourse ensued as to whether or not the illustrator was deliberately symbolizing something phallic.

SYMBOLISM

The theory that underpins signs and symbolism will identify three aspects: the *pragmatic*, *semantic* and *syntactic*. In relation to illustration practice, the pragmatic deals with visual language, its use and the contexts in which it is used. This tends to be a straightforward, objective overview, a denotation of the actual image, its iconography and content, its brief and media placement. The semantic deals specifically with meaning and identifies two strands, the *logical* and the *lexical*. The logical is concerned with sense and reference, presupposition and implication. In other words, this is the contextualized message being imparted by the illustration and the intended impact for its prescribed audience. The lexical will be an analysis of the message and the visual language that imparts it. It will also determine counter-meanings, possible subterfuge, alternative meanings and any relationships that might exist between them. The syntactic deals specifically with visual syntax: an analysis of the construction and depiction of appropriate connections and relationships within elements of illustration and design – in other words, visual literacy. The syntactic will determine an appropriate arrangement of themes and elements within the visual, thus creating well-formed images that communicate effectively and meaningfully.

There can be no doubt that to many illustration practitioners, this theoretical paradigm is common sense; it is often applied when answering a brief and working through the process of image design and production. However, understanding the connotations and potential consequence of having unstated symbolism imbued within an illustration can only help to contrive an alternative narrative, challenge socially accepted criteria and communicate more powerfully and effectively. The power and influence of illustration is often reliant on duplicity, intrigue and persuasion. By the subtle use of symbolism one can go beyond producing the acceptable and recognizably 'good' illustration. The integrity-laden advertisement or the respectful and un-libellous visual commentary can be decontextualized and recast for a different field of knowledge or culture without deviating from the original brief; this can be seen as 'neutralising its *mythical* content'.

Barthes once implied that the way imagery speaks to us is through the *activation of myths*. In other words, 'activation' represents publication or broadcast and the 'myths' contextualized communication such as journalism or advertising. However, this 'communication' will only be 'truthful' to its target audience when applied to the culture from whence it emerged. Semiotics reveals substantial differences regarding the decoding of signs and symbols across a range of cultures, ethnicities and social classes. What might be acceptable to one culture or nationality may be anathema to another. Typically, signals borne by the human hand, such as an upturned thumb, mean something positive in some societies and the opposite elsewhere. Analogies such as this can inspire a vast range of concepts for the illustrator to consider when needing to create tensions, polarize, present controversial ideas and deliberately deceive the audience. This is a strategy often used for hard-hitting promotional or advertising purposes. One such example is a campaign for Amnesty France, which highlighted the plight and brainwashing of children in Third World, war-torn countries: the strapline states, '300,000 child soldiers dream of simply being children'. The image shows children playing, using ropes and the hangman's noose as a swing suspended from a makeshift gallows. Alongside are adult victims of the oppression, their bodies dangling lifeless beside the children, ropes tight around their necks. The power of association or assumed familiarity cannot be underestimated. It is likely that most people would recognize the 'symbol' of the hangman's noose and the children desensitized by the horrors around them; others might see the children as naïve and playing innocently.

INTERPRETATION

The semiotics of signs and symbolism cuts across everything that can be seen and will determine ways in which the human mind can interpret, transpose and recast what is visualized. The shape of a long, curved and pointed blade will immediately remind many people of a sabre or a sword, its association being that of warfare, battle and aggression. However, would anyone associate such shapes, or indeed the vision of the real and material object, with medical and surgical practices, whereby its actual use is for the betterment of the afflicted? For years, surgeons used implements that are identical to those previously used in torture chambers. This is an example of where the symbolism of a negative can be interpreted as a positive.

To conclude, it might be expedient to briefly analyse the context and definition of the term *sign* with regards to semiotics and illustration practice. There are three aspects: icon, symbol and index. An *icon* is signified and its meaning is literal and unambiguous: it represents a pictorial truth in whatever context it might appear. A *symbol* is normally the opposite of an icon and as an image does not represent a pictorial reality. Symbols of a graphic nature will rely on simplistic geometric shapes and strong colour in order to deliver their message or instruction. These representations are used as power symbols: strength, control, influence, rule, supremacy and even energy, as exemplified by the symbolism that was used extensively by autocratic and dictatorial regimes like the Nazis or Soviets. Red

is used frequently as a warning, for example on road signs ordering motorists to stop. More benignly, a map will use a thin, blue, meandering line to represent a river. Symbols are learnt culturally, which explains why some milieus will develop unique traits. The Mars and Venus symbols denoting gender identities will be used extensively throughout the 'Western' world but elsewhere be unknown or take on a totally different meaning. There are many examples such as this, but overall, symbols allow humans to create meaning and decode the mark or sign implied from whatever culture or global location they may be from. Finally, an *index* describes the physical connection between that which is signified and that which is connoted. A communication suggesting literal reality, either by word, sound or image, cannot really exist unless its presence is evidenced by audience reaction through connotation, inspiration or interpretation – in other words, the essence and spirit that is *the power and influence of illustration*.

2.35
The gender-specific signs that are clearly marked on the closed doors as shown in this illustration are obvious and relatable to all, wherever in the world restroom or toilet facilities are designated as discrete for male or female. There is no need for words or any other form of communicable information. However, the scenario depicted in the illustration has deemed it necessary to appropriate these particular signs in order to convey a very determined editorial commentary. The title of this illustration and the article it accompanies is *The Secret Life of a Transgender Airman* and was published by the BBC News Magazine, June 2016. The image is by **Rebecca Hendin**. Transgender people are banned from serving in the US armed forces, yet an estimated 12,800 do. 'Jane, a master sergeant in the Air Force, has hidden her gender identity from the military for 25 years'. ©Rebecca Hendin

2.35

2.36

2.37

2.36
This is a full-page illustration that accompanied an editorial article for the *Sunday Times* (UK). Illustrated by **Patrick George**, the image featured in the 2016 World Illustration awards. A visual concept imbued with connotation, cliché and stereotype, yet still inviting of some interpretation, its remit was to help define the article's subtitle: *Beyond Binary – How to Understand Trans*. The article was written by Nicola Gill. 'First we had Orange is the New Black giving a ground breaking mainstream role to the trans actress Laverne Cox, then we had the androgynously beautiful model, Andreja (formerly Andrej) Pejic, who has modelled both men's and women's clothes with equally sinuous grace, with surprisingly few eyebrows being raised in Middle England'. ©Patrick George

2.37
This is the door of a Freemasons' lodge in the small market town of Langport in Somerset, England. Photographed by the author, it is located at the side of a unique structure called the Hanging Chapel, a medieval building atop a portcullis-type bridge over the road. The silvery, shiny metallic symbol clearly shows the Masonic square and compasses, ubiquitous signage that has given visual identity to Freemasons for centuries. The organization practices its rituals and assemblages in secret, with much intrigue and subterfuge given for their rationale and purpose. This familiar and recognizable icon is synonymous with the guild of Freemasonry. Much more intricate and conceptual imagery will be found as symbols and signs throughout the Masonic Lodge. Many represent the working tools of the medieval or Renaissance stonemason. There are many Masonic jurisdictions across the world, the ritualistic symbolism clearly recognized and identified by both protagonists and the profane. ©Alan Male

2.38

2.39

2.38, 2.39 and 2.40

The human skull has been one of the oldest and most powerful of symbols. Its long and varied history identifies multiple, overlapping interpretations. Since the earliest of times, its principal representation was of death and mortality, ubiquitous in burial grounds and sites of religion and ritual throughout the world. Some of its many explications include that of invoking fear and caution; celebrating the memory of the dead; celebrating life *and* life after death; vanity, machismo, bravery and indifference to danger; and nonconformity, free thinking and rebelliousness. Its presence in literature and entertainment is no less omnipresent, being one of the most potent symbols used in stories, films and the ever-expanding interactive games genre. From Shakespeare's immortal line in Hamlet, 'Alas, poor Yorick' to the heavy-metal rock band Iron Maiden's Gothic style monster mascot Eddie, the skull's potency to evoke drama and a frisson of expectation for the supernatural rarely fails. It is also notoriously associated with Nazism, the SS and the Gestapo using the skull and crossbones insignia as *totemkopf* – 'loyalty until death'. The following were photographed by the author. Figure 2.38 is a skull and crossbones found inside the church Parish of St Anthony of Padua, Cadiz, Spain. Figure 2.39 depicts a symbolic skull embedded with great subtlety into the stonework of an outer wall of St Mary's Parish Church, Bury St Edmonds, England. Figure 2.40 shows a seventeenth-century tomb engraving found on the floor inside the Church of St Mary, Haddiscoe, Norfolk, England. ©Alan Male

2.40

2.41

2.42

2.41 and 2.42

The *swastika* is an ancient religious icon and remains a sacred symbol of spiritual principles in Hinduism, Buddhism and Jainism. It has been found on every continent and appears to have given symbolic identity to rituals, the worship of deities and governance for many peoples and cultures. Its purpose can be exemplified by the original Sanskrit meaning of 'well being'. In Europe it was historically a symbol of auspiciousness and good fortune. However, since the 1930s it has become stigmatized. Today it will induce fear and revulsion, with many people recognizing its association with racism and prejudice, hatred, mass murder and organized genocide. The Nazi Party in Germany adopted the swastika as an emblem for the Aryan race, an icon for white, Nordic supremacy. These figures represent antithetical meanings for its use. Figure 2.41 depicts a swastika embedded in the filigree railings of an entrance to a Hindu temple in the town of Sanur on the island of Bali, Indonesia. Figure 2.42 shows the swastika in a more recognizable context as the flag of Nazi Germany, seen here in the dungeons of Budapest Castle, Hungary; the Gestapo and SS used the site for their regional headquarters during the Second World War. The difference in swastika design may not be immediately apparent, but upon examination it can be seen that the Nazis deliberately inverted the symbol, the reversal of its design thus negating and degrading its original, spiritual meaning. The author took both photographs. ©Alan Male

2.43

2.44

2.43
Symbols have been used for centuries to give identity and recognition to ruling dynasties, social clans, disparate political groups and mainstream political parties, none more so than the early twentieth century in Europe, which witnessed the rise of certain political ideologies resulting in the seizure of power – most notably those of fascism and communism. This led to rule by oppression, tyranny and war, both civil and on a massive, international scale. Arising from the extreme right and left wings of the political spectrum, their 'brand identities' are a reflection of their credo: power, strength and obedience. The hammer and sickle, an example of which is featured here, was originally conceived during the Russian Revolution as a communist symbol, the hammer standing for the industrial labourers and the sickle for the rural peasantry. After the dissolution of the Soviet Union, the hammer and sickle remains commonplace throughout the world, being used predominately for both national and regional communist parties in many countries. This example was photographed by the author on a wall down a back street in Cadiz, Spain.
©Alan Male

2.44
Symbolism will often manifest as visual commentary. By combining recognizable semi-representational elements into a simple graphic construct, it is possible to evoke an immediacy regarding meaning and message. This illustration is by **Hannah Barcyzk**; entitled *Afghanistan Is an Infinite Quagmire*, it was published by *New Republic*.
©Hannah Barcyzk

2.45

2.46

2.45
Although considered conceptual, the symbolic representation conveyed by this illustration does not purport to subtlety. An uncompromising and apposite visual commentary by **Paul Garland**, *The Power of Love over Hate* is from a series of images collectively entitled *Artists and Designers Against War . . . or whatever they call it*. ©Paul Garland

2.46
The interpretation of an image that is symbolic can engender multifarious connotations.

Often, seemingly inoffensive subject matter might in reality be a smokescreen for parody, satire, biting comment or cutting edge humour. Sometimes naivety and innocence lead to ridicule: former British prime minister Margaret Thatcher once famously remarked that 'everyone needs a Willie', referring to her reliance on the deputy prime minister, Willie Whitelaw! That particular example shows how even clichéd and hackneyed utterances can be delivered through blissful ignorance. Transpose this premise to illustration whereby an image is inadvertently decontextualized and understood to mean something completely different from its original intent. This illustration by **Paul Garland** fits easily into that category. To some, it will be a cactus – but to the 'initiated' amongst Garland's intended audience, it will interpret humorously as *Prick*, the image's formal title! ©Paul Garland

2.47
Pictorial and narrative in essence, this highly conceptual illustration was designed and produced by **Chiara Ghigliazza**. Its theme is *Alzheimer Prevention* and it was published by *La Repubicca*. The message purports that interventions like 'brain training' – in other words, undertaking tasks requiring mental agility and stimulation – can improve cognition over short periods. However, research has not yet demonstrated whether this can prevent dementia in the long term. ©Chiara Ghigliazza

2.48 and 2.49

In 2017, McDonald's were identified as the largest fast-food burger chain in the world. Their brand identity is immediately recognizable, the logotype developed as a simplistic letterform along with its accompanying trend-infused strapline 'I'm lovin' it'. The two illustrations featured here present divergent messages, yet both are incompatible with the original brand identity.

2.48

This editorial comment illustrated by **Benedetto Cristofani** is entitled *The Attractive Power of a Brand*. Its use of the McDonald's logo needs no explanation regarding the message being conveyed.
©Benedetto Cristofani

2.49

An illustration by **Paul Davis**, who presents a disparaging and pointed commentary using the McDonald's icon as a vehicle to express an opinion that 'Advertising is the Rattling of a Stick Inside a Small Bucket!'
©Paul Davis

2.47

2.48

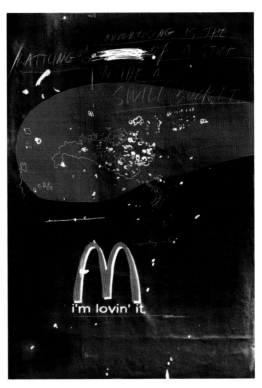

2.49

Allegory, Metaphor and Paradigm

One of the most effective and powerful forms of illustration is that which utilizes *analogical juxtaposition* in order to strengthen an argument, intensify emotion, deceive, clarify ambiguity and willingly confound and entertain. What is meant by analogical juxtaposition? An analogy is a comparison between two things that have similar features and is a way to explain a principle or an idea. Juxtaposition defines placing those two things (or variables) side by side, their contrast or similarity shown through comparison. By juxtaposing two objects – and in the context of illustration, specific key features contained within the composition – the human brain will automatically associate or transfer meaning, often by turning something familiar into something *less* familiar or vice versa. The use of analogy, the cognitive process of transferring information from an original *source* to another subject or *target*, plays a significant role in problem solving, decision making, perception, memory, creativity, emotion, explanation and communication; these are all key aspects related to illustration practice. Analogy is behind basic tasks such as the identification of objects, places and people; face perceptibility and recognition are important characteristics and facilitate the creation of both standard portraiture and caricature. Analogy is the core of cognition and is embedded in allegory, metaphor, comparison, exemplification, simile and parable.

DEFINING IMPACT

The practice of expressing ideas rather than verbatim 'scenes' or 'pictures' has meant that *conceptual* illustration is now the dominant visual language. This can be challenging for some illustrators. If one's style is dominated by ambient figurative realism, it could be considered as being *contextually superficial* – in other words, only suitable for messages or subjects that require no more than a 'veneer' or 'surface' representation, or what some might disingenuously call 'chocolate box'. Conceptual illustration, whatever its genre of stylization – from the representational, such as the presentation of new knowledge related to scientific discovery, to the anti-literal, where the need might be to convey abstract or symbolic meaning – will be interpretative and present the 'texture' of a topic and delve deep into its explication. It will present illusion, be enigmatic, convey fresh ideas and define impact for its audience as opposed to unadulterated ambience. It will be broadly conceived through analogical juxtaposition, with an emphasis on *allegory* and *metaphor*.

A message can be interpreted in many ways, by being *literal* or *allegorical*. In a literal context, there is no hidden meaning or symbolism. However, the allegorical will often present a figurative or obvious treatment of one subject that is under the guise of something else. Typical examples could emerge from both classic literature and science. In George Orwell's novel *Animal Farm*, the farm represents the old Soviet Union and the pigs are the megalomaniac communist leaders, who in turn oppress and subjugate the people, as represented by the other farm animals. The story of the apple falling on Isaac Newton's head made the scientific revelation of gravity well known by condensing the theory into a short, entertaining tale. These are simple and obvious examples. With regards to illustration practice, some of the most well-known and powerfully visual allegorical adaptions may be found in children's literature. The story of 'Little Red Riding Hood' has been told in many different ways and is clearly couched in East European folklore, notably that of Gothic horror and the legend of the werewolf. Far less gruesome versions of the story have been appropriated for young audiences, with key characters greatly adapted for wider and much more 'upbeat' interpretation. Most people are familiar with the unfolding narrative, but would children be aware of the original theme? Whilst retaining their characterization from the former tale, the personas of the main protagonists are acculturated to conceal a scenario of intended paedophilic rape and explicit and brutal murder, all couched in sheer terror and fright.

VISUAL EUPHEMISM

There is also the antithetical approach to communication that reverses the sentiments of appeasement and concealment. In illustration, this is *visual euphemism*, and sometimes it means the production of pleasing or inoffensive images to represent objects, concepts or experiences that are considered distasteful, unpleasant or distressingly explicit. Visual euphemism can also be used for humorous reasons, and Keith Allan and Kate Burridge provide entertaining examples from their book *Euphemism and Dysphemism: Language Used as Shield and Weapon* (OUP, 1991): 'Still photography, film and television are superb media for *deceptive euphemisms*. These media present a world of perfected forms in which there is romance in the toilet bowl cleaner, poetry in the sanitary napkin, temptation in the tampon and beauty in a glass of dentures'. Illustration should be included along with the media stated in this quote as it uses euphemism extensively. For example, both Victorian illustrated literature and satirical 'cartoons' would often feature women enthroned on a 'gentleman's' knee as a visual euphemism for a sexual encounter. The use of euphemism can be exemplified by a quote from Quentin Crisp: 'Euphemisms are unpleasant truths wearing diplomatic cologne' (*Manners from Heaven*, 1984). Euphemism will also substitute an inoffensive expression for one considered explicitly offensive, an approach frequently used by illustrators who present propagandist and prejudicial negative persuasion. R. W. Holder stated in his book *Oxford Dictionary of Euphemisms* (2007), 'We use euphemism for dealing with taboo or sensitive subjects. It is therefore the language of evasion, hypocrisy, prudery and deceit'. The context for communicating euphemistic expressions motivated by fear, distaste, hatred or contempt can be taken one step further. *Dysphemism* presents that which is derogatory and deeply unpleasant; it conveys offence and extreme negativity. Illustration that uses a dysphemistic perspective goes into the extreme by directing humiliation and degradation at its chosen audience.

THE METAPHORICAL

Metaphor is a figure of speech in which implied comparison is made between two different things that actually have something important in common. The word *metaphor* itself is a 'metaphor', coming from a Greek word meaning 'to transfer or carry across'. Metaphors 'carry' meaning from one word, image, idea or situation to another. A common phrase might be that something is 'right up your street', meaning that it is favourable and to be appreciated. With regards to illustration, metaphor plays an enormous part in image conceptualization and message. A metaphorical image is one that is imaginative, but not literally applicable: it is a visual depiction of ideas or theories with the accent on the *conceptual* as opposed to pictorial realism. This approach enables innovative and creative solutions for the most prescriptive of themes, with the conceptual process reliant on a kind of *metamorphosis*, allowing for the interpretation of the brief to morph into adaption. The implication is a process of search and change regarding the development of ideas: a clear signal to strategically deconstruct any visual syntax, either iconographic or compositional. Certain themes related to illustration assignments, particularly those of an overtly commercial nature, can be 'dry', abstract in nature and obtuse. Examples might relate to company finance, corporate management or obscure statistical analyses. The challenge for the illustrator is to convey the essence of the theme appropriately in accordance with the brief, to enable the audience to engage effectively with any text that accompanies the image and most importantly, to present a suitably creative and imaginative illustration that will play successfully on the audience's sense of the metaphorical.

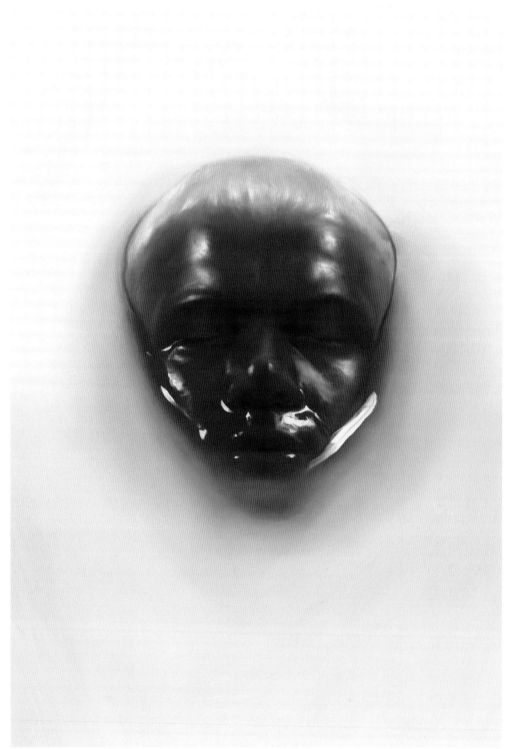

2.50
This rather disturbing image is entitled *The Language of Knives* and was conceived and illustrated by New York–based illustrator **Sam Weber**. Commissioned and published by Tor.com, the context is narrative fiction, produced to accompany a short story written by Haralambi Markov. Its visual impact is uncompromising in both content and theme. ©Sam Weber

2.51
This is an editorial illustration by **Jaime Anderson** published by *Illozine19*, a contemporary publication about drawing, ideas, experimentation and illustrators creating their own personal vision. The theme of this issue was 'Into the Unknown'. The illustration's title is *Go Forward* and exemplifies the apparent message contained in its narrative content: the depiction of women pushing on – perhaps against certain odds – in order to achieve that all-important status of equality and fair treatment. ©Jaime Anderson

2.50

2.51

THE EXTERNALIZATION OF IDEAS

The process for solving problems of visual communication, conceiving ideas that are challenging, original and at the same time, contextually strong, is not something that can be easily taught. The desire for the final imagery to be imbued with allegory or metaphor can be daunting to many, particularly for students embarking on this method of working for the first time. Authors often complain of 'writer's block', and comparative situations can easily arise for illustrators. Taking inspiration and developing this into a creative visual idea is not something that can be done by rote. It cannot be compared with performing a simple, repetitive operation. The blank page in a sketchbook or notebook can provoke psychological anxieties. This, in part, can be alleviated by the instantaneous recording of the first thought that transpires, no matter how trivial or seemingly unconnected with the brief. From plain origins, experimentation can evolve, and from this appropriate associations can manifest. The creative process should start to flow more readily at this point and more concrete and defined ideas could materialize. It is important to maintain freshness and originality even if the brief has a number of restrictions, such as a narrow target audience or seemingly 'uninteresting' subject matter. It is not advisable to dispense with all ideas and purely focus on a single thread that would evolve into the final interpretation. The brainstorming process should provide for some challenging and provocative answers to be considered: review as many appropriate worded metaphors as possible, research other thematic ideas that might have a correlation with the brief, develop into an allegorical narrative and go beyond the expected and excepted boundaries. At completion, whatever its contextual placement, if the imagery fails to evoke reaction and dispense impact upon its chosen audience, then the overall remit for *power and influence* is negated. As an aside, the application of creative processing by being inventive, imaginative and original is intrinsic and inherent to the individual and is something that cannot be given. However, it can be controlled, brought out and directed; it is therefore essential to maintain the integrity, authority and command of one's status and individuality as a creative practitioner.

THE PARADIGM OF ILLUSTRATION

To conclude, where do the intellectual, creative and material processes of illustration lie, and what supports the methodologies for the application of allegory and metaphor? In a nutshell, the answer is the *paradigm of illustration*. This is the philosophical, theoretical and practical framework that determines the definition of the discipline and its influence and impact through cognition, research and cultural hypotheses. It is a paradigm that denotes a clear configuration of practices and provides the discipline with its boundaries and archetypal distinction. The inflected forms of its parameters, its professional, contextual, educational and creative applications, are supported, formulated and debated within this framework. It was once said that science is the paradigm of true knowledge; perhaps *illustration is the paradigm of communicating true knowledge.*

2.52
The world of children's illustrated literature is replete with pictorial representation imbued with hidden meaning. One such example is that of 'Little Red Riding Hood'; ubiquitous throughout the Western world, it has been recast both in text and image away from its original Gothic horror inflections of werewolf folklore into a more light-hearted and upbeat narrative, with all characters 'living happily ever after' – apart from the dastardly wolf! However, this visual interpretation by illustrator **Blaz Porenta** does nothing to conceal the wolf's true intent. Thankfully, there has been some censorship as the whole story is a metaphor for paedophilic rape and murder. ©Blaz Porenta

2.53
The use of analogical juxtaposition in illustration is when two variables are cognate with one another. An example might be the characterization of a recognizable physical entity used as a metaphor for something completely different yet perceptively representative of its meaning. This image by **Paul Garland** is a specific commentary related to cultural competences and purports to the theme of *educating racism* through teamwork. ©Paul Garland

2.54
This image, a World Illustration Award winner for Advertising by New Talent, was conceived and produced by Maltese illustrator **Julinu**. It is entitled *Maia's Morning Malaise* and was used as part of a promotion for a short film called *Loophole*. This is a conceptual image, yet it utilizes much that can be considered representational – a 'dreamlike' composite designed to succinctly encapsulate atmosphere and aura. The overall narrative is centred on an individual's journey, accentuating the protagonist's inner world. ©Julian Mallia

2.52

2.53

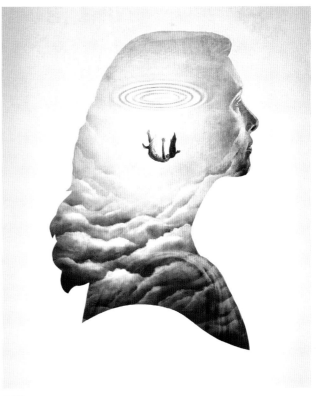

2.54

2.55, 2.56, 2.57 and 2.58
Allegory, in all of its
manifestations, can be
deceptive and enigmatic or
blatantly obvious, bold and
frank. Classic literature has
been demonstrable and clear
by using animals as metaphors
for humans; even in religion,
the Old Testament of the
Christian Bible depicts the
devil as a lowly yet conniving
and manipulative snake. More
latterly, the English author
Kenneth Grahame used well-
known wild creatures from the
British countryside as substitute
humans in his book *Wind in
the Willows* – their characters
and traits representative of
class and social affiliation, such
as Toad of Toad Hall assuming
the persona of 'Lord of the
Manor'. These figures were
conceived and illustrated by
Haydn Symons, concepts that
interpret the meanings imbued
in George Orwell's classic
twentieth-century novel *Animal
Farm*, the farm representing
the old Soviet Union and pigs
as the megalomaniac Bolshevik
rulers, who in turn oppress
and terrorize the proletariat,
as represented by other farm
animals. ©Haydn Symons

2.55

2.56

2.57

2.58

2.59

2.60

2.59, 2.60 and 2.61
The process for conceiving ideas that demands originality and a perceptible and demonstrative frisson of creativity can be fraught with 'stumbling blocks': where does inspiration come from? However, the mental practice of *free association* will often deliver the desired outcome by revealing associations and connections that might otherwise go uncovered. It does not require a linear thought pattern, the aim being to produce a seemingly incoherent stream of unconnected themes and narratives that can gel into an innovative and meaningfully

exciting solution to a problem of visual communication.
The following three images were produced by initiating first-class ideas and visual solutions: they are gold, silver and bronze winners, respectively, of the Association of Illustrators and London Transport Museum's Prize for Illustration 2017. The illustrators were invited to respond to the theme of 'Sounds of the City' and capture sounds heard in UK cities in a single image, from loud and frenetic urban noise to the more quiet and relaxing sounds of nature.
Figure 2.59 is the gold award winner and is by **Chiara Ghigliazza**. The image could be

representative of a great many cities and towns. Ghigliazza stated: 'You just need to turn the corner to move from chaos to silence and change familiar noises into unexpected melodies'. ©Chiara Ghigliazza
Figure 2.60 is the silver award winner by **Julia Allum**, who was inspired by sounds that are unexpected in an urban environment, in this instance, the squawk of parakeets heard above the noise of traffic. These tropical birds are now a familiar sight in many London parks after being 'accidentally' released from captivity a few years ago and having established themselves as 'native'. Allum employs a visual

language imbued with the bold shapes found in Art Deco and the decorative flourishes of Art Nouveau, here infusing the birds with the simple roundel logo for the London Underground network. The piece is critically described as 'elegant and subtle'. ©Julia Allum
Figure 2.61 is the bronze award winner by **Paul Garland**, whose illustration pays homage to London's buskers and street performers. The image combines the London Underground's iconic roundel logo and line colours as alternative machine heads for a stringed musical instrument – strong, simple and immediate. ©Paul Garland

2.61

2.62

2.63

2.63
This is a full-page illustration commissioned by *Monmouth Magazine* and created by **Davide Bonazzi**. Its message is unequivocal and imbued with much symbolism and metaphor – the donkeys and elephants representing the two big political parties of the USA, the Democrats and Republicans, along with the premise that to 'physically sweep away' is a suggestion to replace something unacceptable, hackneyed or disagreeable. The article demands a *focus on facts* rather than ideology to cut through the polarizing partisanship that has gripped political discourse. ©Davide Bonazzi

2.64
The visual language of pictorial representation cannot be described as that which will always convey unadulterated truth. A seemingly literal interpretation will often be loaded with intense meaning, yet shown through subject matter that is explicit and clear-cut. This illustration is by **Sam Weber** and was commissioned by the *New York Times*. It is entitled *My Monster, My Self*. Published around the time of Halloween, the publisher required an image that embodied the illustrator's deepest and most irrational fear. ©Sam Weber

2.64

Irony, Wit, Sarcasm and Perversion

It can be said that most people will conjure up wit, deliver sarcasm and contrive perversion: but what of irony? Irony is normally evidenced through rhetoric and expresses a meaning that signifies the opposite to what is actually meant, typically for humorous or emphatic effect. It defines a gap between reality and expectations. Irony pertains to situations that can manifest anywhere and in any context where people are perceptible and engaged. This means that illustration, and other forms of communication, will deliver messages with an ironic twist in order to emphasize the plotline of a story or accentuate a paradox or perversion pertaining to some cultural or social dialogue. There are many examples across the gamut of illustration practice, but how does irony deliver real power and influence the actions, opinions and behaviours of those targeted? Perhaps the most obvious is to discern those messages that are overtly sardonic, cynical and acerbic – in other words, satire.

SATIRE

Satire has been used in illustration for centuries. Loathed political leaders and other persons of influence were being castigated for 'crimes against the people' as far back as the classical period, the columns and public edifices of Rome scrawled with graffiti. Today, this genre of illustration practice can be described as one of the most persuasive and dominant forms of visual communication. Typically its messages are able to swing national opinion for or against an incumbent government or for dispensing judgement on the misdemeanours of a media-inflated 'star'. Satire holds to ridicule vices, follies, abuses and shortcomings with the intent of shaming individuals, corporations, government or society itself into improvement or, alternatively, into dissolution and ruination. Satire uses mockery to get at more serious truths. Because of this, it is important not to lose sight of the message and its intended impact on its audience. Being forthright and scornful of an individual's blatant stupidity or flaws will often achieve a desired effect. Irony will often come to the fore in the guise of barbed sarcasm. A typical example might be the caricatured profile of a high-status politician that states, 'You are a very humble, hard-working and caring member of Parliament who operates with immense integrity'. The more discerning in society – which often means the majority – will understand the underlying comment as meaning, 'You are a self-righteous, dictatorial, immoral hypocrite and should be impeached for your criminal actions'.

There are many applications capable of delivering substantial and vigorous indictments, including the use of parody, spoof, skit, scorn, derision and even burlesque. These approaches are evidenced across the majority of visual communication contexts from advertising and commerce to entertainment and literature. The other and most obvious example is journalistic commentary, where all aspects of social, cultural and political life are held to scrutiny and critique by way of publication and broadcast. Illustration is used in several ways. The British publication *Viz* has utilized the comic strip format to present a regular monthly series of 'situation comedies' that lampoon and satirize all aspects of society. It has been suggested that its popularity is due to contents that comprise strictly adult material and a total disregard for political correctness. Every social stereotype is ridiculed, including its audience: in some instances, certain *Viz* characters or scenarios will offend, a strategy used by the BBC television comedy troupe Monty Python's Flying Circus, who claimed it was their intent that at least one sketch from their film *The Meaning of Life* would offend someone. This approach can be potent when communicating power and influence; controversy will always incite debate and argument, a stratagem worth considering by illustrators, irrespective of context and subject matter.

DEVIANCE AND OFFENCE

It is useful to observe the overall visual language employed by illustrators working within this genre; there are standard comic strip formats without any dramatic 'break-outs' or contemporary graphic novel extremes, and characterizations reminiscent of bygone times, an almost 'cosy' 1940s to 1950s pastiche, not unlike the bawdy, yet stereotypically recognizable figures created by the British 'saucy-seaside' postcard illustrator, Donald McGill. This approach negates any precious attitude towards one's personal iconography, a type of 'inverted snobbery', disregarding 'cutting edge' stylization as content, message and audience reaction supersede style.

Another publication renowned for its cutting edge satire is *Private Eye*. Founded in London in 1961, it established itself as the *enfant terrible* of the British establishment, having been the frequent subject of lawsuits and libel charges. At the core of these 'misdeeds', which include charges of bigotry and blasphemy, lie a succession of illustrators who have contributed regularly over the years, some household names with considerable reputations for political comment: Gerald Scarfe, Ralph Steadman, plus the late Wally Fawkes (Trog) and William Rushton. Such is the influence of illustration, a *Private Eye* cult comic strip called *Celeb* featured a character called Gary Bloke, the ultimate 'wrinkly' rock star, drawn and devised by cartoonist Charles Peatie. Peppered with innuendo, comic paradox and irony, it inspired a BBC situation comedy in 2002.

This genre of illustration, with its potential for offence, debasement and deviance, came into its own regarding public notoriety in 1971. It was targeted by the then Obscene Publications Squad and centred on a law writ known as the *Oz* Obscenity Trial. *Oz* was a typical 'underground' magazine, one of several that were published without any formalized editorial control. It presented what was considered sexually explicit illustrated imagery that challenged convention with a remit to deliberately shock and offend the establishment audience – an antidote to the wit, facetiousness, waggishness or repartee prevalent across establishment media such as *Punch* magazine and the television programme *That Was the Week That Was*. It went 'full on' with articles of a highly sexualized and perverse nature. One infamous example featured morphing the much-loved anthropomorphic children's character Rupert Bear into an extreme 'porno-graph': a collage underpinned by drawings created by the American illustrator Robert Crumb. Crumb had a reputation for producing controversial imagery; a prolific cartoonist, he was a prime mover in establishing the *underground comix* genre. One of his best-known creations is *Fritz the Cat*, a comic book and satire on contemporary American society that spawned the first X-rated animated film, owing to its explicit and morally challenging content.

THE IRONY OF IGNORANCE

There is *irony* embedded in satirical illustration. Generally speaking, this is illustration that deliberately presents laughable incongruity regarding the attitudes and actions of society at large, particularly its mainstream establishment elements, the 'respectable' middle classes, the Church and all those adherents wanting to maintain the cultural and political status quo. The sarcasm and satire being dispensed become paradoxical, often revealing contradictions. The distorted fictionalized scenarios that visually pour scorn often prove to be well founded and true. Self-denial only increases the hypocrisy – those being lampooned for their 'moralistic', conservative behaviour and views being 'found out'.

There are paradoxes of faith and religion. The satirist wishing to expose the many contradictions and anomalies of the believers, in their 'lifestyle' and their dogmatism, has much material to draw from. One of the greatest ironies ever presented by an illustrator was the *Wanted* poster of Jesus, conceived and produced by the American political cartoonist Art Young. Highly controversial, it was published in *Good Morning* magazine in 1921. It contained a standard, bearded portrait of Jesus. However, the accompanying hand-rendered text composed by Young caused outrage and offence, particularly amongst America's more pious and evangelical Christian communities, who damned the poster as blasphemous and corrupt. Young's thesis was simple: he would undermine and challenge the closed mindsets that stereotyped members of the established churches and denominations. He presented the facts

2.65

2.65

underpinning Jesus' character, way of life, associations and visionary ideas and did so by using populist terms and phrases without any 'supernatural' or spiritual references to traditional Bible stories. The ultimate irony is that the words displayed on the 'wanted' poster revealed the truth: 'Reward for information leading to the apprehension of Jesus Christ. Wanted for sedition, criminal anarchy, vagrancy and conspiracy to overthrow the established government'. There was no inherent blasphemy intended, just a slight at ignorance and superstition.

THE ABSURD

Associated with the ironic, the witty and the satirical is the *absurd*. In illustration, this can often appear totally baffling, nonsensical, preposterous, farcical, illogical, ludicrous and idiotic. The adjectives are many and to the point; however, overt satire, sarcasm and perversion are contextualized and have a message to deliver requiring audience attention and reaction. On the outset, it would suggest that the absurd in illustration does not communicate through any defined context. In fact, it can be asked, what is the point of such 'illustration' and what is its raison d'être – ambient, zany humour, perhaps, or intellectually light, discard-able entertainment? Today, absurdity is considered synonymous with *nonsense*, but is there a difference? It would appear that traditionally there is. The seventeenth-century English philosopher Thomas Hobbes said that 'absurdity is viewed as having to do with invalid reasoning, while ridiculousness or nonsense is to do with laughter, superiority and deformity'. This is a quote worth considering when applying absurdity to an illustration. Hobbes's definition of nonsense would certainly pertain to light entertainment, although contemporaneously it is not expedient to feature human conditions, physical or mental, that society might consider in need of empathy and compassion.

The presentation of inoperative reasoning can be applied to most contexts. An illustration that utilizes absurdity as a stratagem can on the surface appear surreal, risible and incongruous, whether it depicts something that is physically tangible and interacting within real space or a 'wild' and outlandish juxtaposition.

A seemingly absurd image can present deep meaning through commentary or narrative. By way of analysis and interpretation, irony, satire, wit and paradox can manifest and biting comment be appropriated. Broadly speaking, there are some themes best represented by absurdity, such as the ethereality of dreams, mysticism, abstract thought and outlandish ideas, either serious or satirical. Illustrators from the past who are associated with the absurd are William Heath-Robinson, Edward Lear, Mervyn Peake and Roland Emett.

To conclude, irony, satire, sarcasm, perversion, paradox and the absurd can all be associated with the notion of expressing or intending to promote a particular cause or point of view, especially a controversial one. This form of promulgation is known as tendentiousness. Freud concluded that *tendentious* jokes 'provide a means of undoing and retrieving what was lost' and that 'they allow us to take pleasure from sources that we have repressed. Tendentious jokes may be hostile, sexual, morbid, blasphemous or any other "pleasure" that we may have repressed'. The illustrator or commentator wishing to broadcast or publish a contentious argument may well take note of this theory: drawing on one's own experiences, ambitions and beliefs can result in original and innovative concepts, challenging way beyond the parameters of expectation regarding any brief or assignment.

'There's terrific merit in having no sense of humour, no sense of irony, practically no sense of anything at all. If you're born with these so-called defects you have a very good chance of getting to the top'. This sarcastic witticism from the late satirist, comedian and writer Peter Cooke epigrammatically sums up this context of communication and illustration.

2.66

2.67

2.68

2.66, 2.67 and 2.68
The Spectator is a UK–based magazine that comments on politics, economics and current affairs. Its political leaning and affiliation could be described as centre-right; consequently, it will broadly support the British Conservative Party. Like many other news journals and publications, it uses *satire* to lampoon, ridicule and insult those politicians whose recent actions have incited unfavourable comment and opinion from the editorial team. However, the mockery is really in place to hold those responsible to account and get to the serious truth. The 'political cartoon' comes into its own: used for centuries as a tool for dispensing damnation upon those in power whose actions were deemed 'unacceptable', today the context for this realm of illustration remains broadly the same. The illustrations shown here are by **Jake Abrams**. Figure 2.66 is a comment from 2009 referring to the then prime minister Gordon Brown's commitment to an impending G20 summit; the illustration was used on the cover and was accompanied by the strapline 'Pull the plug on Brown's Summit'. Figure 2.67 was also used on the cover, depicting the then leader of the Conservative Party, David Cameron, revealing his 'superior status' over Labour Party Prime Minister Brown. The comment imbued in Figure 2.68 needs no real explanation regarding US President Barack Obama. ©Jake Abrams

2.69

2.70

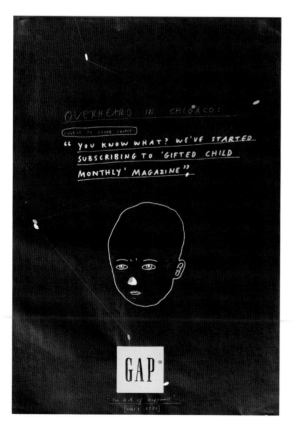

2.71

2.69, 2.70, 2.71, 2.72, 2.73 and 2.74
The six 'posters' reveal substantial parody, spoof and scorn poured upon the organizations being 'promoted', most of whom are multinational companies of considerable status and prestige: American Express, Disney, Dodge, Gap, GSK and Tiffany and Co. The originator of these is artist and illustrator **Paul Davis**, who has been described as 'an opinionated satirical illustrator whose work contains bleak humour, bad relationships and foolishness'. Much of his work is inspired by overheard 'off-cuts' of conversations and shards of revealed thoughts picked up along the way and subsequently infused into his work as the basis for substantial comment. He is known for turning clichés and platitudes 'back on themselves'. He stated, 'Corporate use of language is just lazy, the language is ugly and the tone is smug and patronising. I find the whole thing grating'. ©Paul Davis

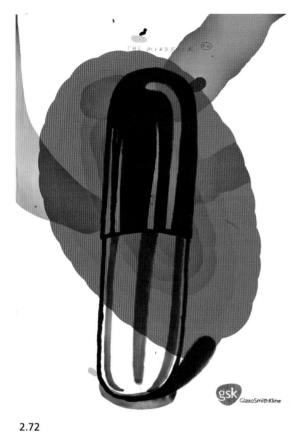

2.72

2.73

2.74

2.75, 2.76, 2.77, 2.78, 2.79, 2.80, 2.81 and 2.82
This sequence of images are stills taken from an animation entitled *The Spirit of Christmas*. Conceived, designed and produced by illustrator, graphic designer and animator **Cyriak**, they would undoubtedly be considered both deviant and offensive by many. In some respects, this project could also be seen as *dysphemistic*, a derogatory and deliberate slight at those who hold dear the values originally inspired by the religious meaning of the festival. However, it is more likely that the intent is contemptuous disdain for the way in which Christmas has been usurped by rampant consumerism, gluttony, decadence, greed and the inflated commercialism of what is supposedly a Christian holy celebration. ©Cyriak

2.75

2.76

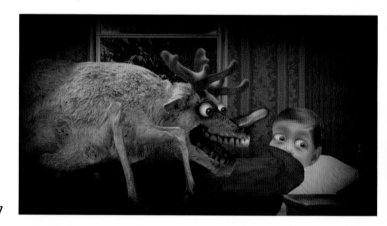

2.77

2.78

2.79

2.80

2.81

2.82

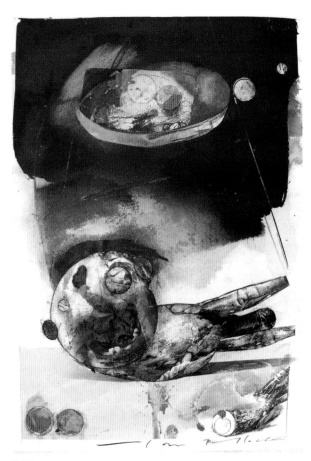

2.83

The Genealogy of Jesus

2.84

2.83, 2.84, 2.85 and 2.86
Religious belief will always incite parody, criticism and ridicule – from total unbelievers such as atheists, but also from adherents of alternative faiths wishing to pour scorn. Blasphemy can take many forms, not always intentional but sometimes deliberate and defamatory. Christianity has often borne the brunt. However, offence can be misplaced owing to a total misunderstanding of the actual message or the platform of presentation. One such example was the 1970s film *Monty Python's Life of Brian*. Castigated for being blasphemous and degrading of the Christian faith, it was banned from many cinemas throughout the UK. However, it was never the intention of the filmmakers to insult any religious believers; the film was basically pure comedy. The four illustrations shown are from a collective series entitled *Pollock's New Testament*. The whole project was conceived and illustrated by **Ian Pollock**. Figure 2.84 is *The Genealogy of Jesus* (Matthew 1:1–17), figure 2.83 is *The Birth of Jesus* (Matthew 1.18–25), figure 2.85 is *The Death of Jesus* (Matthew 27.27–50) and figure 2.86 is *The Resurrection of Jesus* (Matthew 28.1–10). These illustrations were produced in 2004, but in keeping with Pollock's ideas and feelings regarding his reworking of this overall subject matter, he stated in 1999 after illustrating the biblical parables, 'This has always been my way of keeping my edge rough. Sometimes I feel quite in awe of the parables. They are nasty stories, damning and unforgiving. The Bible addresses the harshness of nature, the culling of the inferior, the condemnation of the failure to procreate. I like the idea. It's so wicked'. ©Ian Pollock

2.85

2.86

2.87

2.88

2.89

2.87
Frequently, there is an *irony of ignorance* immersed in satire, more often than not, by comedic incongruity, dispensed at the beliefs, attitudes and behaviours of society. This happens when the adherents of all of those wanting to protect and uphold the religious, political, nationalistic and cultural status quo are 'found out' – the so-called establishment, the Church, and as this illustration so blatantly reveals, 'those gun-toting, God fearing, good 'ol boys from America's Deep South and Mid-West'! The sarcasm and satire being disbursed become paradoxical, often bringing to light glaring contradictions. The illustration was produced by London-based American illustrator **Rebecca Hendin** and needs no explanation. The distorted scenario visually pours scorn, but in reality it is well founded and ostensibly true. ©Rebecca Hendin

2.88
Entitled *Pear Fisher*, this illustration by **Sam Weber** is rendered traditionally in acrylic and watercolour. There are some people who would claim that this image is explicit and revealing. A counter argument might suggest an irony of ignorance and that the illustration reflects the innocence, yet harsh realities of life on remote tropical islands. ©Sam Weber

2.89
The *absurd* in illustration can manifest by way of a number of disparate contexts, none more so than in advertising. Usually associated with baffling, outlandish and nonsensical imagery, this example is pure *fashion* promotion. Undoubtedly to focus attention on the trend-infused eyewear, the model has been absurdly and humorously appropriated by what can only be described as 'ocular overkill'. The illustration was published in *Eye Republic Magazine*; the eyewear is by Delalle, the coat by Homo Consommatus, the top by Darling London and the jewellery by MAWI London. **Lola Dupre** is an illustrator and collage artist based in Scotland. ©Lola Dupre

2.90

2.91

2.92

2.90, 2.91 and 2.92
The three illustrations shown are by **Mr Alan Clarke**, an illustrator and artist from the Republic of Ireland. Figure 2.90 is entitled *The Martyr*, 2.91 *Weird Scenes in the Meadow* and 2.92 *The Armchair Empress*. Drawing on surrealism, whimsy, humour and above all absurdity, Clarke approaches his work totally free and unhampered by convention or truth. Utilizing a visual language that dispenses scenic credibility and an implied narrative, some of the characterizations and their interactions are reminiscent of either music hall farce or dark and dreamlike fantasy. ©Mr Alan Clarke

2.93

Absurd, surreal, humorous, enigmatic, preposterous – these are possible adjectives that might describe this illustration by **Anita Kunz**. Indeed, many people would ask, 'What does it mean?' Perhaps that is its intention. Originally published by *LA Style Magazine* in 1991, the image delivers much to ponder: the quizzical but seemingly knowing expression, with a gaze that looks straight at the viewer. And why is she naked, certainly from the waist up? Her caricatured visage and form – rounded shoulders, a slightly submissive body language – also suggest a person not entirely at ease with herself. However, the real intrigue lies with the lighthouse so strategically placed on the top of her head, and it is this that provides her with some implied status. Lighthouses are rich with symbolism and conceptual meaning. They can symbolize the way forward to help us navigate through rough metaphorical waters, problems that might be financial, personal, business or spiritual. They can also be interpreted as representing some of the lofty ideals of contemporary humankind. The lighthouse on her head is clearly glowing. Might she be quietly suggesting an adherence to certain humanistic values, values emanating like the valuable light that shines from the lighthouse? Or is the whole image just a whim of complete absurdity . . .? ©Anita Kunz

2.94

Paul Slater is renowned for creating imagery that is ludicrously humorous and farcical. He employs a style of painting that is reminiscent of Rene Magritte and the 'genre' of nonsensical surrealism. His compositional and pictorial visualizations are also evocative of Norman Rockwell and Edward Hopper. This illustration is entitled *The Riddle of Playtime*, its meaning and context totally figmental and fanciful. However, it does entertainingly invite the viewer to conjure up what might happen after Wild Bill Hickok has indulged in the 'activity' thus presented. ©Paul Slater

2.93

2.94

Rhetoric and Visual Bombast

How does illustration convey characteristics such as grandiloquence, hyperbole and ostentatiousness, and how pertinent is it for this type of imagery to lack sincerity or meaningful content? In order to answer these questions, one must consider the context of the brief and the manner in which such work is contrived and delivered. The context of advertising, sales and promotion will often demand an approach that is impassioned and persuasive by making grandiose statements – cryptic, effusive or otherwise – by using exploitative rhetoric and bombastic visual linguistics. Rhetoric suggests that the use of oral or written language as illustration in this context tends to be driven by a campaign strapline. However, illustration *is* a visual language, a language 'linguistically' embroidered by the need to effect an exaggerated embellishment of the subject matter. This is done by creating an appropriate ambience and atmosphere, by using either vigorous or frail mark making, semiotic contrivance, compositional theatricality – or alternatively, deliberate passing insignificance.

THE UNCOMPROMISING APPROACH

There are many aspects to consider when conceiving ideas and producing imagery for 'rhetorical' contexts. The principal deliberation should determine an uncompromising approach to both message and visual language, particularly when the illustrations set out to sell, persuade or 'preach'. Power and influence can be best achieved when the imagery is memorable and 'to the point'. It is unlikely that an advertising or propagandist campaign will rely on narratives that conceal 'clever' ironies or extreme metaphors; there needs to be a visual immediacy, with the audience/ viewer left in no doubt as to what is being said. A typical example is the work of Sue Coe, whose messages are delivered using a style of illustration often described as powerful and thought provoking – but also 'aesthetically challenging'. Themes such as terrorism, animal rights and the excesses of capitalism show no quarter, with explicit visualizations of torture and death, drawn with angry, passionate and vigorous mark making. The opposite can be said of the 'chocolate box' approach to image production. Whilst equally strong on message, it relies on a visual rhetoric that plays on sentimentality and crassness. Whether depicting cuddly kittens advertising chocolate cookies for children or risqué adult themes such as those derived from the world of glamour, the visual language will always be figurative and excessive in thematic overstatement and pictorial embellishment.

THE RHETORICAL MODE FOR ILLUSTRATION

There are certain patterns of development when applying a rhetorical approach to illustration, as there are with any other form of applied communication. These patterns are often referred to as *rhetorical modes*. What is the rhetorical mode for illustration? When applied generally, it does not mean 'drawing' or any other form of technique-driven strategy; this mode reflects specific contextual applications such as demonstrating, proving, exhibiting, revealing, showing and exemplifying – all necessary considerations for producing successful visual communication. Formally, this pattern can be broken down into the process of research, conceptualization and production from which detailed questions and methodologies will emerge.

2.95
The question often arises as to how far one might go in embellishing a story that is explicitly violent, bloody and disturbing. Does one adopt an *uncompromising approach* in order to convey the physical barbarity of certain human actions? Examples might be a factual account of warfare or a fictional drama of great fantastical bloodletting. How far is it acceptable to go? It might be expedient to look towards theatre and film. Director Quentin Tarantino is certainly uncompromising regarding extreme violence in his movies, to the point of choreographing the bloody action. Shakespeare's plays can be described as being even more extreme; his sixteenth-century audiences were suitably desensitised by watching torture and executions for real, so no need for theatrical compromise there! This illustration by **Sam Weber** can be described as psychologically nuanced and disturbing, the blood intimated rather than explicitly gory or obvious. It is part of a series of images for *Vanity Fair Italy* to accompany a set of horror stories. A woman wakes to find herself covered in blood, dripping from a small wound on her index finger. ©Sam Weber

The subject to be communicated can be anything as long as its provenance and genealogy can be identified. It can be something abstract, physical, living, or just an idea. The first aspect of rhetorical development is that of *description* and *narration*. This determines a definition for the subject, its classification and its chronological placement: what is it, when did it occur, why does it occur, what does it look like and how does it work? The next step is *process analysis*: what message is the subject commissioned to convey, who are the recipients of the message and what is their demographic, how can this message be told and how powerfully and memorably can I get that message across? Finally comes *cause and effect*, an analysis of the intended consequence and its repercussions regarding the subject: what might the advantages or disadvantages be and how does it compare and contrast with others of its own class or outside of its class?

In conclusion, to many, imagery communicating extreme rhetoric and bombast is considered extravagant, pretentious and pertaining to 'low culture'. How accepting society is of that viewpoint by commercial illustrators, or the 'authorial' illustrator elite, remains to be seen. What is clear, though, is that this context of practice will flourish as long as the advertising, broadcasting and publishing media continue to use illustration.

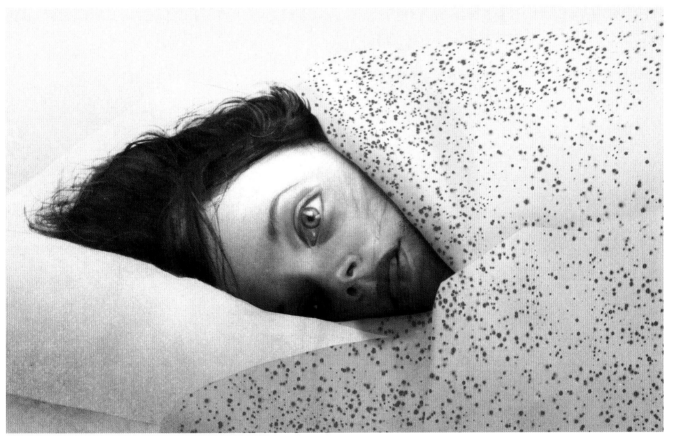

2.95

2.96

2.97

2.98

2.96, 2.97 and 2.98
Uncompromising or not? The so-called artistic depiction of death is always a matter for individuals to decide. These images are part of a series entitled *Forgotten* and were originally published by *Dark Beauty Magazine*. They were conceived and produced by international award-winning photographer **Maria Svarbova** from Slovakia. The images present people who have become forgotten 'under the layers'. Each image represents 'another layer, another place'. ©Maria Svarbova

2.99

How compromising can it be *not* to depict the potential heinousness of a truly hateful and destructive crime like paedophilia? This is an editorial illustration by **Mario Minichiello** and is entitled *Easier with Whoever You Want*. It does not require any analysis or explanation! ©Mario Minichiello

2.100

This is a detail of a large, imposing mural-type image that once dominated the interior wall of St Peters Church, Wenhaston, Suffolk, England. Truly grandiose, these visually bombastic illustrations are known as *dooms* and broadly depict the Last Judgement, when Christ judges souls to send them to either Heaven or Hell. The paintings, such as the *Wenhaston Doom* shown here, were encouraged by the early medieval Church as an instrument to highlight the contrasts between the reward of Heaven and the agony of Hell, so as to guide – or to threaten – Christians away from misbehaviour and sin. The congregation at that time would have been present by lawful obligation, as severe and brutal punishment awaited those who did not comply. The image would have been a constant reminder of their afterlife fate if they strayed from the narrow path of righteousness. This is a detail, photographed by the author, showing the mouth of Hell, represented by a monstrous sea creature. There are damned souls inside, all naked and mainly women, plus various devils, one of which is mauling a woman and dragging her down and into the mouth of Hell itself. ©Alan Male

2.99

2.100

2.101

2.102

2.103

2.102 and 2.103
It has been said that the context of advertising, sales and promotion will often demand an approach that is impassioned and persuasive by making *grandiose* statements using exploitative rhetoric and *bombastic visual linguistics*. The illustration shown, designed and produced by **Rebecca Hendin**, does well to exemplify that description. Reproduced as a massive hoarding and displayed aloft the premises housing the world-famous bookstore Foyles in London, its remit was to reassure the public that the shop was fully operational in spite of substantial reconstruction work to the building. The strapline accompanying the illustration was 'All paths lead to Foyle's'.
©Rebecca Hendin

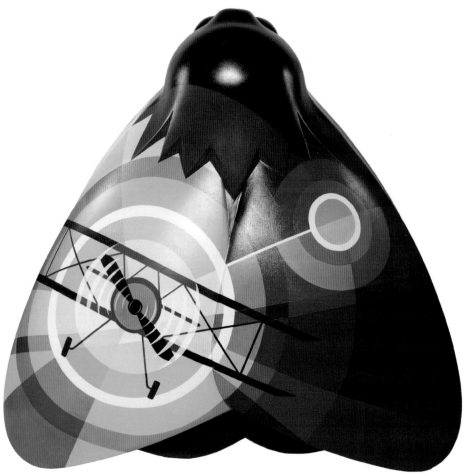

2.104

2.104

Public space is frequently exploited by every professional design and communication context with an audience comprising a potentially broad multicultural demographic. Town and city centres, landscapes and countryside rarely escape some form of advertising, propaganda, retail or public branding and identity.

The need for visual immediacy will never be greater and the platform for delivery accessible to all in the vicinity. The image shown is a three-dimensional 'sculpturesque' production classed as 'public art' but in reality an illustration to promote the Amy Johnson Festival, held in Kingston-upon-Hull, England, 2016. Shaped as a giant moth, it was placed in the public

domain. Amy Johnson was a celebrated early twentieth-century British aviator who was born in the city. Her first aircraft was a de Havilland DH.60 Gipsy Moth – hence the artwork's shape and its symbolic, illustrative representations. The image was illustrated by **Julia Allum**. ©Julia Allum

Subject Matter

It has been said that without subject matter there can be no illustration. Also, the essence of any communication delivered by illustration will be embedded in subject matter. This could be something physical and perceptible by touch; an action or process; something conceptual or abstract in thought or deed; or the ethereal and imaginative either in fact or make-believe. Illustration can be used to depict or represent anything, in any visual language from the pictorially realistic to the anti-literal, and in any context from pure commercialization to the presentation of new knowledge.

VISUAL UNTRUTHS

How a subject is represented will be driven by the brief and the message needed to be imparted. The notion that illustration wields *power and influence* is largely dependent on this precept. The subject in question needs to appear 'larger than life' in order to achieve this. However, that does not just imply sublimity or an over-dramatic portrayal; visual subtlety and quiet subversion will also achieve the desired effect.

It has been said 'the camera never lies'. In fact, photography has a tenuous relationship with reality, as both amateur 'happy snapping' and professional digital manipulation will deliver distorted and unrealistic characterizations. The camera often lies, and in order to communicate its messages effectively, it will need to. This applies similarly to illustration. A typical example is where the author, when engaged in a paleontological research project in conjunction with Leicester University, produced a highly detailed and ultra-realistic representation of a newly discovered marine organism from 500 million years ago. The overall image also depicted the creature's underwater environment, scientifically proven to be dense and extremely murky, making visibility impossible. The organism, *Keurbosia susanae*, was shown clearly and in full focus in spite of field perspective and the nature of its surroundings; integrity for the research demanded nothing less.

UNDERSTANDING AND EMPATHY WITH SUBJECT MATTER

It is essential that the illustrator is able to engage fully with subject matter. This engagement will often need no more than a slight empathetic glance at the reference source, but there can also be a need for the illustrator to have an authoritative specialism, the result of high-level study or practice. In this context, it is not uncommon for the illustrator to have an undergraduate or higher degree in a subject or discipline some way removed from art and design practice. This can include an innumerable and disparate range of subjects from humanities and cultural studies to science and technology. This will automatically provide mastery in subject matter, with the illustrator able to assume a professional and respected status associated with his or her specialism. It is not unusual for certain practitioners to claim job descriptions like illustrator-archaeologist, journalist, anthropologist, zoologist, media creative director or academic.

> " LITERALLY ANY OBJECT, OCCURRENCE OR MATTER KNOWN TO HUMANKIND CAN BE SUBJECT TO THE ILLUSTRATOR'S ART: BOUNDLESS AND ILLIMITABLE SUBJECTS FROM THE WORLD OF ARTS AND ENTERTAINMENT; THE GREAT SWEEP OF HUMAN AND GLOBAL HISTORY; EVERY CONCEPT, PROCESS AND DETAIL FROM THE REALM OF SCIENCE, TECHNOLOGY AND THE NATURAL WORLD; THE UNRELENTING VICISSITUDES OF CONTEMPORARY SOCIETY AND CULTURE. "

ALAN MALE, *ILLUSTRATION: MEETING THE BRIEF* (BLOOMSBURY 2014)

Applied disciplines like scriptwriting, advertising, journalism and literary authorship will command expertise in *both* written and visual language. Writing and illustration are more than just proximate – they are one and the same. This link is intrinsic, as exemplified by the large percentage of author-illustrators for children's books, general fiction and other forms of creative writing, editorial and reportage, copywriting, specialist non-fiction material for children and adults, academic journals and research literature.

RESEARCH AND THE ACQUISITION OF REFERENCE

An essential methodology underpinning an illustrator's understanding and empathy with subject matter is the strategy of information gathering and research. Reference material can be as varied as the parameters of visual communication itself, with the potential to encompass virtually any subject or theme required and context in which it sits. More important is what constitutes good, appropriate reference material and how that material should be evaluated and used. Sometimes a glancing overview of the subject may be sufficient, or it may be necessary to delve deeply into the complexities of the subject in order to achieve real factual accuracy. Illustrations are dependent on the direct use of this reference material or on a mental recollection of references previously consulted. Even imagery born out of pure fantasy or avant-garde distortion is influenced and underpinned by a reality that has been researched and referenced. In the majority of instances, it is visual reference that needs to be sourced.

There can often be difficulties in acquiring the most appropriate reference material. An awkward, rare or obscure subject, a specific or isolated location, or the need for an expert opinion in order to get it right can all present challenges. It is important to think around these problems. The ability to go and confidently seek out the required references is often the best practice – for example, sourcing one's own photographic imagery or sketchbook work, as well as networking and arranging consultative and advisory interviews. Such meetings can result in potential collaboration between the illustrator and consultant, with the potential for new and innovative projects, beneficial for both parties.

OBJECTIVE DRAWING AND REPORTAGE

Drawing is an essential visual language for research and reference acquisition. One such approach is determined by the epistemological value of objective drawing. Observation and learning to see are part of the illustrator's education; it has been said that *we draw to understand our subject matter*. This is a crucial skill, essential for illustrators, when recording information and establishing concepts and should go beyond the ability to render an attractive drawing based purely on surface mark making. The drawings should represent the subject matter faithfully yet distinguish between important details such as shape, form, surface texture and colour and the unnecessary anomalies that are often present – visual intrusions, defacements and unneeded ambience.

In order to have complete knowledge and understanding of the subject matter, the drawings should determine its cultural or contemporary placing. There are three key questions that an analytical drawing approach should address, and they can be applied to most objects that are tangible and real, whether natural or constructed by humans. The first is to discern exactly *what* it is: its morphology and how it was conceived or made. Secondly, learn *why* it exists: what its 'ecology' is, where it exists, when and with what and how it interacts with or impacts on its surroundings. Finally, explore *how* it works: what is its 'biology' and what does it do? The successful application of these criteria implies that there is a knowledge-based discourse held within the drawings and that it can be a significant strategy for an empirical approach to research.

Sketching as visual note taking is a relevant and important skill, especially when documenting references on location. A less formal approach to mark making and visual language, this particular method can provide an immediate reference of an environment, a sense of place, recording atmosphere, character and ambience. It can also operate journalistically and chronicle an unfolding narrative, depicting all relevant aspects of dynamics, scale, movement, gesture, human body language, interaction, setting, time and place. Often such work will be published as *reportage* illustration, a journalistic-style commentary that could be of any event anywhere in the world.

SUBJECT MATTER IN CONTEXT

The context of commentary provides a platform for all forms of conviction, view, sentiment, belief, feeling, judgement and preconception to be broadcast and published via the editorial and journalistic framework of the media. Illustrators who are frequently commissioned to produce editorial work will need only a negligible and surface understanding of subject matter related to lightweight themes such as lifestyle and popular entertainment. However, much editorial business is dominated by topics of importance and gravitas, and the imagery should not only reveal a significant connection but also firmly and substantially expound the message. A typical example is politics and current affairs. Many illustrators will be required to produce an image representing their own account of the news in question. The views and opinions expressed must come from a working conviction that is knowledgeable, up-to-date and above all opinionated.

Whilst narrative fiction might inherently be the world of make-believe, the intended audience should be able to connect with the setting and backdrop for the story, particularly if it is contemporary. Subject matter needs certain credibility, whatever the age range or culture of the audience. The customs, fashions and mores shown should not be out of step with audience perception. As with most literature, the fiction will emerge from a basis of fact. Illustrations for narrative fiction, even for very young audiences, should convey colours, textures and atmosphere matching the environment and setting of the story, no matter how stylized the visual language. It is also important to understand the period in which the story is set, whether historic, contemporary or futuristic. An example brief might require an American Civil War dramatic reconstruction; it would be essential to ensure accuracy and authenticity for the period.

There is such a diversity of theme and subject. The following is a range of topics frequently subjected to illustrative interpretation or representation: architecture, botany, classic literature, current affairs, fairy stories, fashion, Gothic tales, history and archaeology, maps and vistas, medicine and anatomy, music and performance art, mythology and religion, palaeontology, science, science fiction, sex and lifestyle, sport, technology and transport, urban culture, world culture and zoology.

> **THE PURSUIT OF KNOWLEDGE AND INFORMATION IS A PREREQUISITE TO EMINENT, PROFESSIONAL ILLUSTRATION PRACTICE.**

ALAN MALE, *ILLUSTRATION: A THEORETICAL AND CONTEXTUAL PERSPECTIVE* (SECOND EDITION, BLOOMSBURY 2017)

2.105

2.106

2.105 and 2.106
As subjects, maps are usually given for providing pure cartographic reference within the context of education and information. Visually, many will assume different forms such as being richly decorated and imbued with associated themes and scenarios, often for promotional or editorial purposes. This map of Africa was conceived, designed and illustrated by **Coque Azcona**. Figure 2.110 is a detail. Its remit is to promote and celebrate the tenth anniversary of Africa Digna, or Foundation for the Dignity of Africa. It is an organization that raises awareness in Spanish civil society regarding matters of health and education in Africa and carries out medical and educational interventions of deep impact. Transversal objectives are the defence of human rights, environment, gender policy, the culture of peace and the strengthening of local, national and international democracy. ©Coque Azcona

2.107

The field of natural science is an area of practice and study that has initiated some of the most celebrated and important works of illustration. By its attention to detail, scrutiny and regard for values held regarding scientific integrity and research, it has educated and enlightened a great many, not only today but also from the Classical period, through to the great Age of Discovery of the eighteenth and nineteenth centuries. This is a botanical illustration by **Victoria Fuller** and is of *Asclepias*, more commonly known as the milkweed, a North American perennial garden plant. It is seen with the milkweed bug (*Oncopeltus fasciatus*), an insect that feeds on the milkweed seeds. ©Victoria Fuller

2.108

Reportage is visual journalism: it offers an opportunity to bear witness to events and storytelling on a myriad of levels. Reportage also unfolds as the drawing is being produced, and it has that indefinable allure of immediacy regarding the subjects and the drama associated with the scenario in question. The completed image should always convey a sense of 'being in the picture', the essence of one's visual endeavours providing both truth and comment – a sense of emotion, opinion, atmosphere, instinct, awareness and understanding. **Melanie Reim** produced this drawing in the midst of a street protest in New York City prior to the American presidential election of 8 November 2016. ©Melanie Reim

2.107

2.108

QUOD ME NUTRIT ME DESTRUIT

2.109

2.109
The presentation of knowledge can take many forms. As well as the traditional concepts of morphological truth (form and structure) and ontological truth (actuality and being), it is often expedient to explore alternative avenues of visualization. Sometimes, an experiential insight or a deep-rooted understanding of the subject, such as medical science, can better exemplify subjects and themes that are associated with emotion and direct human circumstances. This illustration is part of a series entitled *Stickman: The Vicissitudes of Crohn's*. It is the overall winner of the prestigious 2017 Wellcome Image Awards and was conceived and produced by illustrator **Spooky Pooka**. Crohn's disease is a chronic condition caused by inflammation of the digestive system, its cause yet to be discovered. The images are based around the character Stickman, a proxy alter ego of the illustrator, who suffers from Crohn's disease. He is made of sticks rather than bones and references the associated symptoms of weight loss, the body's fragility following a flare-up and the abrupt, transformative nature of Crohn's. This image carries the sentiment *Quod Me Nutruit, Me Destruit*, the Latin for 'What nourishes me, destroys me'.
©Spooky Pooka

2.110

2.110 and 2.111
Architecture, including its broader context of the *built environment*, provides the illustrator with innumerable themes and opportunities – as backdrops and real-space scenarios for fictional narratives of all description, specialist subject matter for knowledge-bearing contexts, and inspiration and reference for a great many visual language expositions, such as composition and atmosphere. Sometimes, even when presented as a visual truth, the overall image can be economical in detail and invite the audience to imagine its broader placement and wider interpretations. The architectural style of an anonymous building can, however, provide a cultural clue to its country or location of origin. The two images shown are by the author: Figure 2.110 is of a house in Aveiro, Portugal; figure 2.111 is a bandstand in Eastbourne, England. ©Alan Male

2.111

2.112

2.112
This highly complex image was conceived and illustrated by **Rod Hunt**. On close examination, the attention to detail is immense and reveals a myriad of scenarios, themes and subjects that relate directly to contemporary domestic life. The illustration was commissioned for IKEA Russia and is called IKEA KVARTIROVEDINE

Apartmentology. A cross-media campaign, the image presents ten different families and their apartments, with IKEA furniture solutions used to suit each family's lifestyle. The illustration was also used in the book by Russian children's author Grigory Oster and as an online game. The campaign won the Craft for Design Award at D&AD 2015. ©Rod Hunt

3

CONTEXT, IMPACT AND CONSEQUENCE

Ethics, Censorship and Moral Responsibility

Will an increase in multiculturalism, globalization, political and environmental change bring about adjustments in the way illustrators think and approach their work. And might this in turn have an adverse effect on the way illustration exerts its potential for power and influence?

Like all other human beings, illustrators will have a personal threshold regarding ethical practice, moral standards and conviction. And, as with the vast sweep of humanity, these thresholds will differ and sway dramatically from one individual to another. To a large extent, all people are directed by customs and conventions laid down by the societies they inhabit, by the formal governance of those societies *and* cultural diktats – which are broadly of our own choosing – religious, artistic, ethnic or otherwise.

Today, one such principle of moral 'guidance' (and expected line of protocol) is that of political correctness. Some think it is a 'curse' and others think it underpins a functioning, modern society. However, if no one went *beyond* the limits of what is acceptable, then no one would *push* at the limits of what is acceptable. In a homogenous world, where everyone is on alert for a reason to feel outraged, we may need to defend those who (even perhaps for a joke) are not totally shackled to the concept of propriety. Typically, these could be illustrators whose work deliberately bastardizes the sanctity of certain themes and individuals, all for the purpose of providing shock and damning comment. Offence and insult can be read into any form of communication, either through broadcast or publication, and as the history of illustration has shown, this is a discipline capable of delivering the most controversial of messages.

DANGEROUS PRECEDENTS

One of the most controversial themes tackled by illustrators in the latter part of the twentieth century and the early decades of the twenty-first is that which pertains to religion, most notably Islam. The growth of Jihad and subsequent terrorist atrocities carried out around the globe have given rise to both intemperate and reactionary outpourings: 'Islamic terror cannot be stopped by the security and intelligence services alone. It has to be fought culturally and economically. We had culture once that would have done the job just fine. But multiculturalism came along and destroyed it'. This is a quote published by *London Revisited*, 11 January 2015. It means that if Europe and rest of the 'free world' are to overcome 'Islamic terror' (a term refuted and despised by the peace-loving Muslim majority), then they need to fight for the values they hold dear. Many will say that illustrators employed by the Paris-based satirical magazine *Charlie Hebdo* paid with their lives when *holding those values dear*. The world expressed horror and revulsion at the *Hebdo* murders. However, there is still a substantial number who think that the magazine in question publishes imagery deliberately inciting distress, anger and grief.

Perhaps it should be observed that thresholds of acceptability regarding how far illustrators can go when producing satire of this kind vary from country to country and community to community. This applies particularly within those blocs that declare common parameters for freedoms of expression to be upheld, such as Europe, North America and the Antipodes. Nevertheless, as single nations, the UK and the United States have a more prescribed notion of how far religious intolerance can be expressed. A few years prior to the Paris atrocity, Danish media published 'cartoons' that inflamed outrage throughout Islam, leading to the perpetrators being threatened with a *fatwā* (assassination). Many people, particularly those from *non*-Scandinavian countries, were prepared to uphold the cartoonists' 'right' for freedom of expression, but broadly condemned the imagery as 'going too far'! However, feelings of revulsion and offence given by satirical illustration come from a great many quarters – and not all religious. Many were angry at the lack of respect shown for the victims of the London terrorist attack of 3 June 2017, imagery published by *Charlie Hebdo* magazine clearly challenging the demarcation lines of moral acceptability regarding the causing of deliberate emotional pain and revulsion.

FREEDOM OF EXPRESSION

But where does this leave the role of the illustrator? What is meant by freedom of expression in the context of global media? And does the illustrator have an ethical and moral responsibility, especially when delivering for a global audience? Broadly speaking, illustration is judged by its impact and influence. However, to many it might seem that illustration itself is being impacted upon by the strictures of a worldwide cultural sensitivity mindful of the need for religious and perhaps political toleration.

To many, *freedom of speech* is a necessity, a given and essential prerequisite of democracy and toleration – the acceptance of everyone's point of view, no matter how unpalatable their views might seem. 'If the freedom of speech is taken away then dumb and silent we may be led like sheep to the slaughter. I disapprove of what you say, but will defend to the death your right to say it. People demand freedom of speech to make up for the freedom of thought which they avoid'. This famous (if now rather clichéd) quote by one of America's founding fathers and first president, George Washington, is a tenet that is deeply embedded in the constitution and social consciousness of the United States. Similarly, it applies to other countries with historic traditions of democracy and liberty, such as Great Britain. But these values are being questioned and in many instances challenged, impacting on all whose work is published or broadcast, and illustrators are no exception.

UPHOLDING STANDARDS

This can be exemplified by the advertising industry. For many years, it was governed by organizations such as the Advertising Standards Authority, which monitors complaints, regulates content and establishes a code of practice. However, some people would like to see the thresholds regarding these criteria significantly raised. For example, there has been a backlash against certain products and services, and the banking sector falls into this category, with its seemingly relentless and unscrupulous promotions, tempting potential customers with products they would never be able to afford. Coming in the wake of the international banking crisis, blamed largely on greed and financial mismanagement, it is a practice seen as immoral and avaricious. But, in a society where *freedom of speech* can be applied to persuasive messaging, will a more robust degree of censure be enforced?

The 'intolerance' directed at this type of campaign does not just come from society at large. Advertising agencies, illustrators, graphic designers and photographers are becoming vociferous about their own ethical and moral position. It is worth noting that in recent years, the recipients of international awards for design and illustration, particularly in the context of advertising, have been dominated by themes associated with public awareness campaigns and charitable trusts. Typical organizers for granting such awards are the British-based D&AD (Design and Art Directors Club of Great Britain), their familiar 'yellow pencils' given on an annual basis for the most outstanding work. Clients such as Amnesty International, Save the Children, the New York Society for Ethical Culture and many environmental and wildlife conservation groups have all had promotional and awareness campaigns featured in these awards.

PROFESSIONAL PRACTICE AND MORAL CONVICTION

What is the impact on the way illustrators operate professionally, particularly when faced with a potential commission that is highly lucrative, but questionable regarding its aim and campaign thrust? Since the 1990s, there has been a progressive change in attitude towards subjects like the environment, health, race and gender. Increased awareness and a willingness to present and discuss these issues mean that in the eyes of many, it is no longer acceptable to purely 'take the money and run'. Many illustrators and graphic designers will work in a freelance, self-employed capacity, therefore being responsible for their own business practices and income. Therein lies the dilemma: many will be at the early stages of their careers and not financially secure – family pressures, along with rent or mortgage liabilities, will undoubtedly bear heavy on some. Does one accept the assignment in question, an undertaking that conflicts with conscience and ethical standing, or do the job and accept the large fee on offer? Many will not be fazed, but these questions present a consistency regarding the growth of principled feelings within society at large.

Many of these 'feelings' manifest by way of social media. This is a platform that itself unwittingly provides a certain censure regarding many aspects of cultural and political life. Vast numbers of subscribers will 'come together' online to protest and broadcast their views unabated without any vituperation or editorial control. The *Sky News* correspondent Katie Spencer suggested that in 1977, social media would have 'put a stop to the Sex Pistols'. This band defined the punk era with their extreme anti-establishment sentiments by releasing their 'version' of 'God Save the Queen'. The iconic record sleeve design was by illustrator and self-proclaimed anarchist Jamie Reid and has been identified as establishing the distinctive punk aesthetic. Aided by Reid's imagery, the 'offence' given by the Sex Pistols was the ultimate publicity stunt of its time. Music writer David Hepworth insists that 'one of the reasons you can't have rock stars nowadays is they'd spend most of their time apologising for stuff. If there were Johnny Rottens today, it'd be very difficult for them to get their message out – it would be all diffused by social media: as soon as they made any outrageous, provocative statements, they would very quickly be called upon before the court of public opinion and forced to apologise. It's a different world'.

This high-profile, albeit anecdotal example shows that whatever subject is broadcast, performed or published today, social media will have an impact on its acclaim or recognition. As a media-based discipline, this clearly has implications for illustration. Illustrators will need to be conscious of sound ethical practices, not just in a pure professional sense but also with regards to their public and personal behaviours. It is prevalent to note the increase in online professional networking services such as LinkedIn, plus other exclusive groups given solely for illustrators, designers and artists. These provide platforms for discussion and cooperation, but can also be a vehicle for unsuspecting members to divulge opinions or actions that may be compromising to the individual in question or anathema to others. Reputation and status in the world of visual communication is no longer confined to pure professional practice; discussion and 'having a voice' is now considered important and relevant, and having the 'right' attitude and conviction carries weight regarding one's prospects.

DISCRIMINATION AGAINST THE PRACTITIONER

It is known that ethical and moral concerns impact on the lives and practices of certain illustrators. One such issue is that of racial discrimination. An example relates to a successful black illustrator, living some distance from his client base in New York, coming into the city to personally deliver a piece of artwork to an agency. He was not believed to be the illustrator when at the building entrance; it was thought he could only be 'the FedEx man'!

Illustrators can encounter mordant prejudice and discrimination regarding the contents of their work, as particular groups become increasingly zealous about protecting their faiths and convictions. The traditions and beliefs of some cultural or national groupings suggest that subjects like religion and politics should be avoided altogether. As previously mentioned, in the United States, some states have made it unlawful for schools to promote the theory of evolution when teaching science without the biblical story of creation being taught in parallel. This can also apply to certain schools in the UK: in spite of its seemingly secular and multicultural stance, Britain still has an inordinate number of single-faith educational institutions across a range of religions. As a result, publishers of scientific material, particularly for children, might become mindful of taboo subjects, so illustrating these themes may be compromised in the future.

There are arguments that censorship can take many other forms. The writer Rachel Cooke stated in an article for the *Guardian* (7 April 2013): 'The idea of "ethical art" is nonsense. We have to separate art from life'. Her thesis was founded on a decision made by the Tate Gallery in London to remove thirty-four prints from an online collection by a certain well-known artist who had been found guilty and imprisoned for indecency and indecent assault on a child. The Tate's reasoning for this was that it considered 'wider ethics'. Cooke questions 'what is meant by wider ethics' – if the thirty-four images do not portray the artist's victims, would they be returned to the public domain? Cooke insists that they must: 'For if it is unethical to show work by a paedophile, what are they going to do about all the other artists who had dubious sex lives? What was art last month must surely be art this month. You can't un-do art'. However, a pertinent

3.1

3.2

3.1 and 3.2
Illustrators have long depicted ethnic variance in humankind, from ancient Egyptian hieroglyphics to the detailed, pictorial engravings of the Enlightenment era showing the 'glorified' cruelty and subjugation of African slaves and the patronizingly repressive 'educational' images of *black savages*, *barbaric redskins* and various other *uneducated and heathen* 'primitive people'! The twentieth century has faired no better. For example, the children's illustrated storybook *Little Black Sambo* by Helen Bannerman became an object of allegations of racism. There are too numerous examples to cite here, but illustration has been at the core of this controversy for many years. Today, the debate continues incessantly. Academic and illustrator Sabrina Scott states in an abstract for a published paper, 'If we take illustration seriously as a form of intellectual and cultural production that influences, reproduces and reinvigorates public and private discourse, what do the pictures we make and the way we represent human bodies within them say about our personal (as private persons) and public (as creative professionals) understandings of race and gender? Do most of today's award winning illustrators challenge dominant power paradigms, or consolidate oppressive hegemonic representations as common sense? What happens when illustrators try to depict The Other? How can we avoid these pitfalls and their consequences?' (taken from *Drawing the Other: Illustration and Representation*). The two illustrations shown are by American artist **Andrew M Kish III**. Kish is renowned for producing work that confronts both suggestive and controversial issues: themes of a socio-political nature, often imbued with ethical, thought-provoking messages. Figure 3.6 is entitled *Divided We Fall* and figure 3.7 is called *Gravity*.
©Andrew M Kish III

3.3

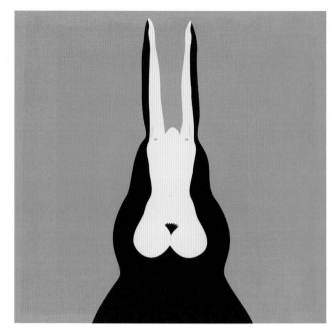

3.4

3.3 and 3.4
The two illustrations shown would probably incite controversy if published in a context deemed reverent, decorous and seemly – such as educational material or media aimed at religious or pious audiences. However, publications delivering content for occidental subscribers considered liberal thinking and 'broad minded' might still be charged with fomenting offence by those wishing to uphold 'moral standards'.

3.3
Oral Sex; Sex Education for Adults, illustrated by **Chiara Ghigliazza** ©Chiara Ghigliazza

3.4
Easier with who ever you want!, illustrated by **Benedetto Cristofani** ©Benedetto Cristofani

3.5 and 3.6
The representation of religion by illustration has been widespread and ubiquitous for centuries, giving whichever faith, creed or denomination a visual identity by iconography and/or narrative glorification. However, in recent years and through the context of commentary and editorial media, the message has changed dramatically. Depending on which country or region the publication originates from, it is not uncommon for the most irreverent and intemperate content to be expounded with Islam and in many cases Christianity bearing the brunt of the offence and criticism. Many would claim that the growth of Jihad and subsequent acts of terrorism lies at the door of Islam generally and the faith as a whole deserves the stoutest of condemnation. This is a theme that illustrators have and will continue to tackle.

3.5
Is this Islam? Fundamentalism distorts representation of Arab Culture, La Stampa, Italian news journal, **Benedetto Cristofani** ©Benedetto Cristofani

3.6
Artists and Designers Against War . . . or whatever they call it, **Paul Garland** ©Paul Garland

3.7
This is an illustration conceived and produced by **Mario Minichiello**; it was commissioned to accompany an article entitled 'The Frank Approach to Titillation', published by British daily newspaper the *Guardian*, April 1992. Considered perceptive and provocative, a published review stated that it 'takes us to places we fear to go and forces us to confront issues, sometimes directly through what we see, sometimes through the gaze of the "lookers" who pack these images'. Dr Pat Kirkham, professor of design history, Bard Graduate Center, New York. ©Mario Minichiello

3.5

3.6

3.7

question should be asked in relation to this story: can you 'un-do' illustration? Again, the answer must be no. Irrespective of an illustrator's perceived misdemeanours, the broad nature of practice covering the spectrum of broadcast and publishing contexts plus its remit for objective communication will suggest that little or no connection can be made between the imagery and any crime or malpractice undertaken by the illustrator.

CARICATURE AND THE CULT OF PERSONALITY

Illustration will deliver the most felicitous caricatures of individuals, either as extreme distortions or by being flatteringly realistic. However, in the context of satire, caricatures can denounce well-known (and not-so-well-known) individuals by having their integrity taken way beyond the edge of 'acceptable comment' to vicious personal insults. But is it right to do so? What if an illustrator is required to go beyond his or her threshold for ethics and responsibility? Would the illustrator accept the commission?

Perhaps a distinction should be made between material that is broadly acceptable – even if portrayed in an unpalatable fashion regarding public interest – and that which is not. Unsurprisingly, those news reports that pour scorn, deliver vicious insults and uncompromising offence would not be censured if aimed at the sympathizers of terrorist organizations and the denigrators of norms within society. Also, few would disagree with sentiments denigrating the character, ideology and actions of a heinous individual like an oppressive and cruel dictator.

However, there are those individuals regarded as 'harmless' but media inflated: superstar personalities whose only 'crime' is to influence fashion and trend. However, they incite derision and ridicule from certain quarters such as the media and those not culturally aligned – but idolization from their 'adoring fans'. Degrading and extreme critical portrayals are often castigated as being intrusive, immoral and totally unnecessary. The press and other news organizations are sometimes chastised for their invasive and unethical behaviour in order to 'get a story'. The paparazzi (photographers) receive the most objurgate criticism, but illustration is just as blameworthy when it comes to personal slights of this nature. US President Donald Trump is no exception, being the recipient of a great many insults and degradations, courtesy of a global array of renowned cartoonists and illustrators!

CIRCUMSPECTION FOR FUTURE PRACTICE

To conclude, if illustration is to thrive in the future, it will *not* have to do with the superficiality of trend and the vicissitudes of visual language, but more to do with compliance and toleration regarding content and message and an increasing acceptance for audiences and their thresholds of moral and ethical sympathies. Extreme violence, particularly in video games, so often developed and visually conceived by illustrators, has become exposed and subjected to much criticism. This, along with other themes inciting discomfort within certain enclaves of society – targeted religious denominations or patronizing comments about certain cultural practices – may curb broader debate. Subjects once considered fair game for vigorous 'dissection' will probably become taboo. It remains to be seen how this will impact on illustration in the future, but as the *Charlie Hebdo* outrage has already shown, caution and deliberation will have to be administered.

3.8

3.8
This illustration comprises a powerful commentary that challenges a contemporary perception that particular socio-economic, religious and political communities in the so-called free West are 'poles apart' regarding attitudes and actions espoused by the very terrorist groups they might rail against. In reality, many would suggest that there are worrying similarities, such as the love and indiscriminate use of firearms and an uncensored adherence to the most extreme aspects of rival faith beliefs. Illustrators that present and publish such views could be seen as 'treading on dangerous ground', the offence felt by those targeted likely expressed with uttermost anger and distain. However, it is likely that the vast majority of those who view and read imagery such as this will wholeheartedly agree with its message. The image was conceived, written and drawn by London-based American illustrator and designer **Rebecca Hendin** and was published by Universal Uclick via GoComics.com. ©Rebecca Hendin

3.9

3.12

3.10

3.13

3.11

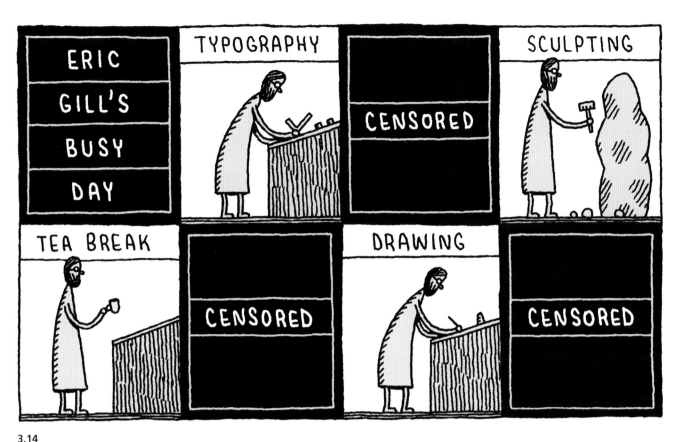

3.14

3.9, 3.10, 3.11, 3.12 and 3.13
With regards to upholding standards, it has long been the case that the advertising industry has been subjected to harsh criticism, particularly over those campaigns considered unscrupulous and amoral. However, it is prevalent to note how many campaigns today relate to public awareness or are charitable in nature, with many environmental and conservation groups featuring strongly. This case study comprises a campaign for BirdLife International, widely recognized as the world leader in bird conservation. The campaign was created by advertising agency Saatchi & Saatchi Singapore and was the recipient of a D&AD Graphite Pencil Award in Crafts for Advertising and Photography in Advertising, 2017. The campaign was devised on the premise

that forest fires in Indonesia are becoming an annual occurrence in order to clear land for farming; palm oil companies burn virgin rainforests, resulting in severe habitat loss for animals, especially birds. Indonesia's birdlife is critically endangered. The agency recreated the most endangered species, many on the verge of extinction, from charred and burned leaves. Each bird is formed from the trees that in nature provide them with shelter but ultimately threaten their existence. The chief creative officer was **Dominic Stallard**, illustrator was **Ming Bong** and photographer was **Jeremy Wong**. ©Saatchi & Saatchi Singapore ©BirdLife International

3.14
Certain illustrators, artists and designers from the past led reprehensible lives that would undoubtedly land them in prison today. Does this mean we should value their work less? This illustration by **Tom Gauld** makes reference to both the private and professional life of Arthur Eric Rowton Gill, English typeface designer, artist, sculptor and printmaker. Gill's reputation has been severely marred over the years by revelations of sexual abuse, particularly of his daughters, plus stories of other heinous sexually related misdemeanours. Opinion is strongly divided regarding the divarication between 'art and life' and to what degree it should be separated. Some people believe that personal biography is irrelevant and that the work should speak for itself. There

are others who vehemently hold opposing views and suggest practitioners such as Gill and any others having lived or living 'darkly' should be castigated and condemned, their work never to be seen again. It has been argued that museums and those publications considered responsible and objective have a duty to present and talk about 'difficult issues' and be a platform for critical debate, allowing society to draw their own conclusions. ©Tom Gauld

3.15

3.16

3.15 and 3.16

The craft of caricature has been prevalent in illustration for centuries. Possibly the earliest examples of note were Leonardo da Vinci's famous – or infamous, depending on one's take – fifteenth-century series of grotesque heads, the 'perfect deformities complimentary to an ideal of beauty'. Also, at that time elsewhere in Europe, the new printing revolution helped to spread widespread discontent by publishing pamphlets caricaturing despised religious and political leaders. In late eighteenth-century England, illustrators and caricaturists such as James Gillray and Thomas Rowlandson lampooned the ruling classes with great irreverence, and a century later the likes of George Cruikshank popularized the *political cartoon* in newspapers and magazines. During the 1960s, British illustrators Peter Fluck and Roger Law created notable three-dimensional caricatures photographed for publication in the *New York Times* and in the 1980s devised the television satire *Spitting Image*. Today, unflattering insults and degradation through caricatured imagery continue unabated.

Figure 3.15 was illustrated by **Anita Kunz** and commissioned for the cover of *Variety* magazine to promote an article entitled 'Hollywood and Politics: *Media Monster*'. The presidential candidates star in TV's weirdest reality show'. ©Anita Kunz

Figure 3.16 is an illustration created and drawn by **Jake Abrams** and produced for the cover of the British current affairs magazine the *Spectator*, 25 April 2009. The figure shown is of Boris Johnson, mayor of London at the time of publication, celebrating the anniversary of his first year in office. Johnson is a member of the British Conservative Party, politically centre-right. The *Spectator* broadly supports that wing of politics, and it is worth noting that the caricature is one of endearment rather than overt castigation. ©Jake Abrams

Globalization and Audience

Effective and meaningful visual communication requires a complete understanding of the audience. This is a fundamental requirement of any brief. Across the key contexts of illustration, any subject, message, comment or persuasive prod can be delivered. This implies that anyone anywhere can be targeted by visual communication, from society at large to narrow focused groupings defined by age, gender, cultural background, socio-economic status, income, profession or personal interests such as hobbies. Advertising agencies and the marketing divisions of retailers and service providers will employ complex methods of classification to identify their particular target groups and will use these sociological and demographic studies to determine their strategies.

AUDIENCE APPEASEMENT

Subject matter and context will determine the audience. The advertising industry has become extremely adept at knowing where, when and how to target their potential customers. Campaigns developed for television broadcast will fill time slots appropriate for their message; for instance, expensive life insurance and quality motor car advertisements might screen during the commercial breaks of a late evening documentary, whilst the latest computer games and other 'younger generation' products might be shown during popular or mainstream early evening programmes. Strategies such as these apply across all aspects of the media where advertising space is sold.

Magazines, journals and newspapers that offer political or social review and analysis will aim to satisfy their regular readers – whose opinions are akin to their own. The editorial stance is prevalent throughout the media industry, with certain publications known for their political leanings. Collectively, a range of opinion is represented in all directions from far left to reactionary right. Specialist magazines given to defined social or cultural groupings such as religious or economic organizations will also expect illustrative imagery to comply with the slant given to the issues explored.

YOUNG AUDIENCES

In children's literature, the age range of the target audience, their cultural backgrounds and learning needs all need to be taken into consideration when it comes to a book's content. It is not unusual for publishers to use school grading systems or curriculum measures to identify the needs of a particular age group, to ascertain their abilities. This also gives an idea of their literacy and visual comprehension of illustrations. Children's age ranges determine specific levels of publication.

Picture books are identified for the youngest children, from six months to very early readers, and comprise novelty products such as floating bath and board 'shape' books with simple text and traditional stories, or repetitive content narratives with either no text or very simple text. With regards to any power or influence that the illustrator might exert in this context, the audience most likely affected will be the adults who buy these products. Originality regarding 'illustrated' physically interactive material that enables very young children to connect with and learn even the most ubiquitous and simplistic of elements, such as texture, shape, colour and even sound, will inspire many parents or guardians. Chapter books are for older children, generally in the five- to eight-year-old age group, and are technically picture books of a more sophisticated nature, with more regard given to the complexity of both imagery and language. Materials for children eight to twelve years old are known as first novels, while publications for teenagers are considered young adult material. In the latter two instances, illustration is used less frequently, but the great range of picture and chapter books for young readers places considerable emphasis and importance on the illustrative content, with themes and messages being largely conveyed by visual means.

Similar classifications for age range and aptitude are given to non-fiction publications for children. Often, stricter and more rigid criteria are applied to these products because the visualization and presentation of facts to young audiences, usually in an educational context, has to comply with requirements of a national/state curriculum as well as compete in the retail market.

A GLOBAL PERSPECTIVE

The oft-repeated cliché that the world is getting smaller represents how media and communications industries now reach across all continents and cultures. With the rise of web and satellite broadcasting, both industries are experiencing an ever-increasing need for communicators such as editors and commentators, manufacturers and service providers, educators and researchers, and entertainers to expound their messages and promote their products. Then there are the consumers, who are, in the main, willing audiences for and recipients of all this information, entertainment and product. However, there are strictures to be mindful of when addressing a global audience, and illustrators are not excluded from adhering to these codes of practice. What might be acceptable to one culture or nationality may be anathema to another.

Children's book publishing is typically careful to ensure strict adherence to international audience-sensitivity guidelines. This is particularly relevant when representing characters and objects; if the published narrative demands the depiction of human interaction and drama, the physical gestures made by the figures and the appearance of other signifiers of taste such as styles of clothing or aspects of behaviour must conform to all cultural sensibilities. What may be entertaining to the peoples of one society may be offensive to those of another.

International markets, particularly in publishing, will dictate whether or not a product will be developed and produced, and this applies to both children's fiction and non-fiction. For example, some UK publishers will only go ahead provided they have secured deals abroad, especially with companies in the United States. This will greatly affect content, as both image and text will be aimed at a broader, multinational audience. Consequentially, this can affect the nature of the image imparted – with the quirkiness or special essence of a story, born from the idiosyncrasies of a particular culture

or environment, often replaced or tempered in order to suit wider audience comprehension and appeal.

Non-fiction books for young audiences, particularly those published specifically for trade consumerism as opposed to defined national or state curricular purposes, are subjected to ethical scrutiny. Also, when published internationally, where relevant, the content should adhere to precepts of respect and support for conservation, the environment and the welfare of peoples. Books about history and society should be mindful to avoid jingoistic references and prejudices, pursuing themes promoting fairness and equality regarding culture, race and gender.

Countries that once had closed borders and autocratic regimes are not only democratizing, but opening up to Western values and buying Western goods. This is having a significant impact on most contexts of visual communication practice. Images for promoting and advertising a galaxy of Western products and services may well need to be adapted for those new audiences. For example, in China most illustration is heavily influenced by Japanese manga and graffiti-esque urban culture. Indeed, China has even embraced Christmas Day and St Valentine's Day, the icons and ubiquitous semiotics of those overtly Western traditions becoming increasingly embedded in the national psyche.

As far back as the fifteenth century, illustrators and engravers, aided and abetted by the invention of printing, sought to influence and change social and political opinion by depicting libellous satire, ridiculing the actions, deeds and personalities of public figures. Today, in a more regulated journalistic environment and a more litigious world, the ethics around this kind of criticism have shifted and publications must be more cautious about how they frame and substitute their claims. There have been a number of attacks upon international media organizations for publishing and broadcasting 'fake news'. This will naturally have an influence on the content and thrust of journalistic illustration, particularly that which expresses controversial views. To reiterate, *the world is getting smaller*, and through publishing, broadcast and online, there is now a massive global audience.

3.17

3.17
This is a poster created for the Anti Harassment Movement and was designed by **Ashraf Foda** of Vision Advertising, Cairo, Egypt. The nature of its inherent message challenges an issue that is prevalent within certain countries and communities around the world. Being created in Egypt, the poster extends the cultural reach of the problem from Western society to the Middle Eastern. A powerful image, the illustration makes its argument in part through use of negative space through which we see a woman who does not appear until she is defined by the hands that reveal her, letting the audience know that what she *should* think and how she *should* look is controlled by others. The only part of her that is left shown is her facial indignation at being so defined.
©Ashraf Foda

3.18

3.18 and 3.19

The two illustrations shown are by **Emily Johns**, who was awarded a drawing bursary to document the experience of travelling to Iran in 2006 on a Fellowship of Reconciliation peace delegation during a period of international tension over Iran's nuclear programme. Entitled *Drawing Paradise on the Axis of Evil*, Johns created a body of images weaving together the larger international dynamics, the mutual cultural influences and more intimate personal connections of Iranian-British relations. The project is considered as *pre-war art*, an equivalent process for a conflict that is hoped will never take place. It deals with themes that a war artist might deal with but in a period of tension rather than the outbreak of hostilities. *Axis of Evil* is an attempt to use imaginative engagement and provoke a more rounded debate. Figure 3.18 is entitled *Major Gerald Talbot and the Tobacco Fatwa* and relates to a widely obeyed fatwa of 1891 against tobacco use. Talbot had won a concession to institute a monopoly of tobacco trade with Iran. The fatwa resulted in everybody stopping smoking and rendered the monopoly of tobacco trade useless. ©Emily Johns

3.19

3.20

3.20
Illustration for children will be always be scrutinized to ensure adherence to international audience-sensitivity guidelines. This is particularly relevant when depicting characters, objects, pictorial drama and human interaction. Gestures, appearance and behaviour must conform to all cultural sensibilities. This illustration is by **Briony May Smith** and was commissioned for *Highlights for Children* magazine. There is a diversity of characterization shown, along with a scenario that conveys wonderment and awe rather than any sense of threat or overt danger. ©Briony May Smith

New Knowledge

The presentation of new knowledge has through the ages caused consternation, fear, ridicule and disbelief as well as wonderment, excitement and awe – this knowledge comes from the great scientific discoveries and pioneering voyages of exploration, technological advancements and invention, plus the many cultural and social challenges that defy the norm. These challenges in particular have perpetrated angst and outrage, typically because of potential threats to religious belief, economic stability and that general sense of a need to maintain the status quo. Even fear of invasion from outer space has been spawned from information regarding all things astral and cosmic! However, there are aspects of new knowledge that have generated intense interest and amazement, with many people 'gripped' with exhilaration and anticipation – an impending expectancy to discover life elsewhere in the universe and progressive research leading to the advancement of medical science are typical examples. Nevertheless, from the earliest civilizations right up to the present day, it is the craft of visual communication that has largely facilitated this immediacy of impact and reaction upon society, irrespective of its underlying medium, from the cave paintings of our Palaeolithic ancestors to online state-of-the-art CGI.

What is meant by new knowledge in the context of illustration practice? An initial overview will reveal that it broadly delivers the following: reference, information, education, documentation, instruction, research and most significantly, new and original knowledge. Topics, themes and concepts will be comprehensive and multi-various, from subjects studied at the very apex of educational and industrial research to all that is considered non-fiction and delivered via popular broadcast and publication. Typically, everything that touches humanity can be served from culture, science and technology.

ACTUALITY VERSUS MISREPRESENTATION

So, with regards to the vast context of knowledge, where does illustration affect true power and influence, and does it deliberately distort the truth? The question raises a clear divergence of direction for a range of knowledge-bearing themes: *actuality* versus *misrepresentation*, or in other words, literal reality versus the covert and the preposterous.

The history of art for science and learning is illustrious and influential, from Euclid's first ever published diagram in 300 BC to the great polymaths of the Renaissance to twenty-first-century audiences thirsting for new knowledge via the ever-expanding creative and media industries. But, over the years, the representation of subject matter and message has been subjected to dictate, sometimes resulting in a battle for moral supremacy. For example, both church and state prescribed the agenda for depicting nature and the 'forces of God'. A typical case is the creationist vision of the antediluvian landscape, featuring Nordic-Aryan 'Adonis-like' Adam and Eve figures, far removed from the theories expounded by the likes of Darwin and Huxley. At this juncture, it is worth appraising the porous demarcation between science fact and science fiction, the blurring between the visual representation of ontological truth with fantasy – and why factual and evaluative speculation can be distorted in order to emphasize cultural, political and religious conviction. Also, these 'distortions' are frequently the subject of populist, journalistic sensationalism.

ONTOLOGICAL TRUTH

This is the frame of reference that delivers the obvious – in other words, all that is actual, proven and real. *Ontology* is the study of things that are seen as tangible and true; it is associated with *morphology*, the scientific study of form and structure, particularly that of living organisms. In a scientific context, it cannot be argued against; in a basic sense, 'all is there to see', whether before one's very eyes or through other means that are proven and verified. In a visual arts capacity, it can be applied to anything that is understandable regarding its physical tangency and reality. There can be no argument; factual evidences outweigh any suppositions or discrepancy.

The validity of any research that claims to present new or original knowledge has to be couched in as much authentication as possible, particularly when derived from an *empirical* research methodology as opposed to a theoretical one. It will have come from a procedure that relies on observation, experimentation or sensory experiences: the detection of the presence of black holes in far-off galaxies, the taxonomy and zoological classification of a newly discovered species, the development of a cure for a previously untreatable disease. Illustration used in this context will be state of the art 3-D animation. NASA (the National Aeronautical & Space Administration) will be a typical client, perhaps needing to show the latest flypast of a remote moon within the solar system. Other thematic examples could be a street-by-street journey through an ancient Roman town, recently discovered by archaeological field research and realistically brought to life, or the procedures undertaken by groundbreaking surgery, all of which are broadcast by newsreels, television documentaries and digital apps or published in subject-specific research journals or magazines such as *Nature*, *The Lancet*, *National Geographic*, *New Scientist* and *Scientific American*.

Research outcomes that have been formulated by analysing pure theoretical evidences can be more difficult to quantify and are usually subject to intense scrutiny: un-corroboration will meet with opposition. Even a positive response from the peer review process will not quash the scepticism and derision from the popular press, social media and public at large. If the thesis being expounded does not deliver any form of meaningful proof or purpose in terms of 'usefulness' to society, then its raison d'être is quashed.

Illustration associated with representing ontological truth can be extremely varied with regards to stylization and subject matter. For example, a picture portraying *real space*, such as believable placement, delineation and spatial dimensions, scape perspective and interactivity, will satisfy any ontological factors providing its message and theme is proven and validated. Surprising to some, this can include children's non-fiction books; an example could be a book about nature whereby animals are represented semi-abstractly, interacting within a lively, fanciful setting – yet clearly identifiable regarding their morphology, character and behaviour. Also, historical reconstructions can be autographically rendered in dramatic compositional fashion utilizing an impressionist and painterly style; the work of the twentieth-century American illustrator Tom Lovell comes to mind, with his masterpieces of technical accuracy and stunning, cinematic compositions. Lovell was particularly well known for portraying Native American history and the American Civil War.

Innovative approaches to visual language and representation have been controversial regarding the publication of facts. In this instance, it could be considered that the parameters of pure ontology and of commercially driven publishing or broadcast become distinctly blurred and overlapping; the children's series *Horrible Histories* is a typical example. However, the alternative viewpoint suggests that illustrations considered an embodiment of thematic accuracy are produced with the utmost integrity and authority, and allowing artistic licence to 'run amok' would invalidate the credibility of the work in hand.

PHENOMENOLOGICAL TRUTH

In a general sense, the definition of *phenomenology* suggests the study of human experiences in which any consideration for ontological and objective reality is *not* taken into account – in other words, something known to be believable, even experienced through the senses, but not necessarily seen. So, where do knowledge-bearing illustrations rest within this context, and what implications are inherent in the development and production of such work?

Whatever subject is in question, such as a timeline through a specific period of history, the evolution of life, photosynthesis, or the birth of a distant star system, the essence of these concepts is both abstract and illusory. Largely, the illustrations will convey concepts known to be proven and real, but devoid of any direct morphological being. The outcome will be a *visual denouement* whereby strands of the concept or process are drawn together and matters are then explained and resolved. The finished imagery can be diagrammatic or conceptual and will need to be designed in such a way as to accurately depict the physical and behavioural manifestations borne as a consequence of these 'unseen' processes and concepts, such as the ebb and flow of life throughout the duration of the Roman Empire, the gradual changes in animal form and behaviour as a result of 'the means of natural selection', tree growth and ecology, or the forming of galaxies and solar systems over billions of years.

The most ubiquitous form of illustration used in this context is the *diagram*. It has, over the centuries, been a pivotal means to explain, elucidate and educate. In its earliest form, it was drawn on natural edifices such as cliff faces and caves by the peoples of prehistory. Imbued with hieroglyphics, these diagrams informed of astronomical and other natural formulations, cultural dictates, hunting and agricultural procedures. Today, the diagram – in all of its manifestations – can be an innovative and richly colourful image that goes far beyond the basics of pure information graphics as seen in the drab and formal graphs and charts used in education or the corporate boardroom. Instead, illustrated maps, detailed cross sections and engaging interactive features, whether online or in the form of a 'pop-up' book format, will convey knowledge with great authority and contextual appropriation.

FANTASY

The integrity for producing knowledge-bearing illustration will often be compromised. There will be several reasons, most commonly because of scant research, poor referencing or ill-informed 'factual evidences'. Also, in some cases there will be an adherence to alternative cultural-belief systems, often driven by religious diktat; here, the imagery presents a distorted viewpoint, borne out of a need for taboo avoidance and a denial of the 'truth'. One such example could be a narrative, couched in an uncompromising faith-belief and presented as a historical fait accompli about the supernatural healing powers of a former deity on earth.

There will also be those illustrators who will unwittingly deviate from the principal aim of producing factual accuracy, purely for the sake of 'artistic licence'. This is done by making the imagery as engaging as possible, enhancing any dramatic effect and generally 'making it look good'! The resultant illustrations can *at best* be described as 'romantic', idealized and idyllic, overtly aesthetic suppositions – such as colourful, unrealistically composed scenes within a rainforest, teeming with luminous, attractive fauna and flora, 'birds of paradise, giant iridescent birdwing butterflies and beautiful flowers'.

Because of stringent reviews and editorial control processes, mainstream and specialist-educational publishers will deliver material with probity and rectitude. However, there is much that is in the public domain, either online or in print, that falls short of these virtues. Some magazines, particularly those aimed at 'sensation-seekers' or the 'studiously obsessive', deliberately thwart undisputed factual evidences, usually in the guise of 'popular science'. For example, highly detailed and dramatically convincing illustrations will frequently appear, showing the latest incarnation of the Yeti, 'Bigfoot' or the 'Abominable Snowman'. Images of this nature over-dramatize and deliberately distort, and this is where the fine line between fact and fiction is crossed, usually for the sake of commercial success. Typical examples of this abound in the first *Jurassic* Park movie, whereby the so-called raptor dinosaurs never actually existed, being based on the much smaller velociraptor.

To conclude, any visual language associated with the communication of knowledge will broadly fall within one of two categories: the *elegant* or the *didactic*. The elegant utilizes aesthetics in order to 'charm and seduce'. This type of image can be associated with anything that relies on 'drawing the audience in' by using emotive or bombastic visualization: 'charismatic' subject matter representation, making the principal aspect appear 'larger than life'. It is also a form of stylization that will rely on enticement by choice of colour, compositional presence and allure. The didactic form is purely instrumental in communicating raw, factual information. Early published examples are the 'dry', and poorly designed, black and white diagrams and simple pictures that were found in nineteenth and early to mid-twentieth-century educational textbooks. However, an engagement with learning and research or the acquisition of reference material, whether in an educational, professional or recreational context, can be considered a more palatable and enjoyable experience if one is acquiring knowledge by ways that entertain, provide interaction or amuse. In order for this to occur, the source of information must transcend the role of basic provider. This, in part, can be facilitated by the creative and innovative use of illustration: a synthesis of both the *elegant* and the *didactic*.

> AN INVESTMENT IN KNOWLEDGE PAYS THE BEST INTEREST.
>
> BENJAMIN FRANKLIN

3.21
From the very dawn of human civilization, the night sky with its myriad of stellar configurations and galaxies has held fascination and wonderment, given religious instruction and meaning, influenced culture and dictated lifestyle through early paganism and astrology. Ancient peoples from the Aztecs to the Palaeolithic hunter-gatherers created a locus for images that depicted star systems, planetary motion and astrological fantasy and magic. In more recent times, space illustration has become intensely sophisticated, from 1940s and 1950s painted reconstructions of planetary landscapes and envisaged spaceship exploration to the state-of-the-art animated CGI of moonscapes and flypasts. A leading protagonist was the American Chesley Bonestell, with his paintings of Saturn and its moons and his inspiration for space travel science fiction. The illustration shown is by the author and is of Trappist-1, a red dwarf star forty light years from earth in the constellation of Aquarius. Trappist-1 is fractionally larger than Jupiter in diameter and is known at the time of writing to have seven earth-sized terrestrial planets in its orbit. This image shows the star as it might appear from the surface of its most outermost planet: simplistic, yet starkly dramatic with its diffused atmosphere, the star and bare rocks. ©Alan Male

3.21

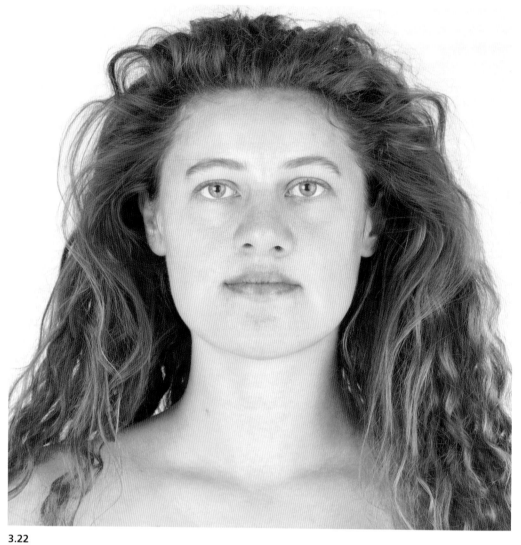

3.22

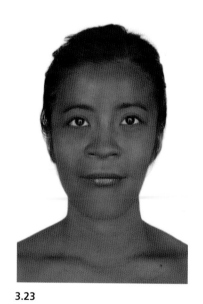

3.23

3.24

3.25

3.26

3.22, 3.23, 3.24 and 3.25

The presentation of new knowledge has been augmented significantly in recent years by the production of superlative hyper-realistic illustration. Presented here are examples of facial reconstruction taken from the skeletal or fossilized remains of individuals who lived millennia ago. This form of illustration has provided society at large, educators and scholars, historians and archaeologists a remarkable insight into how our ancestors actually looked. Figure 3.22 is a young woman aged between eighteen and twenty-two years and standing at 5 feet 5 inches tall (1.65 metres). A member of the Bell Beaker culture, she lived more than 3,700 years ago (in the Bronze Age) in the Scottish Highlands and is dubbed Ava, after the place she was found by archaeologists. This image caused a sensation when first exposed via the international media. It was created by forensic illustrator **Hew Morrison**, who used sophisticated software and tissue-charts to digitally add muscle and skin to Ava's bones. Her facial features were then photorealistically applied. Figure 3.23 is a female from the Iron Age Khmer Empire of Northeast Thailand, figure 3.24 an early Christian Swedish Viking king and figure 3.25 is a female from medieval Edinburgh. All three were reconstructed by Hew Morrison. A great deal of research and facial reconstruction work is carried out by the Centre for Anatomy and Human Identification at the University of Dundee. ©Hew Morrison

3.26

Natural science illustration will encompass not only every aspect of organic life but also those that are inanimate and dubbed *mineral*. Usually couched in the broad remit of earth sciences, this will include geology, meteorology, oceanography, volcanology, ecology, palaeontology and atmospheric science. All of these are subject to illustrative representation that is contextually classed as educative and knowledge bearing. The image shown is by the author and is part of a research project related to the *Coastal Geomorphology of North Cornwall*. From Perranporth, the rock formations reveal exposed greisen veins and are part of the Porthtowan Formation of Devonian rocks. ©Alan Male

3.27

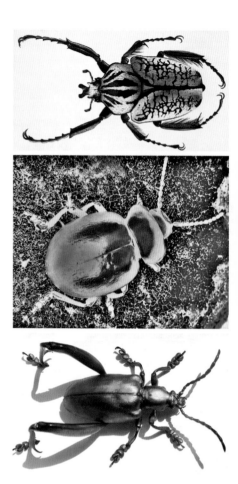

3.28

3.27 and 3.28

Natural history illustration is one of the most ubiquitous regarding non-fiction publication and documentary. Animal and plant life has been visually represented since our Palaeolithic ancestors produced paintings of the wildlife they encountered on rocks and the walls of caves. Since then, vast and innumerable tomes – ranging from scientific treaties of significance and research-laden integrity to the layman encyclopaedias of all things to do with nature – have been provided by this branch of illustration practice much that is informative, scholarly and enlightening. Insects form the largest class of animals, with more species than any other form of animal life put together. The two images shown represent contrasting styles of representation, yet both are contextually informative and educational.

Figure 3.27 is a school poster aimed at young children. It was designed and produced by **LouLou&Tummie**, a creative partnership from the Netherlands. Whilst decorative in nature and having a simplistic and symmetrical design, the insects are recognizable as species and given character and life. It is expedient today for educational material of this kind to be engaging and entertaining, ensuring that the audience is receptive and involved. ©Loulou&Tummie

Stylistically the antithesis of figure 3.27, figure 3.28 is a representative plate of beetles, or *coleoptera*. Produced by the author, the specimen at the top is an autographically rendered image (painted illustration), the centre image is a photo-solarisation produced to convey how it would appear to nocturnal predators and the base specimen is a standard photograph. ©Alan Male

3.29

3.30

3.29 and 3.30

It has been said that natural science illustration demands an approach that ensures the imagery in question is as true as possible to its subject. However, today as with the past, it can be expedient to 'stray' from this premise and produce work that will be broadly an accurate morphological representation, yet 'elegant' – in other words, imagery that utilizes an aesthetic that is seductive rather than that which is purely 'didactic'. The two illustrations shown are representative of this context. Avian subject matter has 'charmed' audiences for many years through exquisite illustration, with American naturalist John James Audubon (1785–1851) considered the original great natural science illustrator, whose attention to detail and characterizations set new precedents for birdlife art.

Figure 3.29 is a wallpaper design to be seen as part of a Georgian interior decoration in the stately home setting of Felbrigg Hall in Norfolk, England. Produced as original paintings, mural style, the imagery conveys a superlative attention to detail yet is highly decorative and in keeping with its historic milieu. Photographed by the author. ©Alan Male

Figure 3.30 is a contemporary study of the bittern (*Botaurus stellaris*), a Eurasian wading bird of the heron family. Illustrated by **Julia Allum**, its pose and habitat is typical of the species. The colours, shapes and other details have been reconstructed to form a more simplistic overall graphic depiction, yet the animal's character and principal forms have been retained. ©Julia Allum

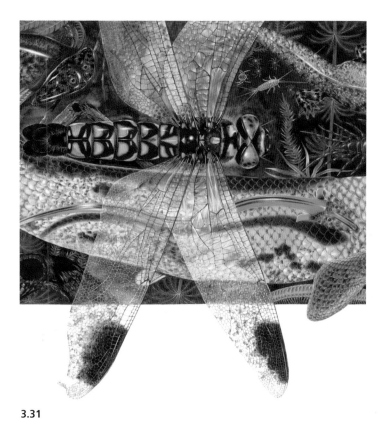

3.31

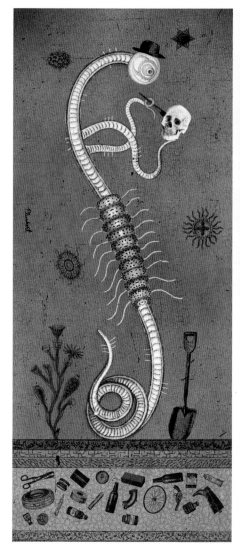

3.32

3.31 and 3.32

The subjects of prehistory and future life are often intrinsically entwined. Frequently, primitive organisms from the earliest epochs of the earth's geologic timescale are utilized to convey the origins of life and subsequent evolution, plus be the inspiration for futuristic science fiction narratives or predictions of how life will become and eventually disappear.

Figure 3.31 is a detail from a much larger illustration produced by the author entitled *A Carboniferous Faunascape*. It shows a close-up of the largest known flying insect to ever exist. Called *meganeura*, it had a wingspan of over 3 feet (1 metre) and inhabited the ancient swamps of the coal forests 350 million years ago. ©Alan Male

Figure 3.32 is an editorial illustration produced by **David Plunkert** for *Chronicle Review* entitled *The Future Belongs to Worms*. Science theory that is embedded in validated research can be supplemented by imagery that is either phenomenological in essence, or tantalizingly conceptual, thus providing additional meaning and comment. ©David Plunkert

3.33 and 3.34

The subject of human evolution has inflamed much argument and debate since it was first brought into the scientific spotlight in the early nineteenth century by the likes of Darwin and Huxley. Even today, certain societies and communities throughout the world are either offended or bemused by the whole concept because of religion or culture.

Figure 3.33 is by **Andrew Selby** and is a clear reference to the controversy associated with the 'Apeman' theory that has pervaded and fomented opinion throughout society. From its earliest reference, published in *The Origin of Species* by Charles Darwin (1859), there are fresh scientific evidences that further strengthen the story of the 'missing link' through recently discovered anthropologic fossilization. ©Andrew Selby

Figure 3.34 can be considered a provocative and unnerving image. Conceived and produced by the author, its remit is to convey the notion that the origin of all life began in ancient primordial seas about 3.8 to 4.1 billion years ago as a chance natural process that synthesized various chemicals into self-replicating molecules, the upshot being the proposition that all living organisms share the same genetic source.

3.33

3.34

So, in spite of many people's revulsion regarding certain reptilian and arachnid forms, humans, centipedes, scorpions, dragonflies, frogs and snakes all share the same biological ancestry. ©Alan Male

3.35
The vocation of *medical illustration* can be traced back as far as the Middle Ages. This was the time of the Renaissance, with considerable advances being made regarding the study of anatomy through direct, objective and primary observation that bound original research with effective drawings and woodblock reproduction. This brought medical practice out of the age of superstition and unproven theory. As time progressed, the attention to detail and pragmatism regarding content and manner of presentation intensified. This illustration does not need any description. It was photographed by the author as part of a display in the Thackray Medical Museum, Leeds, England. Although only dating from the 1950s, its essence can hardly be described as 'aesthetic' or pertaining to 'visual good taste'. The accent is purely to do with providing accurate information and instruction, aimed purely at medical practitioners. Thackray Medical Museum

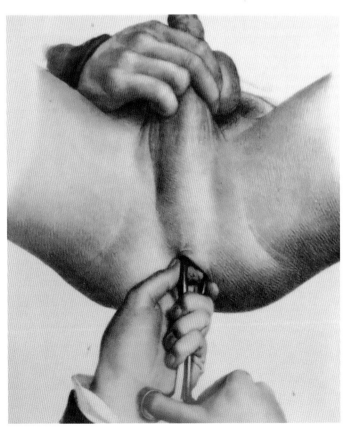

3.35

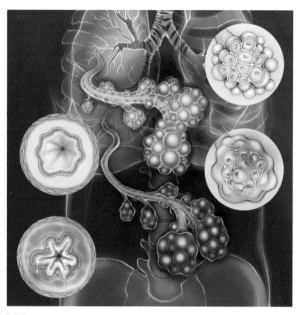

3.36

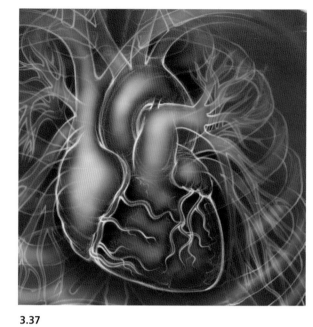

3.37

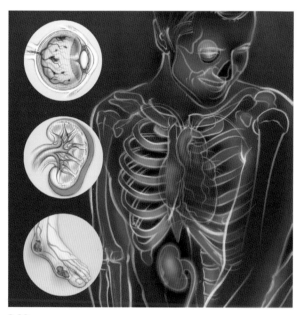

3.38

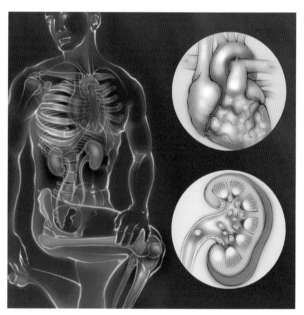

3.39

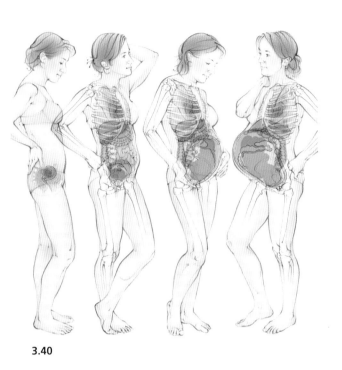

3.40

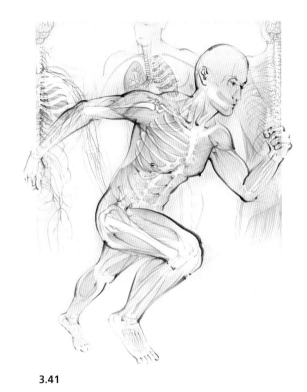

3.41

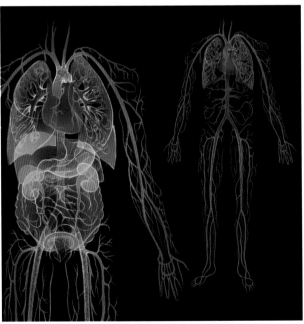

3.42

3.36, 3.37, 3.38, 3.39, 3.40, 3.41 and 3.42
Contemporaneously, whilst the accent is on the provision of accurate information, the visual language of medical illustration can be a much more 'sumptuous' form of stylization, as opposed to the 'frugality' of purely educative material – rich and colourful, highly detailed literal *and* conceptual images rendered to the highest standard of autographic or digital finish. Much emphasis is placed on ensuring an adherence to 'good taste' regarding the presentation of subject matter and aesthetics with visual language. The human subjects are represented as healthy and fit; it is no longer acceptable to depict cadavers with exposed internal organs removed for exposition amid shreds of peeled-back skin and flayed muscle! The days of glorifying a bloody autopsy by painting or illustration are a thing of the past. These illustrations are by leading science and medical illustrator **Juliet Percival**. Percival is professionally engaged at the highest level in subject matter and visual arts practice, having first-class honours degrees in physiology (Edinburgh University) and illustration (Falmouth University). Extremely experienced and diverse in output, she has painted directly onto the naked bodies of living humans for a Channel Four television programme entitled *Live Autopsy*. ©Juliet Percival

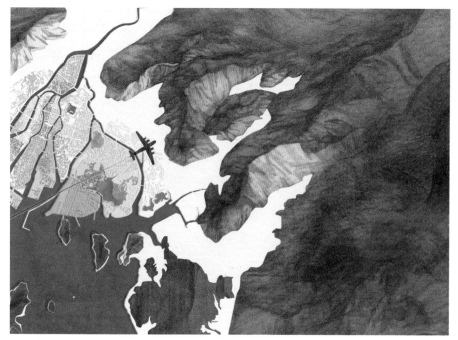

3.43

3.44

3.45

3.46

3.43, 3.44, 3.45 and 3.46
There has always been a need to visually reconstruct subjects associated with human history. The ability to give resurrection and life to the past through the discipline of illustration will be forever in demand. Even when there is photographic evidence of the theme or period in question, illustration can go much further and recreate events with much more detail, emotion, comment and exposition. The four illustrations shown are by illustrator **Nancy** **Liang**. The series is entitled *Junko's Story: Surviving Hiroshima's Atomic Bomb*. The imagery is inspired by the personal testimony of Junko Morimoto, an eighty-three-year-old survivor of the bomb. The work forms part of a responsive website to the story and was made for the seventieth anniversary of Hiroshima in 2015. The illustrations were featured in the 2016 World Illustration Awards. ©Nancy Liang

3.47

3.47
Technological subject matter is multifarious and extremely diverse and offers the illustrator who specializes in this area a boundless list of ontological material as well as an ever-expanding array of concepts, processes and theories. This image is by **Spooky Pooka**, created to package and give identity to an online journal entitled *IEEE Xplore Digital Library*, volume 37, *Architectures for the Post Moore Era*. This is a guest editors' special edition that explores how Moore's law, a techno-economic model enabling the $4 trillion IT industry to double its performance, has started to fail and to predict what the technological drivers for the digital industry might be in the future. ©Spooky Pooka

3.48 and 3.49
Architecture and the urban and built environment are subjects that have engaged visual artists, designers and illustrators for centuries. Think of the magnificent vistas of Venice and other cities created by Canaletto, the *Ascending and Descending* of Escher, the evocative sketches of Paul Hogarth and Yang Yongliang's Chinese landscapes that make poignant statements about post-industrial urbanization. There are far too many great examples to mention. The two examples shown are by the author. Figure 3.48 is a composite study of contrasting architectural forms comprising a contemporary design indulgence, twentieth-century dilapidation and a medieval townscape – all from the north Portuguese city of Braga. Figure 3.49 depicts various aspects of Liverpool Metropolitan Cathedral, England. ©Alan Male

3.48

3.49

3.50

3.50, 3.51, 3.52 and 3.53
Emma Lewis has conceived,
researched, written, designed
and illustrated *The Museum
of Me*, published by Tate (UK)
2016. Truly polymathic by
practice and approach, the
author has produced a project
that is commercial in nature
and aimed specifically at a
young audience. The product
makes no pretence regarding
its contextualized remit and
rests comfortably within the
knowledge-bearing realm of
children's non-fiction. The
content is educational, yet fun
and engaging. The story follows
a little girl's journey of discovery
to find out what museums
are and what they contain.
Brimming with anticipation,
she finds a myriad of artefacts
and natural history specimens.
However, she eventually
discovers that her favourite
museum is her home – the
Museum of Me. This piece
was the winner of the Bologna
Ragazzi Opera Prima Award
2017 and nominated for the
CILIP Kate Greenaway Medal
2018. ©Emma Lewis

3.51

3.52

3.53

3.54

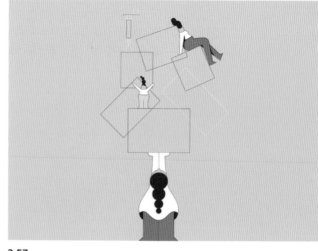

3.57

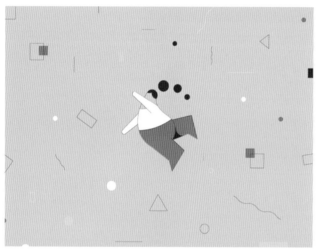

3.55

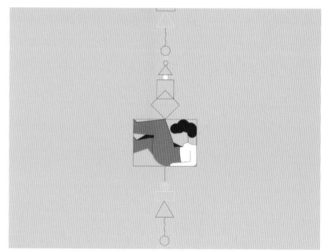

3.58

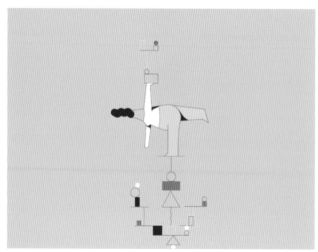

3.56

3.54–3.58
What defines a diagram? It is usually an illustration or series of illustrations that depicts the features of an object, a system or a manufactured or organic process by way of an exposition that goes far from pictorial reality and is normally associated with 'dry', black and white, overtly scholarly and formal images. However, contemporary diagrams can be innovative and highly conceptual, and convey material that historically would not be considered appropriate or capable. This series of images has been conceived, designed and produced by London-based Swedish illustrator **Linn Fritz**. The overall theme is *anxiety* and considers aspects such as feeling trapped, losing control and then finding a balance.
©Linn Fritz

Politics and Propaganda

Illustration that purports real power and influence is well represented within the parameters of politics and propaganda. Indeed, when one's work is at the cutting edge, it is expected that the imagery you produce will deliver messages vigorously exploiting the vulnerabilities, weaknesses and prejudices of your intended audience. You will make them feel either empowered, subjugated or offended according to what it is you want them to believe. You and/or your sponsor (client) have something to say that is *not* negotiable, and you must be unyielding, resolute and unafraid of the backlash. You have a contentious argument that is contemporaneously relevant and critical and will be totally dismissive of any opposing viewpoint. You are communicating pure, unadulterated *propaganda*; the 'information' that you are giving is biased, misleading and loaded in order for you to promote the political cause, ideology or belief system in question.

POLITICS AND EDITORIAL ILLUSTRATION

Many people would find this particular way of thinking abhorrent, as there is no apparent sense of seeking 'common ground' or compromise. But how often do we see a conciliatory, 'softly softly' or editorially diplomatic approach when it comes to the publication of imagery commissioned to communicate raw opinion and criticism? Hardly ever, as exemplified by the illustrators of the French satirical magazine *Charlie Hebdo*. Indeed, a glance through most newspapers, periodicals and magazines from around the world will reveal a rich array of what are popularly termed *political cartoons* lampooning the actions of government and institutions, damning and ridiculing their decisions. Also, any form of deference or respect afforded the so-called ruling classes no longer exists: individual politicians of all persuasions and credo are subjected to the most toxic vituperation. Other individuals considered fair game for the illustrator to caricature, condemn and revile are foreign leaders and other non-native characters that have some form of influence over one's own country or society. Presidents, prime ministers and dictators often fall into this category. But is this *propaganda*, or just an intense form of criticism, satire or vitriol?

The distinguished academic David Welch states in his book *Propaganda: Power and Persuasion* (British Library, 2013), 'Exclude purely religious and commercial propaganda, it is a distinct political activity and it is one that can be distinguished from related phenomena such as information or education'. Politics and propaganda are symbiotically entwined. But, what of everything else that is covered within the vast gamut of editorial broadcast and publishing? Illustration serves this context with meaningful zeal in fashion magazines, newspaper colour supplements, popular culture, specialist journals and periodicals, sport, television, cookery, gardening and travel, even to the ubiquitous and decorative ambience of the horoscope page. But, the original raison d'être for editorial illustration is *visual commentary*. Its principal function is *not just* cognate with journalism – it *is* journalism. The best illustration couched in this context is thought provoking and contentious; it cannot purport any notion of power and influence if it is not. Its principal remit is political, economic and social commentary: it challenges both popular and alternative opinion, it poses questions and leaves them unanswered, it makes provocative statements. It disregards aesthetics or notions of 'good taste' regarding subject matter or visual language, with drawings rendered with passion, force, energy and bite.

PROPAGANDA IN A CONTEMPORARY CONTEXT

How does illustration work today within the remit of politics and propaganda, and is it as effective as it has always been? In order to evaluate this, one must look at how propaganda is changing in a world dominated by social media, the net and online news publications. It can be said that we are all propagandists now. However, the new media has not freed those citizens living under the tyranny of oppressive regimes; the only imagery commissioned and published in these countries is that which is state controlled and strictly monitored, like the illustration produced at the behest of the fascist dictatorships of the twentieth century. However, the cyberspace has allowed those living in the democratic world to more freely hold the established and elite media to account by demanding viewpoints and perspectives across the compass of public opinion, promulgated by the open and divergent instruments of communication. But, as Noam Chomsky once said: 'Propaganda is to democracy what the bludgeon is to a totalitarian state'. Even in the so-called free world, political propaganda serves as a conscious and deliberate attempt to influence the mindset of an audience by either direct or indirect obedience to the self-interest of the propagandist. Here, the propagandist can be anybody, from a nation's governance, a political party or movement, a commentator, an illustrator, a documentary film maker, or any individual seeking to perpetrate a virtual online global campaign, which could be of a personal nature or otherwise. These are generalized examples, but the aim of the propagandist is to package a message, dressed up as facts, in order to evoke a certain response. Education, at least in its free and unorthodox tradition, teaches people how to evaluate and be discerning, whereas propaganda tells people what to think and in some instances is controlling, indoctrinating and threatening. Two examples in recent UK history will exemplify how political propaganda in a so-called democratic country can be designed to 'frighten' and be of concern to the public. The 1979 pre-election posters promoting the British Conservative Party claimed that 'Labour isn't working' by showing a long line of dishevelled, unemployed people. More latterly, there were threats to the British public prior to the European referendum in 2016 that if they voted for the UK to exit the European Union, the government would deliberately impose a 'punishment budget'. These are common examples of propaganda using 'highly charged' language to produce an *emotional* rather than a *rational* response to the message being delivered. David Welch concludes: 'Information and education are concerned to broaden the audiences perspectives and to open their minds, but propaganda strives to narrow and preferably close them. The core distinction lies in the purpose'.

DEFINING AN ENEMY

Throughout history, most societies and more latterly established nation-states have identified 'enemies' that are real, implied or totally false. They are often seen as the perpetrators of war, social or economic disruption, revolution or just critics of an incumbent government, and these so-called enemies will have generated a clear 'them and us' mentality within the body politic. Often, this feeling against a defined 'enemy' is completely justified, particularly if a country is threatened with invasion or suppression. However, there are many and varied manifestations of 'enemy'. Frequently, a society will ostracize a certain group of citizens because of cultural, racial or religious discrimination. In this instance, a different sort of 'enemy within' is identified. Also, the 'war on terror', as perpetrated by the 9 September 2001 attacks in the United States, has created a symbolic and immediately recognizable image of an enemy within. The illustrations, which are numerous and drawn by a considerable number of different cartoonists from around the world, visually convey an array of commentaries and outright damnations and have been published in practically every newspaper and media outlet that is editorially in agreement with this line of opinion. They present *visual stereotypes* of a certain cultural swathe of humanity, the majority of whom are in despair and loathing of their own 'enemy within', with their violent, 'death cult' ideology. However, many people who live in the 'free world' will view these images as legitimate, because so many democracies are under the constant threat of terrorism.

ILLUSTRATOR PROVOCATEUR

Illustration has played a significant role in bastardizing the 'enemy' for centuries, often by using ridicule, offence and extreme humour, thus deflating the enemy's presumed power and authority. Alternatively, the enemy will be represented as a brutal and horrific caricature, created to elicit feelings of hatred. It will be essential for any illustrator operating in this context to be highly informed and intellectually embedded in political and world affairs commentaries:

- To have strong opinions and be forthright in producing an image that will satisfy audiences in agreement with one's own sentiments and not to hold back from controversy

- To make those people opposed to your viewpoint baulk at the explicit and condemning nature of your drawing
- To be capable of deep analysis and discern between agreeable or disagreeable viewpoints

An illustrator working in this capacity will deliver an uncompromising and 'memorable' verdict on the individual in question and his or her 'crime', no matter how trivial or earth shattering it might be. It is also important to be 'immune' regarding the effects and impact of issues being disclosed and discriminated. This is a practice that inexorably defines the notion of *illustrator as provocateur*.

> **OVER THE YEARS, AND IN ONE WAY OR ANOTHER, THE POLITICAL CARTOON HAS STIRRED UP MASS HATRED, INCITED BLOODY REVOLUTIONS, KEPT DISCRIMINATED SECTIONS OF SOCIETY OPPRESSED AND SUPPRESSED, SWAYED PUBLIC OPINION AND HELPED BRING DOWN GOVERNMENTS AND INSTITUTIONS. IT INCITES INTENSE IRREVERENCE AND DISRESPECT FOR EVERYTHING HELD SACRED OR DEAR FROM RELIGION TO CULTURE.**

ALAN MALE, INTERNATIONAL KEYNOTE LECTURE 'THE POWER AND INFLUENCE OF ILLUSTRATION', PORTUGAL 2015

3.59

A magazine renowned for cutting edge satire and uncompromising commentary is the British publication *Private Eye*. Published in October 2016, approximately one month prior to the 2016 United States presidential election, the Obama 'Hope' meme was given a revamp to reflect how American politics had evolved since Mr Obama came into power. Presidential candidate Donald Trump appears as a mutation of the iconic image of Obama as created by contemporary street artist and illustrator Shepard Fairey during the presidential campaign of 2008. At the time, Trump denied accusations of 'groping' women and making derogatory and highly sexualized remarks even though a historic tape revealed he was lying. Commentators praised the *Private Eye* cover, stating it exemplified 'how much of a laughing stock American politics had become'. ©Reproduced by kind permission of PRIVATE EYE magazine – www.private-eye.co.uk

3.60

This illustration, with its descriptive and pointed wording, needs no explanation. It addresses another highly controversial topic – *sex trafficking* – embroiled in the complex machinations and manoeuvring of US politics. This hard-hitting piece of journalistic illustration and cutting edge commentary by **Rebecca Hendin** was published by Universal Uclick via GoComics.com. ©Rebecca Hendin

3.59

3.60

3.61

Religion and all of its complexities and manifestations will always find a place within the broad remit of political current affairs commentaries. This image, by **Caroline Macey**, is a section from a large, intricate image entitled *Flock*, which comprises a circular composition of twelve constituent parts, placed symmetrically around a single central image. Six of the twelve are the same and entitled *Clash of the Religions* – the example shown here. These are interspersed by a series of six highly detailed narrative composites: Evangelical, Jewish, Orthodox, Islamic, Church of England and Catholic. Macey is an award-winning artist who has exhibited nationally. She creates her work in the printmaking studio and is based in Hastings, East Sussex, England. ©Caroline Macey

3.62

Benedetto Cristofani makes an uncompromising plea through this illustration for the end of the death penalty across the United States. Many would say that this image is too optimistic; whilst the electric chair is no longer the preferred option to 'dispatch' those deemed no longer worthy of 'earthly existence', many states now use lethal injection. At the time of writing, some states give offenders a choice: electrocution, firing squad, gas inhalation or hanging. Interestingly, there was a hiatus, with no executions in the United States, between 1967 and 1977. Amnesty International opposes the death penalty on moral grounds. ©Benedetto Cristofani

3.61

3.62

3.63

3.63
A barbed commentary that could easily reflect on the relaxed gun laws in America, this image was conceived and produced by award-winning illustration partnership **Anna and Elena Balbusso** to accompany an article entitled *One Summer Day* by Sonia Sarker and published by *Hopkins Bloomberg Public Health Magazine*. The illustration captures a sequence of events related by the article's author: 'I watched as a skinny kid in a yellow tee shirt came up behind the group that was on the lawn and reached for a gun that was in his waistband . . .'
©Anna+Elena Balbusso

3.64
The First World War (1914–1918) was the largest military conflict in human history right up until the outbreak of the Second World War. To this very day, it is charged with a stigma and consciousness like no other conflict before or since for the senselessness of its outbreak: ten million military dead. It was fought principally from lines of trenches and supported by artillery and machine guns, infantry, assault tanks, early airplanes and poisonous gas. And yet, it provides a milieu for numerous stories and anecdotes, poems, films, novels, visual art and illustration. Much is based on fact: enemy soldiers playing football on Christmas Day, for example. However, a lot of the damning comment regarding this subject manifests as satire imbued with narrative absurdity, such as the BBC television series *Black Adder Goes Forth*. The illustration shown is entitled *Piano Attack* and was conceived and produced by **Paul Slater**.
©Paul Slater

3.64

3.65
This illustration provides a sentiment that will undoubtedly resonate with a great many people. Entitled *Erase Terrorism*, it is by **Paul Garland** and forms part of a series of images called *Artists and Designers Against War . . . or whatever they call it*. ©Paul Garland

3.65

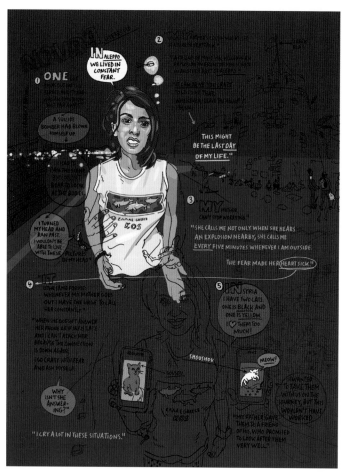

3.66

3.66, 3.67 and 3.68
Reportage drawing becomes international journalism. These images are by **Olivier Kugler** and are from an extensive project commissioned by Médicins Sans Frontières and published by Harpers, Annabelle and Internazionale. The drawings, produced ostensibly on location, tell the story of Syrian refugees seeking protection on the Greek island of Kos. Many of the refugees have lost homes, family members, jobs and possessions. The drawings along with their handwritten annotations manifest superbly as single-image narratives of great power and poignancy. ©Olivier Kugler

3.67

3.68

3.69
The illustration on the cover
of this magazine is by **Davide
Bonazzi**. Its essence and
message are unequivocal. Many
would claim that tensions and
hostilities between certain
powers are increasing and
pose as great a threat to peace
and stability as never before.
©Davide Bonazzi

3.69

3.70

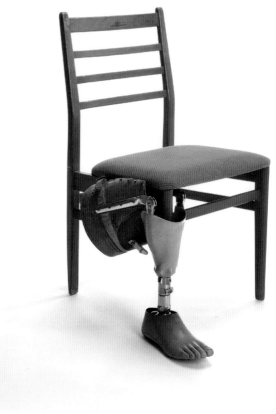

3.71

3.70 and 3.71
President George W. Bush's declared War on Terrorism, enacted after the September 11 terror attacks, resulted in widespread condemnation for the lack of planning regarding how the political, social and physical infrastructures of Iraq and Afghanistan would be 'repaired' and made good for the future. Thousands of innocent civilians were killed, maimed or made homeless. These two images are life-size models and conceived and produced by British illustrator **Jake Abrams**. Figure 3.65 is entitled *Afghanistan Chair*, or more sarcastically, *Dining Chair and Crutches*. Figure 3.66 is called *Triumph in Iraq*, or *Chair with Prosthetic Leg*. ©Jake Abrams

3.72
This powerful message was created by **Paul Garland**. Commissioned by the Council for Advancement and Support in Education and published in *Currents Magazine*, the illustration accompanied an article entitled 'Access for All' and questions, 'Is your campus truly welcoming to students with disabilities?' It was shortlisted for a World Illustration Award in 2017. ©Paul Garland

3.72

3.73

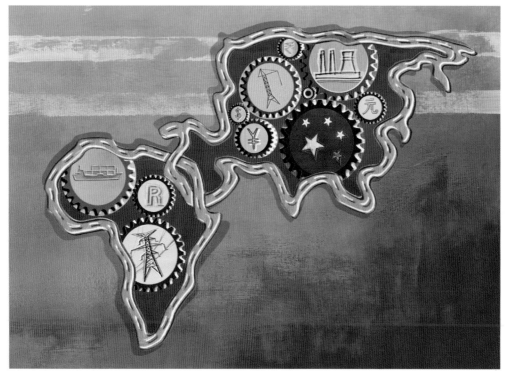

3.74

3.73, 3.74 and 3.75
Not all political themes incite commentaries that are damning and derisory. These illustrations are by **Sue Clarke** and were commissioned by Newsweek International. They reflect on the agenda and outcomes related to the annual World Economic Forum (WEF) meeting held in Davos Klosters, Switzerland. It remains the foremost creative force for engaging the world's premier leaders in collaborative activities to shape the global, regional and industry agenda at the beginning of each year. For over four decades, the WEF's mission – to improve the state of the world – has driven the design and development of the annual meeting programme. ©Sue Clarke

3.76
A satirical, amusing and possibly portentous illustration by **Tom Gauld**, *Dystopia* could also be considered a fitting conclusion to this particular chapter section! Imbued with connotations of George Orwell's *Animal Farm* and *1984*, Margaret Atwood's *The Handmaid's Tale* and even a nod to Charlie Brooker's television drama series *Black Mirror*, the message could be construed as a disturbing prediction for the future or a 'sideswipe' at the doom mongers. It was commissioned by *Guardian Review*. ©Tom Gauld

3.75

3.76

Entertainment and Literature

Broadly speaking, this is the context of narrative *fiction*. It is distinct from any other form of contextualized communication, as whatever theme, content and characterization is dispensed, the story will conform as a conventionally accepted falsehood. Everything – or indeed, practically everything – is feigned, imagined or invented. This differs significantly from other contexts. For example, whilst based on truth, current affairs commentaries and propagandist literature will present extreme distortions, even blatant lies, with a remit to 'hoodwink' an audience into believing that the message is sincerely meant. Not so with fiction: the audience is never in any doubt regarding its principal objective – to entertain, to distract from reality and to engender an escapist, mental and sensory experience. In fiction, every human emotion will be touched upon, from exhilaration, joy, sadness, humour, sensuality, anger and excitement. It will challenge and engage every cerebral and cognitive function, from pure mind-relaxation to blasting a frisson of psychological and intellectual curiosity and empowerment. Every demographic, culture, race and creed will engage with narrative fiction in some way. It is also the most ubiquitous and diverse context for the creative practitioner to work within. Whilst the knowledge-bearing environment will deal with every subject known to humanity, its aim is to deliver documentary facts. Fiction will also utilize every subject known. However, it enables authors, scriptwriters, illustrators, artists, performers and filmmakers to conceive ideas, stories and situations that can 'go any place and do whatever thing' – its possibilities are infinite!

DEFINING GENRE

This context is vast and immensely diverse, providing substantial opportunities for the illustrator, either by commission or by authorial practice. Some of the most creative and innovative illustration has been generated here. Its influence has a monumental bearing on published and performance entertainment, including animated films, games and movies. Over the years, characters and events conceived and originated by illustrators have given rise to many clichéd and ubiquitous representations: the Disney stable, the superheroes originated in comics, the famous and the infamous literary villains, philanthropists and benefactors, the celebrity heroines and champions, and the various anthropomorphized characterizations and monsters.

The parameters of fictional genre are porous and overlap with at least one other. However, it is prevalent to define the genre as they all have specific characteristics and audience preferences. Also, as an illustrator it is essential to know the milieu of one's chosen genre: the environment, backdrop, setting and context, location and element.

- Mystery focuses on making a discovery, typically regarding a crime of some description. The appeal for the audience is to determine who committed the 'crime' before the 'detective' in the story does so, and before the 'big reveal' at the end. The novels of Agatha Christie are classic examples. There are numerous subgenres, from the *police procedural*, the *historical*, the *caper* or comic approach and the *noir*, which features dark characters and situations, with graphic sex and explicit violence being the norm.
- Thriller and suspense is about what might happen and what has to be done to prevent a catastrophe. The storyline usually involves action, with emphasis on occurrence and incident rather than any depth of characterization. The main protagonists are 'larger than life' personalities and face danger from the beginning and throughout – think Ian Fleming's James Bond. Readers and audiences will be gripped, anticipating the next – usually far-fetched – occurrence. The story accentuates prevention

3.77

3.78

3.79

3.77

Nursery rhymes and traditional children's literature have given rise to numerous fictional interpretations. 'Three Little Pigs' is a fable, written for a young audience and originating from England in about 1840. Later adaptations have included animated versions by the likes of Disney. It uses the literary 'rule of three', a concept that enables children to anticipate a positive outcome: the third pig's house, which is constructed of bricks, is able to withstand the 'dastardly wolf'! This visual interpretation is by **Blaz Porenta** and intended for an adult audience. ©Blaz Porenta

3.78 and 3.79

These two linocut style illustrations by **Vladimir Zimakov** are both narratives in their frame of reference, with an overall visual language devised to create harmony and balance between the text and imagery through expression, message and graphics. Figure 3.78 is an excerpt from Nikolai Gogol's nineteenth-century tale *The Diary of a Madman*, a diary written by a man who is slowly losing his mind. The tone of the diary entries changes dramatically over the period of the story. Figure 3.79 was created as a single entity in print and poster form. ©Vladimir Zimakov

of some kind, such as death, the overthrow of a country or the destruction of the planet. There are several subgenres: the *political*, such as spy and Cold War tales, and the *historical*, which are based on a recognizable time period. There are also *crime*, *legal*, *technological*, *medical*, the *paranormal* and the *psychological*.

- *Science fiction* deals with possibilities that do not yet exist but might in the future. It deals specifically with advancements in science and technology and their effects on humanity. It will traverse audiences to other worlds – planets and universes that have not yet been destroyed by humankind. It projects hope that we can 'get it right' or at least repair what has been wronged. It pushes our imaginations beyond the boundaries of what we can see in front of us. Science fiction proclaims that it is fine to dream – 'to dream of the impossible'. Subgenres include *aliens*, *time travel*, *space opera* (a type of grand-scale sci-fi soap opera – *Star Wars* is a classic example), *parallel history* and *alternate history* (or 'what if'). There is also *steampunk*, a subgenre with a different appearance and discernment from other aspects of science fiction; some might suggest that it looks 'eccentric'. Here, steam-powered machines drive the world's technology. Many of the stories are an embodiment of Victoriana or the American West, with distinctive fashions and architecture indicative of those times. The novels of Jules Verne and H. G. Wells fall into this category. Today, it is found predominately in graphic novels and films, such as *Grandville* by illustrator-author Bryan Talbot and *Gulliver's Travels*, as directed by Rob Letterman.
- *Fantasy* includes magic and the supernatural. Its predominant theme features mythology and incorporates *dungeons and dragons* and *swords and sorcery*. It often conveys the medieval world, if not in setting, most certainly in style. The HBO drama production *Game of Thrones* is firmly embedded in this genre. Other subgenres include *urban fiction*, the *Arthurian* and *quest*.

- *Horror* is a broad and diverse genre. Whatever milieu, it will accentuate fear, dread, terror and abomination. It will feature psychological terrors, such as in the Thomas Harris novel *Silence of the Lambs*. It originated as *Gothic horror*, with inspiration from east European folklore and classic tales such as Mary Shelley's *Frankenstein* and R. L. Stevenson's *The Strange Case of Doctor Jekyll and Mr Hyde*. It now features a ubiquitous array of monsters and other terrifying manifestations such as ghosts, vampires, werewolves, demons, Satanism, gore, torture, vicious animals, evil witches, zombies, cannibals, serial killers, psychopaths and natural or man-made disasters. Audiences and readers seek fright, and horror facilitates a way for us to face our fears and then conquer them.
- The *Western* is set in the late nineteenth-century American West, popularly known as the 'Wild West', with an early generic title of *cowboy*. It has been extremely popular since the first published stories appeared, with literally hundreds of Hollywood movies since. Characters can be frontier lawmen, Native Americans, gunslingers, saloon keepers and preachers, the chief protagonist often being a loner: think of Clint Eastwood's 'Man with No Name'. The story will emphasize a swift application of frontier justice, the audience left in no doubt as to who will live and who will die!
- *Literary fiction* is an embodiment of what can be regarded as the best of traditional classic fiction. It represents much that is studied as literature in school, college or university. Its principal focus is to reveal insights into a character's emotional growth, experiences and concerns, and to facilitate an empathic connectivity for the audience. It will divulge journeys of self-discovery incorporating both torment and positivity. Typical examples in classic literature are the works of Thomas Hardy, Evelyn Waugh, George Orwell and Margaret Atwood. Also, Charles Dickens conceived some of the most well-known protagonists of this genre, such as David Copperfield, Oliver Twist and Pip from *Great Expectations*. Literary fiction contrasts overtly with other genres; instead of concentrating purely on plot and action, it aims to deliver a deeper and more meaningful understanding of universal truth.

- *Romance* is a genre that presents and recounts the relationship between two main characters, with an emphasis on love – finding it, recognizing it and keeping it. Classic examples are *Jane Eyre* by Charlotte Brontë and *Pride and Prejudice* by Jane Austen. Modern romance varies considerably in tone and explicitness, from innocent depictions of young love to hard-core sex. Subgenres include the *inspirational*, where religious faith and pious attitudes dominate the storyline, and *suspense*, where romantic relationships are impacted by social tensions and conflict, mystery, danger and intrigue. There is also the *erotic*, where sex plays a massive role and is a major component of the story.

- *Adventure* is principally the genre of action and danger. Couched in 'lightweight' popular culture, its principal remit is to dispense thrills and excitement without fatalism, melancholy or covert cynicism. Consequently, its contents are *not* infused with any form of character introspection – think Indiana Jones!

- *Young adult* is aimed at the specific age group of twelve to eighteen years. Any genre can feature, but it is customary for the lead protagonist to be of teen age and having to deal with life-changing issues that might overwhelm the character. A principal theme reflects the transition into adulthood, with dilemmas including school, jobs, friendships, sex, family, separation from parents, fear of the future and death.

Audiences can engage and interact with entertainment and literary fiction through diverse media: motion pictures, animation, games, comics and graphic novels, classic literature and compilations, specialist books such as contemporary creative writing and poetry, children's picture and chapter books, performance and theatre, installation and exhibition.

ILLUSTRATOR AS AUTHOR OF FICTION

Narrative fiction is the contextual domain offering the illustrator the most significant opportunities for authorship. Children's book publishing can present substantive openings for progression as an author-illustrator: approximately 50 per cent of young audience fiction is written and illustrated by the same individual. An examination of contemporary children's books will reveal a multiplicity of imagery and fictional genre. Many illustrators are singularly associated with this field of practice, providing pleasure and inspiration for young audiences and influencing many aspiring commercial artists. Because of the inventive possibilities afforded by the fantasy and imagination given, many visual communicators are attracted to its inherent creative outlet. The graphic novel and other sequential forms such as script writing, storyboarding and conceptualization for films and games, provide further opportunities.

Initially, one's ownership, personal expression and choices made as creator and author can be given precedence over any notions of being commissioned in a standard commercial manner, as this is where the publisher merely oversees the production of prescribed and often heavily art-directed images. Any form of narrative fiction conceived by an author-illustrator, whatever mould envisaged for publication or broadcast, will generally manifest comprising imagery with words – either as voice or text. However, it is the content and essence of the invented story, its plot, characterization and setting, that are of paramount importance.

The conception of narrative fiction is a process that can allow one's imagination and creativity to 'fly' free and unhampered. But it is important not to lose sight of one's strengths and limitations regarding interests, inherent general and specific knowledge and sources of inspiration. These are factors that can initiate and facilitate a 'spark' of ideas and concepts for a potential story. The creation of the storyline setting, plot and characters can be borne out of the drawing process. However, one cannot invent a fictional narrative 'out of thin air'. There has to be inspiration or a desire to undertake the bidding. It is much more advantageous to proceed with a topic that holds a strong personal interest. This can make the subject unique and confers it with animate bearing.

CHARACTER AND SETTING

The author-illustrator should empathize with the setting of the story. If an audience is unfamiliar or confused by a setting, its credibility is destroyed. Each setting has unique advantages and disadvantages, and it is important that all is completely understood. If the setting is of a historic period, ensure the facts surrounding it are correct. A contemporary setting should provide a backdrop for your characters to think and know in a way the present-day audience would understand or even relate to. Each generation has a 'language', even a culture of its own, and whereas human nature does not change, customs, fashions and mores do.

The favourable development of characters is paramount to the successful creation of any story. A guiding principle is to ensure that the characters are believable to oneself. If this can be attained, then it is very possible for them to be real, or at least credible, to the audience. It is also important to ensure that they do not 'act out of character'. One cannot successfully maintain credibility with characters if they are manipulated to behave in a manner they would not in reality. Reference must be made to how an individual has been developed in terms of his or her personality and disposition, appearance, family and peer situation.

Whatever visual language employed from caricature, distortion or the representational, every character should be conceived from painstaking observations of body language, gesture, expression, movement, individual idiosyncrasy and eccentricity. Accurate visual studies of this nature can be pushed into whatever exaggerated or realistic poses are necessary to make the character 'do' what is required. Personality, trait and emotion must also be convincingly portrayed. Mood and sense of being can be presented by an appropriate representation of physical gait, hands and facial expression.

There is also the question of what is acceptable for presentation to young audiences. This particular domain of practice has over the years provided illustrators with immense scope to 'push the boundaries' regarding the conception and visualization of 'extreme characters': monsters, ghouls, ogres, witches and many more frightening entities that have pervaded the pages of children's literature, animations and films. However, there are often editorial checks and balances regarding content and how it is visualized. Much of this is related to the main characters within the plot. It would seem that an essential ingredient to infuse into one's characters is 'appeal'. Western publishing and broadcast will insist that stylized and distorted facial features must not make the character unpleasant or threatening. The size, shape and placement of the eyes, nose and mouth are all important considerations.

The representation of animals and their subsequent characterization is also an important aspect of children's fiction. Here, the process of character conception is the same as before. However, because of the diversity of species within the animal kingdom and the scope for distinctly different stylistic approaches, this area can provide immense creative and inventive opportunities. The animals 'play out' scenarios that are either fantastical or a replication of reality associated with the broad sphere of humanity. Over the years, animals have been portrayed to be both good and evil, with certain species stereotyped as one or the other. The visual representation can vary from the 'cute' to the contemporaneously challenging and from familiar 'fluffy' domestic creatures to outrageously distorted invertebrate monsters. Anthropomorphism is a method of stylization that has been utilized for centuries. Ever since the early east European woodcuts and engravings depicted legendary lycanthropes, Beatrix Potter's rabbits and friends along with Bestall's Rupert Bear have given animals distinct human physical characteristics, almost to the point of being people with animals' heads. This way of character development is still considered and used today. However, it is also important to recall audience perception and receptivity. Animals as substitute children within a narrative, often in anthropomorphized form, will engage the audience with empathy and imagination.

THE PLOT

With regards to the storyline, it is essential to know where one is proceeding and to firmly establish, for example, how the mystery is going to be solved at its conclusion and, as the narrative unfolds, how seemingly impracticable barriers will be overcome throughout. If the conceived narrative is fantasy, it is important to abide by the laws that your fantasy dictates. There is nothing in fantasy to suggest that a 'miracle' will ensure that everything will 'turn out okay' because the world of one's story is imaginary. From classic fairy and folk tales to psycho-horror, fiction is based in some actuality, and the events and outcomes abide by the strictures of credible reality. It is too easy to concoct a story that is 'far-fetched'.

Textual and visual dialogue and interaction are key aspects of maintaining an appropriate pace and flow throughout. This immediately alludes to the important relationship between words and imagery. These two elements should articulate in a simultaneous manner, without duplication, and be complementary to one another. An example might provide for a component of surprise, the imagery depicting one suggestion or direction and the words alluding to something completely different or unseen, furnishing questions, subtle nuances and twists to the underlying message contained in the illustrations.

CREDO AND PROVOCATION

The author-illustrator has complete, uninhibited freedom to create. It is also not necessary to feel compelled to pursue a theme, plotline or genre seemingly dictated by contemporary fashion or trend. The most original and challenging stories often 'buck the trend'. In this context, it is possible to create a story that will be a disruptive influence on the established hierarchies of power and control in society and help 'change the world for the better'. Themes related to the environment, discrimination and inequality are embedded in all forms of entertainment and literary fiction. By either discrete or blatant use of psychology and semiotics – whichever is most appropriate in accordance with one's target audience – it is possible to provide solutions to problems, remediate experience, promote clarity of thinking and encourage creative ideas.

Narrative fiction and its iconography wield considerable influence. Over the years, pilgrims and religious adherents have worshipped before the icons of their faith. Today, millions flock to the shrines of a different form of deity to enthral and 'worship' before the icons of popular entertainment, icons conceived by illustrators – for example, at Disneyworld and the film studios of Harry Potter. But, some might say, rather than promote mindless celebrity, consumerism and self-interest, illustrators can continue to develop the human capacity to meet the challenges of the future and influence how people in any society think and behave – another pertinent example of the power and influence of illustration.

3.80

3.80

Science fiction and its 'dungeons and dragons' fantasy counterpart are dominant genres within the world of contemporary gaming, a branch of entertainment whereby the audience interacts with the story and determines its outcome. The essence of nearly all themes and stories is truly couched in the world of make-believe. Consequently, the illustrator or 'concept artist' is at liberty to create and innovate the most outlandish scenarios and characterizations. This image was conceived, designed and produced by **Simon Dubuc**, concept artist at Riot Games, Los Angeles, California, USA. The figure is Zoar the Solomancer: 'to the drifting images of the upper strata, the sun's light was not a privilege, it was a birth right'. ©Simon Dubuc

3.81 and 3.82

Dave Palumbo is a Philadelphia-based illustrator whose work is largely embedded in dark fantasy and Gothic horror, using a visual language that is distinctly pictorial yet painterly in style. Palumbo utilizes dramatic, almost cinematic visualizations to create his narrative concepts. The two illustrations shown depict scenarios that clearly convey 'action', yet nonetheless are full of intrigue, aided by unnerving compositions that fly in the face of traditional pictorial convention. Figure 3.82 is entitled *Fed* and is a Spectrum Fantastic Art Gold Medal winner. Where is the woman running? What or who is she running from? Why is she naked? Is the man dead, and if so, who killed him and why? Figure 3.81 is entitled *Seven*. ©Dave Palumbo

3.81

3.82

3.83

3.84

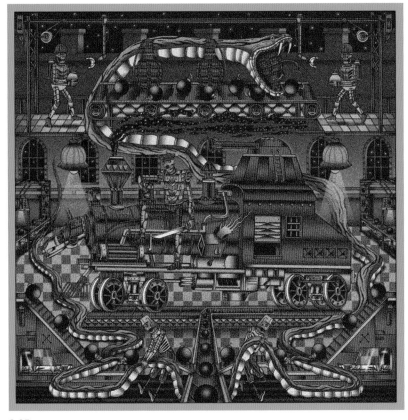

3.85

3.86

3.83, 3.84, 3.85 and 3.86
The Four Horsemen of the Apocalypse were first described in the last book of the New Testament Bible, *The Revelation of Saint John the Divine*. This Christian vision is that the four horsemen are setting a divine apocalypse (catastrophic destruction) upon the world as harbingers of the 'Last Judgement'. There have been hundreds of artistic interpretations throughout history, notable artists including Saint-Sever Beatus (eleventh century), Albrecht Dürer (1513) and Gustave Doré (1865). The Bible contains some of the most creative narrative concepts ever written, mostly metaphoric in context, with much hidden meaning imbued. However, it is largely considered a work of fiction. These images are by Switzerland-based illustrator **Dexter Maurer**. Figure 3.83 represents *Conquest*, 3.84 *Famine*, 3.85 *War* and 3.86 *Death*. ©Dexter Maurer

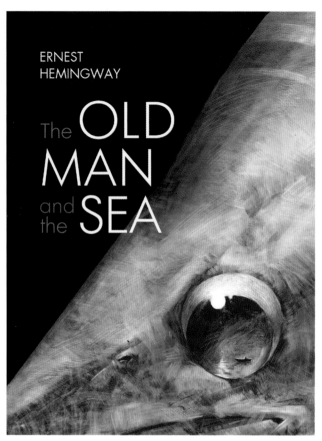

3.87

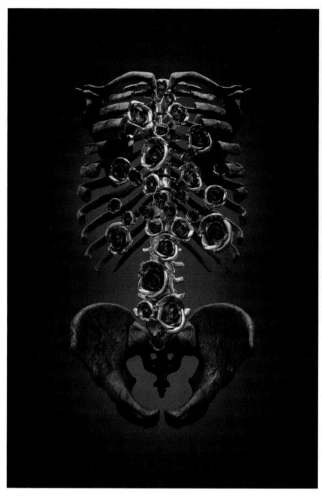

3.88

3.87
This book cover was designed and illustrated by **Slava Shults**, an illustrator from Kharkiv, Ukraine. It is for the author Ernest Hemingway's most celebrated work, *The Old Man and the Sea*, first published in 1952, a short novel that tells the story of Santiago, an aging Cuban fisherman who struggles with a giant Atlantic blue marlin far out in the Caribbean Sea off the coast of Cuba, only for it to be devoured by sharks. It is said that Hemingway wrote this novel to prove that he 'wasn't finished as a writer'; his most celebrated work prior was *For Whom the Bell Tolls*, from 1940. However, Hemingway was awarded the Pulitzer Prize for Fiction in 1953 and the Nobel Prize for Literature in 1954. Permanently in print, the book cover has had many illustrative representations over the years. ©Slava Shults

3.88, 3.89 and 3.90
The American science fiction writer Isaac Asimov once said that 'life is pleasurable, death is peaceful, its' the transition that's difficult'. Horror and Gothic imagery will never lose its appeal as long as humankind maintains its fascination with death. For illustrators, artists, filmmakers and writers, it is a 'playful' way to seek a reactive frisson from their audience. This series of images is entitled *Infestation* and is by digital artist, illustrator and art director **Billelis**. ©Billy Bogiatzoglou

3.91
The Birds is a 1963 American horror-thriller film directed by Alfred Hitchcock and loosely based on the 1952 novel of the same name by Daphne du Maurier. It focuses on a series of sudden and unexplained violent bird attacks on the people of a California coastal town. This is an illustration for a contemporary movie poster by **Davide Bonazzi**. It is an intelligent and conceptual interpretation, an overt counteraction to the pictorially sensationalist imagery that had gone before. ©Davide Bonazzi

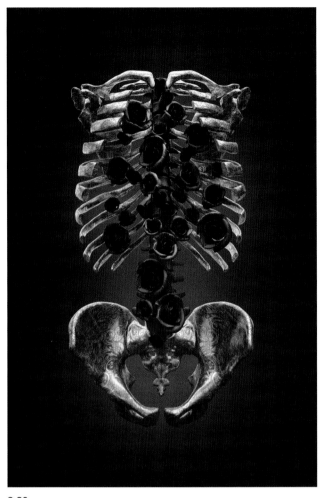

3.89

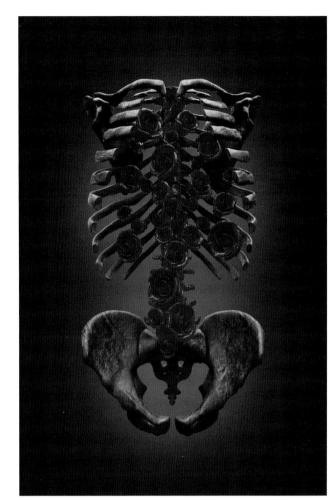

3.90

3.91

3.92

3.93

3.94

3.95

3.96

3.97

3.92, 3.93, 3.94, 3.95, 3.96 and 3.97
Illustrated by **Neil Webb** in collaboration with Studio Sutherland, these are a set of stamps commissioned by the UK postal service Royal Mail to mark the 2016 centenary of Agatha Christie writing her first detective story, *The Mysterious Affair at Styles*. Each stamp is based on a pivotal point in a different Christie novel. In the spirit of crime fiction and detective work, by using conceptual twists in the imagery, the stamps contain hidden secrets, with clues to point to the murderer. The 'hidden clues' are revealed with exposure to ultraviolet light or heat and by using a magnifying glass to read the microtext. The project was recipient of a D&AD Yellow Pencil Award 2017 and 'Best in Book' Prize Creative Review Annual 2017. Stamp designs illustrated by Neil Webb, Debut Art Ltd ©Royal Mail Group Ltd

3.98

3.99

3.100

3.101

Within the image:

guardian weekend 21.12.13

Winter fiction special
New ghost stories by
Lionel Shriver
Ned Beauman
Jeanette Winterson
Chimamanda
Ngozi Adichie

3.102

3.98
This is an illustration by **Anna and Elena Balbusso** for a dark fantasy novella entitled *Of Sorrow and Such* by Angela Slatter and published by Tor Books, 2015. Mistress Gideon is a witch. Her neighbours suspect it of her but prefer to remain silent. Eventually, Gideon is charged with practicing witchcraft, tortured and put to death by fire. ©Anna+Elena Balbusso

3.99
Among the Thorns is a dark fantasy, set in seventeenth-century Germany. Written by Veronica Schanoes, it was published by Tor.com in 2014.

The illustration is by **Anna and Elena Balbusso**. The story recounts the intent of a young woman to avenge the brutal murder of her pedlar father many years earlier by a vagabond with a magic fiddle. The illustrators recounted: 'We imagined the woman as a tree, her hair a bush with thorns that imprison the vagabond with the magic violin. The hanged man refers to brutal murder'. The image makes reference to several historic sources: frescoes by Giusto de Menabuoi (1320–1391) and paintings by Pisanello (1395–1455), Vincento Foppa (1430–1515) and Leonardo da Vinci (1452–1519). The architecture is inspired by

northern European cities with Gothic spires and churches. ©Anna+Elena Balbusso

3.100 and 3.101
The two illustrations shown are by **Scott Balmer** and are a tribute to a dark fantasy film entitled *Pan's Labyrinth*, written and directed by Guillermo Del Toro. The setting for the story is Spain in the summer of 1944, five years after the end of the Spanish Civil War, during the Franco period. The narrative intertwines the real world with a mystical one centred on an overgrown, abandoned labyrinth and an enigmatic faun creature with which the main

character, Ofelia, interacts. ©Scott Balmer

3.102
Illustration for narrative fiction can take many forms and manifest in a variety of applied contexts. This image was created by artist and illustrator **Su Blackwell**, who works predominantly within the realm of paper by constructing highly detailed and complex structures. Blackwell sums up the thrust of this image: 'Paper has been used for communication since its invention, either between humans or in an attempt to communicate with the *spirit world*'. ©Su Blackwell

3.103

3.104

3.103 and 3.104
This is the cover and interior illustration for the *Guardian Review*, 16 May 2016. Whilst considered by some as editorial illustration, its essence and real context are narrative imbued with humour and irony. Conceived and drawn by **Tom Gauld**, the imagery packages an article written by John Mullan and entitled 'Whatever next? *The joy of plot* – from Dickens to The Night Manager and Line of Duty'. ©Tom Gauld

3.105
This illustration by **Tom Gauld** accompanied a short story by Charles Yu entitled *Fable*. Commissioned for the *New Yorker* magazine, the tale begins, 'Once upon a time there was a man whose therapist thought it would be a good idea for the man to work through some stuff by telling a story about that stuff'. ©Tom Gauld

3.105

3.106, 3.107 and 3.108
In book cover designs and illustrations by **Katie Ponder**, the overriding objective is for the illustrator to conceive and design an image that is consistent with and evocative of the book's theme. These are three very well-known and celebrated works of literary fiction, all having inspired either numerous motion pictures or televised drama adaptions. Ponder has been consistent with visual language in spite of a disparate range of literary genres, each one providing a focused identity for the contents.

3.106
Frankenstein by Mary Shelley is a unique novel in the canon of English literature. Infused with elements of the Gothic and Romantic movements, it has had a considerable influence on literary fiction and popular culture. Shelley was just twenty years old when it was first published in 1818. Ponder's illustration conveys both pathos and 'technical' insight into the unorthodox scientific experiment carried out by Viktor Frankenstein to create a grotesque but sapient creature. It also provides clues as to the book's alternative title, *The Modern Prometheus*;

Frankenstein 'stole' the secret to creating life from nature. Shelley was keenly aware of concerns about how fast technology was progressing during the eighteenth century, and perhaps this novel addresses the issue of advances created by humankind, but which fly in the face of the natural elements and 'divine' plans. ©Katie Ponder

3.107
The Life and Loves of a She Devil by Fay Weldon, published in 1983, concerns a highly unattractive-looking woman who goes to great lengths to take revenge on her husband and his attractive lover. Through surgery, her appearance is gradually restructured as an identical version of her female rival. The story is considered to be about envy rather than revenge. ©Katie Ponder

3.108
The Girl on the Train by Paula Hawkins was the fastest-selling adult hardcover novel in history in the year of its release, 2015. A psychological thriller, it is told from the point of view of three women and is a bleak tale of complex intertwined lives, revenge, deceit and murder. ©Katie Ponder

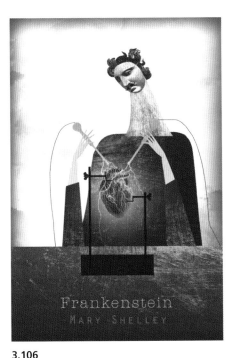

3.106

3.107

3.108

3.109

3.109, 3.110 and 3.111
Illustrator **Orly Orbach**
produces visual work in a
participatory and interactive
way, making narratives come
to life. Orbach is interested in
finding alternative means of
disseminating stories, creating
objects, environments, and
interactive performances
through which stories are
experienced in museums,
libraries and schools,
ephemeral and transient books,
collaborations with theatre
companies and socially engaged
regeneration projects. The
drawings and prints shown are
from various narrative projects:
Figure 3.109 is *Buried Doll*,
Figure 3.110 is *Cage-Birds, and
other Mythological Stories* and
Figure 3.111 is *Grandma Snake*.
©Orly Orbach

3.112
This illustration was
conceived and produced by
Valentina Brostean and was
commissioned for a book
entitled *Hauntings*. This is an
anthology of ghost stories
compiled by acclaimed horror
genre editor Ellen Datlow,
a contemporary collection
of tales 'lyrical and strange,
monstrous and exhilarating,
horrific and transformative'.
Brostean's image is evocative
of the human obsession with
mysteries of the afterlife. Whilst
dark and contemporary Gothic
in style, it nonetheless superbly
transcends the clichéd and
overtly pictorial illustrations
given for previous books of this
category. ©Valentina Brostean

3.110

3.111

3.112

3.113

3.114

3.113 and 3.114

The comic strip format with sequentially arranged pictures has a distinguished history, with hand-drawn illustrations supplemented by 'speech balloons' appearing regularly in magazines and newspapers in the nineteenth century. Today, comics contain narratives of great diversity, from graphic novel–type formats including horror, science fiction, steampunk and fantasy to lightweight entertainment and education for very young audiences. As a visual language, most sequential imagery will be embedded in pictorial reality; even some elements that are wildly dramatic, distorted or caricatured tend to represent 'real space'. The examples shown are from an original and contemporary comic book devised and illustrated by **Briony May Smith**. Entitled *Tam Lin*, the story is taken from a traditional legendary folk tale and ballad, with origins associated with both Scotland and Norfolk, England. The story revolves around the rescue of the main character, Tam Lin, by his true love from the Queen of the Fairies. ©Briony May Smith

Advertising and Commerce

The power of persuasion cannot be underestimated, and illustration has throughout the years contributed enormously to this precept. Visual imagery is the first aspect noticed within an advertisement, whether it is a static image or an animatic or filmed sequence. An essential prerequisite for most advertising campaigns (except audio media) is to produce compelling, distinctive and arresting imagery, produced and delivered at the highest reproduction or broadcast quality. Illustrators create exemplary and innovative visual solutions, conceived, designed and worked to the highest standards of contemporary illustration practice. Indeed, it is one of the disciplines recognized and lauded by way of annual awards given for excellence in illustration for advertising. The Design and Art Directors Club of Great Britain (D&AD), the Society of Illustrators (New York), the World Illustration Awards (Association of Illustrators UK) and Communication Arts (US) are professional organizations providing opportunity for recognition in this way.

THE COMMISSIONING OF ILLUSTRATION IN ADVERTISING

The diversity of visual language employed is vast. There is no particular trend or house style associated with the broad church that is advertising. Campaigns will use styles that evoke whatever is necessary to impart the 'right message', from 'chocolate box' to 'shock'; decorative, whimsical and historical stylization; humour and caricature; and hard-edged technological and contemporary visualization. If illustration is chosen as part of a campaign, whatever its nature, the intention will be for it to aid brand recognition and awareness into the subconscious of society at large. Such is the power of this command: there are examples of illustration not only being effective in product identity and persuasion, but also contributing to a massive cultural vicissitude. The early appearance of Santa Claus in his current guise is one such example. Haddon Sundblom, the illustrator chosen by the Coca-Cola Company in the 1930s to visually 'reinvent' Father Christmas as a benevolent, white-bearded man attired in brand colours, almost to the point of replicating a bottle of the said drink, was undoubtedly unaware of the impact he was about to unleash on an unsuspecting Western society. Some will say that Sundblom unleashed a character synonymous with the excesses of consumerism and gluttony!

In a professional practice context, advertising is the most prescribed and directed form of illustration practice. It can also potentially provide the illustrator with the highest fees, particularly if the client and brand are high profile. However, the negative aspects of this way of working are exemplified by inhibited creative freedom; mostly, advertising agency art directors and copywriters initiate and devise the concepts for the campaign. This implies that an illustrator is selected and employed solely for visual language and proven dedication and adherence to the punishing schedules and deadlines expected. Illustrators must also be prepared to embrace, even if only for the duration of the commission, the culture and attitudes that prevail throughout this sector. There can be a 'hard edged' and unsentimental approach to working practice. Indeed, it has been described as a brutal environment.

Also, the advertising world does not always distinguish between what many might consider good or bad taste. The audiences and potential customers 'played to' by way of advertising campaigns are categorized in a somewhat crude taxonomy that identifies people's social status. This can often be gender specific and is sometimes based on area of residence and placement within a hierarchy determined by wealth (or lack of wealth). However, the vast majority of advertisers operate with integrity and do not set out to offend – but, the overriding objective is to 'sell'. Sometimes, the illustrator might have to confront certain questions of conscience or morality in relation to the thrust of a campaign associated with a certain commission; a product or service may be considered in some way destructive to the environment, or there may be some issue related to animal welfare, religion or some other question of ethical concern. With regards to visual language and any conceptual input that might be expected of the illustrator, the level and degree of art direction will depend largely on the theme and essence of the original ideas initiated by the agency creative team. An illustrator with a particular working knowledge of a subject or topic that is the main feature of the campaign may be expected to develop the concept in a visual sense and be given freedom associated with the design and composition of the image – the placement of elements within space and the levels of abstraction and visual contortion. As an illustrator, one would have been selected for style, and there would be an expectation to remain within the parameters of that style, irrespective of one's own ideas about the overall concept.

THE ESSENCE OF ADVERTISING AND ITS GUIDING PRINCIPLES

What is advertising? The term originates from the Latin *ad vertere* and means 'to turn the mind towards' – in other words, 'to persuade'. Today, it can be defined as *a paid, mediated form of communication from an identifiable source* that is *designed to persuade or encourage action in the short and long term*. Its overriding aim is promote and sell whatever product, idea, service or entertainment at the behest of its client. It is proven that the most successful advertising campaigns combine powerful, meaningful messages, delivered in ways that inspire and captivate their audiences ,with sales outcomes that not only perform to expectation, but also proceed to engender credibility and trust in the brand, product or service provider in question. Advertisers ensure that campaigns are devised to emotionally connect with their audience. Once connected, the advertisements' rhetoric should strongly persuade their potential customers to either want the product or service or to 'buy into' the cause or message being promulgated.

The generative and creative process that formulates the essence of a campaign generally uses ideas inculcating the narrative concept; in other words, the advertisement will 'hang on a story'. Many campaigns rely on a raconteur approach: cogent, understandable and entertaining storylines that have themes and characters that will sometimes remain in the psyche of the masses for years. A typical example was the Heineken lager campaign from the 1970s that was based on an effective and well-conceived strapline, 'Heineken refreshes the parts other beers cannot reach'. The series ran for several years and won many awards with prime time television, billboard and press exposure. It also used a considerable amount of illustration. The next consideration is *simplicity*, based on the idea that a simple story well delivered is easily remembered. Also, a story embedded in *relatable situations* will speak to the potential consumer directly, and the advertisers will devise 'ads that are for "people like me"'. *Humour* will uplift the audiences' spirits and contribute hugely to memorability. Finally, there is *branding*, and here the full essence of corporate identity will ensure that the product, enterprise or service is uniquely recognizable and strongly recognized.

The communication of advertising is mediated by information age technology accessed in the public domain by way of the following:

> On-air media: television, cinema, websites and apps
>
> Print media: newspapers and magazines
>
> Outdoor media: bus shelters, bus sides, roadside billboards and posters, and airports, railway, metro and underground stations
>
> Consumer and retail product branding and packaging

CONTEMPORARY ATTITUDES AND THE MARCH OF PUBLIC AWARENESS

Many people complain about advertisements being intrusive and tiresome by invading our everyday lives. According to a 2015 research report, approximately 90 per cent of television viewers in the UK skip the commercial breaks on their digital video recorders. Further research by Adobe determined a similar trend: only 8 per cent pay attention to online advertising, 14 per cent to billboards and 5 per cent to ads in apps and games. These statistics have meant that advertisers have had to adapt accordingly as to how they engage with clients and audiences. Generally there is a concerted effort not to 'patronize' potential consumers and to communicate how the product or service will fit positively into their lives and work. Also, the advertising industry now tries to ensure that it stands for values above and beyond the product or service itself.

There are now, more than ever before, numerous charities, pressure groups and public awareness campaigns that utilize advertising as a platform for raising support and affecting meaningful change. Some of these advertisements are commercial as they promote financial aid for the body in question, but also effectively champion many social or environmentally aware causes and campaigns across the world. Typical organizations include Amnesty International, the Christian Campaign to Abolish Torture, the World Wildlife Fund and Friends of the Earth. One such foundation is called 28toomany and demands the complete banning of female genital mutilation. Its strapline and series of images depict soiled close-ups of well-known international flags, including those of the UK, France and Italy, with a clear, straight rip down the middle with crude stitching binding it together: 'Female Genital Mutilation Doesn't Only Happen in Far Away Places'. This is one example of many. The inference is that advertising of this nature is on the increase, and illustration will continue to provide that all-important power and impact necessary to mobilize action.

> **ADVERTISING JUSTIFIES ITS EXISTENCE WHEN USED IN THE PUBLIC INTEREST – IT IS MUCH TOO POWERFUL A TOOL TO USE SOLELY FOR COMMERCIAL PURPOSES.**
>
> DAVID OGILVY, FOUNDER OF THE OGILVY & MATHER AGENCY AND KNOWN AS THE FATHER OF ADVERTISING

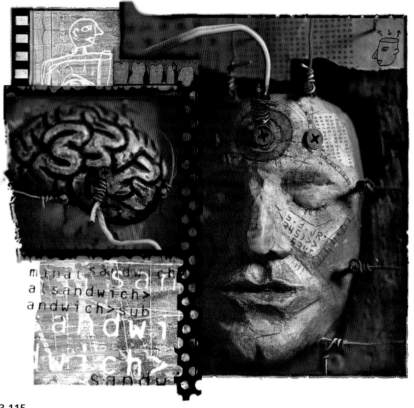

3.115

3.115 and 3.116

The music industry has for many years been synonymous with creative and cutting edge use of visual imagery. The sleeves of original vinyl, long-playing records were considered an essential and iconic representation of contemporary taste and fashion. The pop, rock, progressive and psychedelic protagonists of the 1960s facilitated the design and illustration of record sleeves, evocative of the bohemian and decadent ideals that challenged the established society. Today, illustration continues to promote and advertise music, providing identity and form for the music and artistes. Currently, certain styles of illustration are appropriated because of their contemporary standing and empathetic association with the music, however eclectic the genre might be. Music videos and moving imagery and the compact disc (CD) cover still provide opportunities for illustrators, even though many customers now obtain music by online steaming. The two illustrations shown were designed and produced by **Richard Borge**. Figure 3.115 is a CD album cover entitled *Subliminal Sandwich* by Meat Beat Manifesto and Figure 3.116 is *Life Before Insanity* by Gov't Mule. ©Richard Borge

3.117

Critical and cynical viewpoints have overflowed into the advertising industry, with the banking and insurance sectors falling into this category, having been widely accused of exploitative and unprincipled methods of service and sales technique. However, the balance is starting to be redressed. This is an illustration by **Rod Hunt**, commissioned for the Bank of Scotland 2016 BBC 'Children in Need' fund-raising campaign with schools. It is entitled *Can You Spot Pudsey*; Pudsey bear is the BBC Children in Need mascot. ©Rod Hunt

3.116

3.117

3.118

3.119

3.120

3.118, 3.119 and 3.120
Some of the most acclaimed and memorable advertising campaigns have been those that contain humour. Also, to be effective, particularly if it is in a poster or billboard campaign, the message needs to be immediate and straightforward. This campaign falls into both categories, winning a D&AD Award for Illustration in Advertising in 2016. The brief was to communicate Dabur Gastrina's proven efficacy against flatulence. 'However, considering it is a distasteful subject, it needed to be handled in an inoffensive, yet effective manner'. The idea was to humorously 'bring alive the embarrassing sounds an upset stomach can make'. The agency was McCann Worldgroup India – chief creative officer Prasoon Joshi; executive creative directors Abhinav Tripathi and Pradyumna Chauhan; creative directors Vivek Bhambhani and Sanket Pathare; and art director, designer and illustrator **Mangesh Kavale**. ©McCann Worldgroup India

ENOITALIA LIMITED EDITION 2016

3.121

3.121
Illustration is frequently at the heart of product or company branding and identity, none more so than food, drink and other popular retail items. Italian wine producer Enoitalia launched a series of limited-edition products with the purpose of restyling some of their historic brands. Four illustrators were commissioned to design fresh new labels to facilitate the rebranding campaign. **Davide Bonazzi** designed and illustrated the new identity for Amarone, a typically rich Italian wine, rarely released until five years after the vintage. ©Davide Bonazzi

3.122

3.123

3.124

3.122, 3.123 and 3.124
There are many products that neither provide a useful service nor are deemed necessary; luxury goods and certain victuals and drinks fall into this category. However, the advertising of certain well-known international brands will be generously resourced regarding campaign appropriation. This can mean that agencies will be able to afford 'sumptuous' promotions, such as richly illustrated press and billboard advertising and maximum-length television slots, featuring celebrities and state-of-the-art filming. Nevertheless, with nothing meaningful or positive to say, the agency is at liberty to create entertaining and recurring themes based on a single idea. In this instance, *Great Beer Enjoyed by Great People Since 1589* has facilitated a series of advertisements that could run indefinitely. The illustrator is **Anita Kunz**. ©Anita Kunz

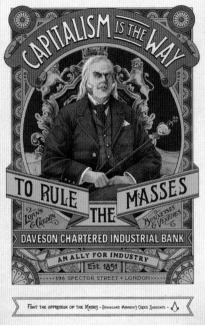

3.125

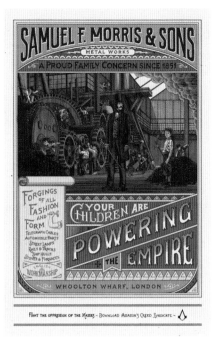

3.126

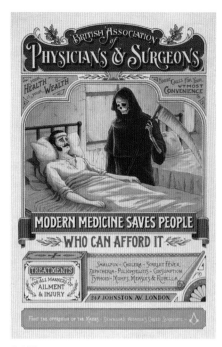

3.127

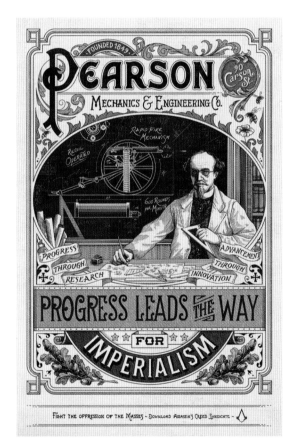

3.128

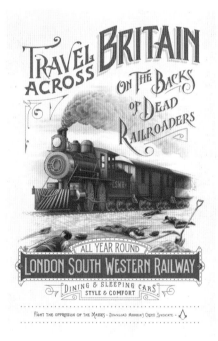

3.129

3.125, 3.126, 3.127, 3.128 and 3.129

This is a series of posters to accompany a promotional campaign for a video game called *Assassin's Creed*. Set in London 1868, the game provokes players into leading the proletariat to revolt against the ruling elite. To immerse gamers in the theme of class inequality, Victorian-style posters were created to depict the different facets of injustice and class exploitation that were prevalent in many important industrial sectors at that time. The client is Ubisoft Canada, the agency Bleublancrouge, the art director Julien Hérisson. The illustrator is **Stéphane Casier**. ©Stéphane Casier

THE FOOL

THE LOVERS

THE MOON

THE WILD CARD

THE BATHER

THE SUN

3.130

3.130
These themed tarot cards have been conceived, designed and illustrated by **Mr Alan Clarke**. They are used as promotional devices for the Body and Soul Festival, held annually, usually around the time of the summer solstice in County Westmeath, Ireland. It is described as 'a bizarre and beautiful banquet of sumptuous surprises for discerning music, performance and art fans'. ©Mr Alan Clarke

3.131

3.132

3.133

3.131, 3.132 and 3.133
German environmental advocacy group Robin Wood recruited advertising agency **Grabartz & Partner** to develop a campaign that aimed to raise awareness around the destruction by humans of fragile ecosystems and animals' habitats. Entitled *Destroying Nature Is Destroying Life*, the series has succeeded in sparking a vigorous discourse that places a searing spotlight on humanity's acquiescence to destructive greed at the expense of our cohabitants and the resources we all rely on for survival. The message is simple, visually powerful and poignant and 'shows that advertising doesn't always have to serve vapid consumerist profiteering'. It is the winner of the Wood Pencil D&AD 2016 Award for Craft and Illustration for Advertising. The creative group director is Florian Kitzing; art director and graphic designer Manuel Wolff; copywriter Katharina Kowalski; account manager Joelle Timores; and illustrator **Illusion** Bangkok. ©Grabartz & Partner

3.134
This is a paper sculpture designed and created by **Sam Pierpoint** to promote 'Bristol as an exciting and magical Christmas shopping destination in 2016'. The brief was to feature some of the city's most-loved attractions. ©Samantha Pierpoint

3.134

3.135

3.136

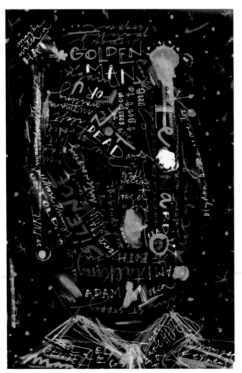

3.137

3.138

3.139

3.140

Figures 3.135, 3.136, 3.137, 3.138, 3.139 and 3.140
It has been said that whatever context and message to be imparted, 'the best posters don't just illustrate history – they shape it! Posters look forward to future events and immortalise the past. At times a celebration, at times a call to action, they are both works of art and printed artefacts of their age'. The best posters are produced with conceptual precision and visual economy. They must also convey their message with immediacy and purpose. However, the intended audience will determine scope and depth of content. Also, the level of graphic or textual

intensity must be appropriate for its physical location, from roadside billboard or side of bus to public institution notice board. Some posters have become iconic – for example, Joost Schmit's 1923 *Bauhaus Exhibition*, Heinz Schulz-Neudamm's *Metropolis* for Fritz Lang's 1927 famous sci-fi of the same name, and Alfred's Leete's *Lord Kitchener – Briton Wants You*.

Figures 3.135 and 3.136 are by Mexico City–based illustrator **Manual Rios**. Figure 3.135 is a promotional poster for the band Guadaloops, and figure 3.136 is an advertisement for Shabu208, a sushi restaurant. ©Manuel Rios

Figures 3.137 and 3.138 are posters designed and produced by Barcelona-based illustrator, calligrapher and musician **Coqué Azcona**. Figure 3.137 is entitled *Respect*, and figure 3.138 is a gallery promotion for Galeria Cromo, shortlisted for the World Illustration Awards, 2017. ©Coqué Azcona

Figures 3.139 and 3.140 are posters and promotional material created by **Cécile and Roger**, a graphic design agency based in Geneva, Switzerland. This is a multidisciplinary partnership, full names Cécile Nanjoud and Roger Gaillard, working with brand identity, typography, motion, web and illustration. Figure 3.139 is for

an electronic music festival entitled Modern. Figure 3.140 is for the Mirage Festival (fifth edition), Art, Innovation and Digital Culture. The theme to consider was (im)materialities – the idea of transforming a perceived truth. To express this concept, the team developed an identity system consisting of round splotches, line patterns and bright hues. The elements are reminiscent of the event's vibrant laser beams that often unite to form abstract faces. The materialization represents the phenomenon of *pareidolia*, the imagined perception of pattern or meaning where it does not actually exist – in other words, a mirage! ©Cécile and Roger

3.141

3.142

3.143

3.144

212 • CONTEXT, IMPACT AND CONSEQUENCE

3.145

3.141, 3.142, 3.143, 3.144, 3.145 and 3.146
These images form part of the award-winning campaign Make a Difference for the Royal Forest and Bird Protection Society of New Zealand. It is the largest independent conservation organization in the country, protecting native species and wild places; it does not receive government funding, relying instead on membership fees and donations. To entice new members, the agency **Ogilvy New Zealand** gave a clear visual demonstration of the difference $5 can make. Print advertisements invited readers to place banknotes on the pages and restore endangered species back to their natural environment. To target people with higher disposable incomes, $10 and $20 were also included, encouraging larger contributions. The campaign won D&AD Yellow and Graphite Pencil Awards 2015. The executive creative director was Angus Hennah; senior art director Martin Hermans; art director Jordan Dale; copywriter Chris Childerhouse; and the illustrator was **Stephen Fuller**. ©Ogilvy New Zealand

3.146

4
CONTEMPORARY AND FUTURE PRACTICE

Creativity and the Challenge of Innovation

Illustration has been a provocateur throughout history by visually dispensing new and controversial knowledge, by commentating and bearing witness, by being a raconteur and cultural standard bearer and most felicitously, by broadcasting propaganda and uncompromising opinion. These are precepts that direct the soul of illustration practice. Are these precepts being eroded, and in the long term, will it matter?

THE EDUCATION OF A VISUAL COMMUNICATOR

The power and influence exerted by illustration can only be upheld and built upon by current and future trends in education, particularly those trends that will determine systems of transformative learning. Whilst this is a process that is fundamentally rational and analytical, the principal objective is to facilitate a deep learning environment, creating a platform for individuals to change their frames of reference by critically reflecting on their assumptions and beliefs to consciously challenge and create new ways of defining everything that controls or influences their worlds, from culture, religion, lifestyle and more appropriately, the applied and professional contexts of visual communication as delivered through and by the creative industry. In the framework of education and beyond, this is the precept that defines 'provocation': the concept of *illustrator as provocateur*. This is a construct that challenges preconceptions, inspires and re-roots an understanding of a given problem. Provocation should be the continuous theme, as acquiescence and pure servility only deliver the status quo. It needs to be a constant throughout the curriculum, 'disrupting' process and challenging convention, positively and for the betterment of the assignment and the wider world, a syllabic and curricular essential in all higher education programmes of study and compulsory at both undergraduate and postgraduate levels.

With regards to illustration and all other disciplines of communication, from journalism to film, the transformative approach to study will develop an individual critical voice in the context of a rapidly changing, complex and accelerating media world, where the ability to create meaningful and effective ideas for business, cultural and societal need is key. The educational experience should ensure a contemporary currency, a journey that delivers the skills, intellectual and entrepreneurial spirit to inspire and shape new practice and subject innovation. Graduates should be critically connected and use the latest insights, critical theories and technologies and become adaptive thinkers whose ideas engage the world.

Foundations previously learnt and embodied, such as those acquired through further education or school, should be strengthened through process, collaboration and human-centred interactions and new boundaries explored through theorized and critical practice. A personal focus should be encouraged to emerge, defined through curating and building a point of view and experimental enquiry – thinking by doing in reaction to complex information and communication dilemmas, with theory and research methodologies interwoven throughout. The key components of *interaction* and *thinking by doing* are pivotal to the conceptual process. Interaction implies understanding the human context in which visual communication is used and consumed and the impact and opportunity for illustration to bring about change. A crucial pillar of the subject is to investigate supporting theories and the behavioural science behind many political and conflicting drivers when communicating for society, the media or industry. Also, thinking by doing defines where the interrelationship between theory and practice can be tested and explored. Here, one can challenge and build skills to tackle potentially complex visual communication questions by exploring completely new forms of making or visualization, whether analogue, performance or digital.

Fundamentally, the educational aims for any programme that delivers the study and practice of illustration should comprise the following:

- Promote imaginative, original, innovative and independent thought
- Foster a well-informed, critical understanding and application of visual communication
- Evaluate, understand and apply advanced research methodologies (the systematic, theoretical analysis of methods applied to a field of study)
- Integrate key social, global, cultural and technological contexts to map innovative futures and practices for illustration
- Creative and innovative use of *risk* as an asset within the working methodology
- Develop leaders and innovators operating at a strategic level
- Reinvigorate and provoke the creative industry, education, research and society at large

AS ILLUSTRATORS WE STUDY THEORY TO STRENGTHEN OUR PRACTICE IN ORDER TO CREATE BETTER ILLUSTRATIONS BY UNDERSTANDING THE WAYS THAT MEANING IS CREATED AND COMMUNICATED TO OTHERS.

PROFESSOR MARIO MINICHIELLO, PROFESSOR OF DESIGN AND HUMAN BEHAVIOUR, UNIVERSITY OF NEWCASTLE, AUSTRALIA

CRITIQUE

The term *critique* usually means a detailed analysis and assessment. Often of an intellectual nature, it is frequently applied to academic theses and theories, such as those of a literary, philosophical, cultural, artistic or political nature. It is also a term embedded in art school tradition and informally recognized by the majority of art students as 'crit': a directive to peer review and deliver a verdict on the quality of an individual's work, at completion or in progress.

At this juncture, it might be expedient to examine the traditional art school method for critique, the most notable being 'Feldman's Model of Art Criticism', conceived by University of Georgia art professor Edmund Burke Feldman in his book *Practical Art Criticism* (1993). Although published fairly recently in the context of how long art schools have been in existence, it nonetheless does reflect a general model that has been in use for many years; Feldman has simply formalized it. His concept surmises four aspects:

- *Description*: List the visual qualities of the work that are obvious and immediately perceived. Ask, 'What do you see in the artwork?' and 'What else?' Includes content and subject matter in representational works and abstract elements in non-representational work.
- *Analysis*: Focus on the formal aspects of art, principles of design and other formal considerations such as composition, exaggeration, etc. 'How does the artist create a centre of interest? How does the use of colour impact the painting?'
- *Interpretation*: Propose ideas for possible meaning based on evidence. Viewers project their emotions, feelings and intentions onto the work. 'What do you think it means? What was the artist trying to communicate? What do you see that supports your ideas?'
- *Judgement*: Discuss the overall strengths, success and merit of the work.

These criteria for assessment are, in reality, couched almost entirely in fine art practice and can only be applied in a superficial manner to professional visual communication. The model itself 'smacks of partiality' and subjectivity; it also suggests being lightweight and intellectually insubstantial, with an emphasis placed on one's taste and appreciation of media-treatment and visual language only. It provides further evidence of the differences between fine art and illustration. The most felicitous criterion in Feldman's model is that of *interpretation*, whereby the question of communication and meaning is highlighted. To emphasize the importance of this, it is the communication process itself that determines the true value of the work in question: context and content. Context defines the reason for the imagery in the first place and underpins the essence of the whole brief – in other words, the 'job of work' assigned for the imagery. Context expounds the message communicated to its intended audience, and content defines subject matter.

Contemporaneously and in the future, successful visual communication, particularly that which commands national and international recognition, will have to satisfy professionally exacting criteria. The following is a general taxonomic breakdown of measurable benchmarks and principles:

- *Impact*
  Cultural, academic and educational value measured by insights with which the public, prescribed audience or user have engaged, measured by evaluation, user feedback or testimony and national or international review; the creation and interpretation of cultural capital in all of its forms to enrich and expand the lives, imaginations and sensibilities of individuals and groups and the level of public engagement measured by critique and repercussion

- *Reach*
  Extent and diversity of individuals, organizations and communities that have or will benefit, engage with or be influenced by the impact; extent of the information and influence to the form and content of education and knowledge transfer to any group in a global context

- *Content*
  Credibility and authoritativeness regarding topic or subject matter; the creation and inspiration for supporting and generating new and original forms of artistic, literary, linguistic, persuasive, propagandist and other expression

- *Standpoint*
  Thematic and scientific uniqueness, thrust, context, argument, opinion, consequence and effect; strength and rationale regarding message, expression, narrative concept

- *Methodology*
  Quality of research; the integration of intellectual, theoretical and practical processes

- *Concept*
  Creativity and originality; appropriate and considered use of ideas; discernment regarding audience receptivity, purpose and appropriation of media and outreach into the public domain

- *Language*
  Quality and appropriate use of aesthetics, design, genre, iconography, visual syntax

- *Technical application*
  Use of media; craft, product or artefact construction, performance, presentation, publication, exhibition or broadcast; drawing skills and image construction; oral and written communication skills; unambiguity of message, connectivity and outreach

AN ART WHOSE MEDIUM IS LANGUAGE WILL ALWAYS SHOW A HIGH DEGREE OF CRITICAL CREATIVENESS, FOR SPEECH IS ITSELF A CRITIQUE OF LIFE: IT NAMES, IT CHARACTERISES, IT PASSES JUDGEMENT, IN THAT IT CREATES.

THOMAS MANN

4.1

4.1 and 4.2
These illustrations were conceived utilizing different styles, yet both are embedded in the context of narrative fiction. With regards to current and future trends, there can be no doubt that traditional literature provides a considerable amount of inspiration for contemporary illustrators. Broadly considered pictorial in essence, the two examples show a well-informed and imaginative use of representative visual communication.

Figure 4.1 is by **Briony May Smith** and is for the classic folk ballad 'Tam Lin'. The whole story has been retold through illustration, much of which is in picture-strip form. ©Briony May Smith

Figure 4.2 is by **Katie Ponder** and is entitled *Feeing Watched*. It accompanies a story entitled 'A Tale from an Empty House' by E. F. Benson and is from a compilation of classic ghost stories. ©Katie Ponder

4.2

Illustration is the most ubiquitous form of language. Seen everywhere, it is visual writing and can communicate messages about anything. The following quote sums up how *critique* is embedded in the framework of illustration practice:

ILLUSTRATION AND RESEARCH

Research is a distinct academic discipline. It can, and should, be applied to any subject taught in higher education, and forms the mainstay of most postgraduate study from master's to doctoral programmes. Its principal methodologies can also be applied across the vast gamut of industrial and commercial enterprise from technology and science, the media and manufacturing.

Research has been the subject of considerable debate in relation to art and design practice. The sphere of higher education in the UK changed in the 1990s: the former polytechnics (higher education institutions that comprised many practice-based, vocational leaning disciplines such as art and design) were incorporated as fully fledged new universities. Suddenly no longer the exclusive domain of the traditional university sector, research became a recurrent and constant challenge for those disciplines. It is now incumbent upon as many as possible to deliver meaningful research outputs, essential to secure funding and provide the necessary esteem, status and prestige required in order for universities to stay viable and competitive.

What is meant by *research* in the context of illustration? In the broad context of illustration practice, there is a distinct difference between *research*, when the inference is solely to do with the gathering of reference materials, and research proper: here, methodologies are tested against academic and intellectual need with conclusions that contribute original and new knowledge. This is where the illustrator transcends the role of being a heavily directed, studio art worker without control or say regarding the work in hand. Instead, the illustrator assumes authority and has command of the intellectual and creative process; the illustration practice becomes holistic and has gravitas and a premier status, be it commissioned or authorial and self-generated. In this context, the research is a systematic enquiry directed toward the acquisition, conversion or extension of knowledge for use in particular applications, such as the provision of material to be written about and illustrated through a published book or editorial commentary. Or, it may be to do with the experimentation, analysis and dissemination of practical processes and visual language development and how that might facilitate new knowledge about a specific cultural or scientific subject. These aspects can be formalized thus:

- Research *through* illustration, by using the discipline to present conclusions and outputs that are directly related to *content* and *context* such as culture, narrative fiction, the contemporary world, society, science and technology. In this instance, illustration is the language being used to expound research conclusions related to subject matter. It is the illustration's content and message that are subjected to critique and review, with the imagery and its conception purely integral to a wider research methodology.
- Research *into* illustration. This is where the discipline itself becomes a focused aspect of enquiry. There are several themes that could be considered, such as *application*; audiences, communication and semiotics: *process*; message conversion, constraints and considerations, drawing, visual construction and dissemination, media, conceptualization: *genre*; visual language and visual literacy, allegory and metaphor, sequence, illumination: *philosophy*; theories and definitions, ethics, traditions, contemporary trends: *history*; illustration and society through the ages, technological advancements.

RESEARCH IN ACTION

Broadly speaking, research is applied when a question needs answering. If the backdrop to one's practice is scholarly, then the output may manifest as a thesis. This will be a compulsory undertaking if embarking upon a research degree programme such as doctor of philosophy (PhD). In preparation, the following questions are paramount for successful completion and must be considered before starting the work: Would the project make an appropriate contribution to knowledge? Can it be achieved by the methods described in the project objectives? Is it appropriate and timely to undertake a project of this nature now? Is the subject matter contemporaneous and/or generic with something that is 'cutting edge', and would that have an impact that could either be positive or negative regarding the project's rationale? Does one have the prior knowledge and the intellectual and practical skills to undertake this work? Is one's prior learning and experience a qualification to undertake this project, and is one's place on the learning curve sufficiently high enough? There are also a number of other questions to consider related to resources, supervision, facilities, practical logistics and timing.

At the start of the thesis, it is important to set out the project's historical, contemporary and theoretical contexts. There should be an identification of the various strands of history that relate to the theme of the project. It may be a history of ideas and concepts that has influenced the subject matter being dealt with, the history of the media, materials or technology on which one proposes to work or a particular part of the history of illustration or visual communication. It is also important to define the contemporary work that relates to the field of investigation. It should be done for the following reasons:

- To demonstrate awareness of the field of work
- To demonstrate that the proposed research will have some distinctiveness and be potentially original
- To form the basis of links with other research work to which there might be a contributing or building upon

- To demonstrate ways in which the work is evaluated and that of peers and other practitioners, and the sources used to inform the evaluation. An element of theoretical context is important for every kind of project, though the degree of theoretical content will vary.
- To help avoid simply asserting a position and support a reflective approach needed for this higher level of study

The next stage is to undertake an archival analysis. What is it that needs to be investigated? Break down key elements of the enquiry and isolate them as individual tasks. Establish a programme of research through action with research methods identified. Outcomes related to these particular methods and tasks should be measured, timed and clearly described, as they will form part of the final critique and analysis. Methods undertaken can be multi-various, both complex and straightforward, from the *empirical* approach – a primary interface engagement that utilizes experimentation, testing or evaluation – to a *theoretical* and speculative approach, using traditional academic methodologies. Initiative and innovation is important. It is essential to think around the problem and all the possible links associated with the subject being researched. Frequently, certain actions deliver insufficient data and do not provide answers to key questions. One could go up a 'cul-de-sac' and not be able to proceed further with a particular line of enquiry. It may register the end of one aspect of research, but it could also have a positive outcome and provide leads and new knowledge to subjects not previously considered, giving the project a new and striking twist.

Whatever the key question or focus of investigation, the project should manifest as authorship, charged with both visual and textual material. This could be a combination of the following: finished imagery within a visual communication context, finished illustrations that present new knowledge by way of primary research, experimental visual work and investigative drawing studies. The project should conclude as a publishable, broadcastable or exhibition-worthy outcome, determined for placement in the public domain – nationally or internationally. Examples could be books, research papers, journal and magazine articles, online interactive packages, apps, films, lectures and conferences. A successful conclusion will also comprise a reflective and critical analysis summarizing the effectiveness of the research undertaken and what originality and potential impact there is to present and digest.

With regards to the teaching of illustration and, indeed, all disciplines resting within the broad parameters of art, design and communication, tutors are no longer just practitioners who 'show students how to do it' – they are academics. This means that the framework of one's remit extends way beyond that of 'doing illustration' supplemented by a cursory amount of teaching. Higher education is evaluative and enquiring. It is therefore important to 'have a voice', to engage in dialogue and debate nationally and internationally, to seek a relevant forum and commentate; a successful engagement with research will facilitate that aspiration. Professional exposure and acknowledgement of one's national and international standing are paramount, and so is ambition. There is tremendous diversity of opportunity. Research will also facilitate ways for full-time practitioners to transcend the rut of 'flat-lining' and escape the trap of style categorization; an engagement with research can generate fresh initiatives and nurture professional development.

Research and practice underpin teaching, and we should strive to present original perspectives on our own practice and the discipline as a whole. As educators, there is a need to adopt a holistic and non-discriminatory overview of all its contexts and cultural applications. That cannot be achieved by an academic delivery of rote learning and repetition. When undertaking straight commissions, present a meaningful and critical evaluation of your work and that of others, past and present. Transcend that 'surface' engagement with 'trend' and make your practice say something mature and relevant.

A MODUS FOR CREATIVITY

Creativity is a given prerequisite, deeply embedded in the paradigm of illustration practice. It is said frequently that when confronted with a given brief, an essential beginning for the whole process of project development is to identify and 'grab' appropriate inspiration, to apply invention, to initiate solutions that are conceived and produced with vitality, rigour, dynamism, energy and flair – to have a *great idea*!

What is creativity? Creativity is a phenomenon whereby something new and possibly valuable is formed. The created entity may be something abstract or intangible, such as a thought, belief or credo, or it might be applied to something more formal, such as a scientific theory or concept. Alternatively, it can manifest as something physical or sensory: an invention, a piece of music, a work of literature or an *illustration*.

Power and influence come from having *radical ideas*, and ideas are borne from creativity.

However, it was once said anonymously, 'If you have ideas but don't act on them, you are imaginative but not creative'. Creativity is the act of turning new and imaginative ideas into reality. It is distinguished by an ability to comprehend the world in a fresh and original manner, to discover concealed arrangements and configurations, to establish connections between allegedly unrelated phenomena and to bring about resolution and results. Basically, creativity involves two processes: thinking and then producing. It also requires a certain amount of passion and commitment, as often that indefinable 'spark' of inspiration will not be forthcoming. First, the 'spark' has to be conceived and then cultivated into a *definable* and realistic solution to the problem in hand. But, it has to be said that taking inspiration and developing it into a creative idea is not something that can be done mechanically. Creativity begins by acquiring a foundation of knowledge, without which one will have no basis to synthesize information. From this, experiment with thought processes, explore and question all assumptions related to the subject and theme of the project being undertaken. Be willing to take risks and be prepared to traverse through 'discomfort' in order to get the finish line.

There are certain key behaviours that optimize the brain for discovery in order for a spark of creativity to materialize:

Association: draw connections between questions, problems or ideas from unrelated fields.

Questioning: pose queries that challenge common wisdom.

Observation: scrutinize the behaviour and attitudes of one's stakeholders, such as audience and clientele, in order to identify new ways of doing things.

Networking: meet people who hold differing ideas or perspectives.

Experimentation: construct interactive experiences and provoke unorthodox responses to see what insights emerge.

An illustration is creative when it is both novel and appropriate. A novel, cutting edge, neoteric illustration is *original* and *not predictable*. The stronger the concept, the *more* the imagery will stimulate ideas and heighten recognition – the *more* the illustration is *creative*.

PROBLEM SOLVING

The *process* for solving a problem of visual communication sits at the heart of creative practice. It also seeks to explore how new methodologies and insights can ensure a communication question is explored to maximize an opportunity for new ideas.

It is important to focus on the *intersections* that exist both in a communication problem and the interface where the message is to be exchanged. Audience receptivity is paramount to a successful outcome: it is expedient to understand fully the idiosyncrasies of the global community and also those of more parochial, unfamiliar and disparate communities. Part of the process is to embrace the possible 'tension' and the unknown nature of coalescence between components of a given brief and the human element.

Understanding how communication relationships 'talk' is central to the project being undertaken, whether

- between illustrator *and* client;
- between emotion and subjectivity *and* experience and objectivity; or
- between transient, organic behaviour *and* 'the white heat' of technology.

It is also appropriate to test one's ability and 'courage' to confront challenging research scenarios. This could include working with an audience in an act of co-discovery by instigating a context for connectivity and interaction by inciting debate, testing controversial opinion, or by inviting participation in workshops, live exhibitions, play or entertainment. It may also include working with a different culture at a distance or a business-orientated competitor or challenger. Engage critical theory around humanness and build insights into behavioural psychology and belief systems, anthropology and the more emotive, sensorial, haptic or political drivers that could impact on understanding an audience or user and the insights that might be gained for communication interactions.

To conclude, the overall aspect of problem solving is to think 'outside of the box' – to break free of conventional design practices and formally accepted and expected constraints and to apply independence of thought, ambition and action. Consider all skills as specific and 'premier league' – intellectual, creative and practical – rather than purely transferrable. Consider all lines of enquiry regarding research strategies, resources and timing. And finally, critically analyse and define the focus and limits of your current practice and fearlessly challenge methods gone before.

4.3

4.4

These images were created by **Zaria Forman**, an artist whose work conveys *the urgency of climate change* by connecting audiences to the beauty and awe of remote landscapes. Her work manifests as extremely large yet traditionally produced drawings, created by drawing with soft pastels on paper. Forman sets out to satisfy exacting criteria by creating powerful, inspirational and impactful work that enriches and informs the sensibilities of all who see it, particularly in its original crafted form. The methodology underpinning its production delivers thematic and scientific uniqueness plus an authoritativeness that transcends the majority of visual art and illustration that is not produced through the highest level of primary research. The three images shown are the result of a four-week residency in Antarctica aboard the *National Geographic Explorer* (November to December 2015). The work was published extensively in *National Geographic*, the *Smithsonian Magazine* and the *Wall Street Journal* and also used in television set design. Forman said, 'I had the opportunity to experience something few people ever do: the ethereal majesty of Antarctica. Although I have travelled all over the planet from Greenland's ice sheet to the Sahara Desert, Antarctica was unlike anything I had ever seen. The towering ice radiated a sapphire blue that took my breath away. Many of us are intellectually aware that climate change is our greatest global challenge, and yet the problem may feel abstract, the imperilled landscapes remote. I hope my drawings make Antarctica's fragility visceral to the viewer, emulating the overpowering experience of being beside a glacier'.

4.5

4.6

Figure 4.3 is of B-15Y Iceberg, Antarctica no. 1 – 72 x 72" (182.8 cm).

Figure 4.4 Risting Glacier, South Georgia no. 1 – 84 x 144' (213 x 365.7 cm).

Figure 4.5 Whale Bay, Antarctica no. 4 – 84 x 144" (213 x 365.7 cm).

Figure 4.6 shows the work being produced and exemplifies the scale of the imagery. ©Zaria Forman

4.7

4.8

4.7, 4.8 and 4.9
This is a research project conceived and produced by **Fang Qi**, a PhD student from Newcastle University at the time of writing. Entitled *The Reversible Future*, this is a video-based installation work that examines ambiguities related to the evolution of life. Fang Qi explores the question 'Does the growth of the mind and body mean "upgrade or downgrade"?' This is a new media exhibition that combines video projection mapping technology with traditional media such as drawing and sculpture in order to create a dialogue of parallels between transformational developments in technology, the human body and art. Fang Qi is a Chinese artist and illustrator engaged in practice-led research, the focus of which examines the relationship between illustration and installation art. The principal aim is to contribute new knowledge related to those visual narrative strategies in illustration that aims to reconstruct the self and identity. The project exemplifies polymathic and multidisciplinary practice. Fang Qi is an international award-winning visual artist whose work encompasses drawing, illustration, video, animation, installation and creative writing.
©Fang Qi

4.9

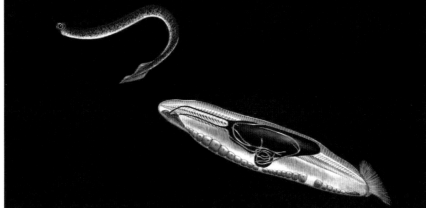

4.10

4.10

Illustration has been at the forefront of presenting new knowledge for all things scientific since the first millennia. In recent years, palaeontology has been a principal benefactor, none more so than the visual reconstruction of prehistoric life, most notably subjects considered sensationalist, such as the dinosaurs. However broader criteria demand the creation and interpretation of the latest research, particularly that related to elements of evolution and the earliest palaeo-fauna to appear on earth. When conducting research of this kind, analyses and subsequent results will often require the presentation of more than one alternative theory or conclusion. Here, the author depicts two correlative images of an enigmatic aquatic organism from the Carboniferous period (350 million years ago), each describing alternative physiology and physical orientation. Called *Typhloesus*, it was approximately 2 inches (50 mm) in length. ©Alan Male

"The heritage problem of who owns what will be
the biggest headache in British cultural history:
warships, fighter jets, nuclear power, the flag,
the poond, subsides, North Sea oil, prescriptions,
the NHS –
Ah could go on."

Robbie Burns
Poet.

4.11

"We need another
Johnnie Walker, ye ken?
A new another.
A £500 increase per person
per annum or liberty?
it's a stupid bastarding question,
Ah'll tell ye"

Adam Smith
Economist

4.12

"I can't vote – I live in London.
I work for the BBC but because the English
can be so horrid,
I want Scotland to vote
for independence. Other reasons too,
obviously."

Mary
Queen of Scots

4.13

"I'm not sure: Union or Independence?
My parents had sex in Edinburgh
so that (and that alone) first made me Scottish,
and I continued to be Scottish thereafter.
To be honest with you, I,m confused as hell about it."

Sir Walter Scott
Novelist, playwright, Poet

4.14

The relentless 'yes or no vote' cold-calling
is really getting on my fucking nerves."

Alexander Graham Bell
Inventor of the telephone

4.15

"It's a momentous decision
and I'm beside masel'
with fear, excitement and trepidation.
Vote for the Union –
ye know it makes sense."

Robert The Bruce
king

4.16

"Don't care anymore.
It's all sound-bites:
Twitter, Facebook selfies
and shallow social media
point-scoring.
Bitterness and bullshit.
Tawdry, fear-based advertising
Either way the vote goes, it won't stop
the bad side of human pride and greed
floating to the surface
like a big nationalistic turd."

Margot, Lady Asquith
Socialite and wit

4.17

4.11, 4.12, 4.13, 4.14, 4.15, 4.16 and 4.17
Amongst the principal criteria for judging successful contemporary visual communication will be its impact and standpoint: the strength, thrust and provocation for argument, opinion, consequence and effect. Politics and current affairs are often a catalyst for snide and condescending satire. Here, the subject of Scottish independence has given illustrator and artist **Paul Davis** a vehicle to produce a series of cartoon-like portraits of famous characters from Scotland's history: Robbie Burns, poet; Adam Smith, economist; Mary,
Queen of Scots; Alexander Graham Bell, inventor; Sir Walter Scott, novelist, playwright and poet; Robert the Bruce, king; and Lady Asquith, socialite and wit. All provide their own 'unique take' on consequences that might befall their country if it is ever given independence. The credibility that underpins this project does not really lie with the quality of the drawings. This is an excellent example of illustrator as journalist and commentator, an exemplification of how important it is for contemporary and future illustrators to create by being wordsmiths as well as image makers. ©Paul Davis

4.18

4.18
Simplistic yet powerfully explicit in terms of its message, this is an illustration produced by **Hanna Barczyk** for the cover of the *New York Times Sunday Review*. Its remit is to communicate the essence of a leader article entitled 'Feminism Lost: Now What?': 'Its amazing to me the lightening speed at which these issues have receded. The story is the total omission of women'. This is a theme that will undoubtedly remain at the forefront of societal concern. In a contemporary context and with the increase in output of opinion-bearing material for illustrators, brazen unambiguity is often the most appropriate approach to visual language and message. ©Hanna Barczyk

4.19, 4.20, 4.21, 4.22, 4.23, 4.24, 4.25 and 4.26
The future of visual communication will be broadly determined by a practice that fearlessly challenges methods gone before, breaking free of conventional design strategies and applying independence of thought, ambition and action – being a provocateur. The work shown here is by Serbian-born **Valentina Brostean**, currently residing in Turin, Italy. Brostean epitomizes visual provocation. It has been said she works 'with a serious passion for the graphic world, strong, expressive, cutting-edge visual language and wild imagination. Some would dare call her a "visual warrior"'. Brostean's style is far removed from 'safe', commercial illustration – in other words, that which is heavily directed and ambient in both message and visual language. However, she has an international

reputation, is critically acclaimed and works across many contexts, from curated gallery exhibitions, children's books, adult literature and magazine editorials. She uses traditional media and the latest technology software, seeking powerful and progressive solutions for creative and 'brave' clients, applying bold aesthetics to 'surprising' outputs across all media platforms. Her work is described as wild, playful *and* serious. The project depicted is a selection of double-page spreads from a graphic novel entitled *Why Ladybirds Eat People*. A complex, 200-plus-page production, it strongly focuses on figurative narration. Brostean said it was 'inspired by the human race and our lives, passions, sins, habits, emotions, situations, states of soul and mind. It reveals to the viewer many weird characters that crawled out of the dark corners of daily life. It is bizarre

and grotesque but on the other side very metaphorical and symbolic with a large dose of naked truth involved. I tried to find the balance between irony and criticism, keeping the whole thing on surreal and narrative ground where the major part of characters simply reflect us – modern society in all its shapes and forms. Yet the only place where we are truly revealed as who we are is from the inside. If you examine the work closely, you might come to the realisation that all the creatures are really kind of self portraits, set in fantastical landscapes of an imaginary world which echoes its own, a bitter, yet sweetly coated prescription for modern life'. All visual aspects are by Brostean: graphic design and art direction, typography, concept and illustration. Words are by Zeljko Katanic. ©Valentina Brostean

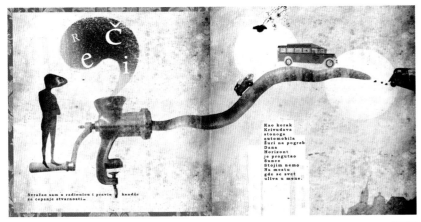

4.19

4.20

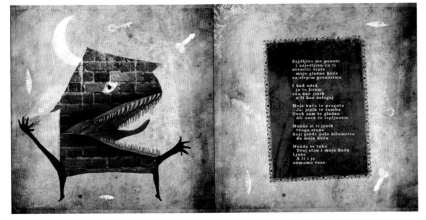

4.21

4.22

4.23

4.24

4.25

4.26

Communication: Effectiveness and Function

This is the modus of illustration that determines its true raison d'être, representing that overarching principle of key directives essential for successful, contemporary, applied, professional communication. It is here that the taxonomic breakdown of measurable benchmarks and principles defining the critique of illustration is 'played out' and put into practice:

- what has to be said and how
- understanding the reactions required from a target audience
- the successful integration of subject matter and the principal line of communication
- the presentation through illustration of an individual critical voice with expectations to be challenging and provocative
- the use of experience and a knowledge base to take ideas and move into new and exciting realms, and where appropriate, confront and contradict the wider communications world
- the application of aesthetic discernment by having a complete and objective appreciation and working knowledge of visual languages and subjects

ENSURING SIGNIFICANCE

Lasting power and influence is determined by significance – a thing is memorable, groundbreaking and controversial, with measurable and recorded impact on the society or culture in question. The history of illustration provides us with thousands of examples, some that have changed the world. But what of today and the future?

It will be essential to create new forms of expression delivering contemporaneously relevant, contextualized and potent messaging. However, some messages will need to communicate themes and directives that are overtly serious, commanding gravitas and purpose; they will also need to offer respect and integrity. But, the world is culturally and ethnically diverse, no matter how increasingly interconnected it becomes. Even within those countries that are historically and culturally aligned, such as English-speaking 'Western' democracies, thresholds of tolerance regarding what is acceptable to broadcast or publish will vary considerably. In order to provoke challenging responses from messages intended to become indelible, celebrated or notorious, all illustration will have to 'go beyond' that which is perceptibly 'real', irrespective of the context. As has been said before, even new knowledge represented in an ontological way has to provide the viewer with a sensory connection produced by exaggerated aesthetics and drama.

CONCEPTUAL LINGUISTICS

There are five aspects to consider, collectively called the *linguistics of narrative conceptualization*. In a certain way, these aspects purport to the *fantastical*. No matter how earnest the knowledge-bearing concept or outrageously crazed in fictional storyline and content, the objective will be for chimeric whimsy and caprice, for a message that deliberately goes beyond its essential core and into a land of positive or negative tantalization.

The first aspect to consider is the *mimetic*: a message and concept where audience expectations are couched in reality – and where everything is explicable. However, as the term suggests, it is the adjective of mime. The imagery will depict a story or concept by 'enactment'. It will be an imitation or reproduction of the real world by recreating the appearance of reality – for example, an autographically drawn image that slightly distorts in order to deceive or a state-of-the-art piece of CGI that exaggerates movement in order to hasten an animated sequence.

The *liminal* delivers messages where expectation is slightly divergent from reality as there are some inexplicable elements. The communication is basically transitional and occupies a position at or on both sides of the argument or threshold of the story. The illustration conveys subjects or concepts that are barely perceptible and incapable of eliciting a focused response from the audience; it is fundamentally impotent regarding its message – or has no message at all, reminiscent of ambient or surface pattern–like imagery.

The *portal* conveys a certain aspect of mystery and intrigue. Crucially, the essence of the message is to do with inviting the audience – perhaps even by temptation – to egress a 'portal', either into a world of fictional fantasy, to sample an aspect of new knowledge that might be morally 'out of bounds' or to explore a morsel of territory previously unexplored and littered with danger. Either way, that part of the narrative, which is seemingly unreal yet inciting much sensory inquisitiveness, does not 'leak through to our side'. There is much that is left to the imagination – an illustration that visually implies and implores questions to be asked.

An *intrusive* message is disruptive, invasive and truly provocative. With regards to fictional narrative, it might be a far-fetched natural or human disaster – or a lycanthropic metamorphosis resulting in a monster, giving chase and about to savage a poor victim. In non-fiction it might be a social or military conflict depicting horrific details and consequences – or the most unpalatable propagandist viewpoints delivered by an uncompromising and 'angrily raw' illustration style.

Finally, there is the *immersive*. This is where the narrative is open and apportioned, the raconteur, commentator or documenter inviting the audience to share his or her assumptions and understandings. Imagery may be interactive, either in a sensory or physical way, or may contain sympathetic messaging with regards to opinion or thematic familiarity.

To conclude, in terms of message and context, one should always apply the most appropriate visual linguistics. By providing a potent audience connectivity with the concept and a frisson of expectation, the outcome will transcend traditional expectation. The narrative can be divergent from reality, even if its essence is couched in all things explicable; it can be speculative, imaginative, anachronistic, futuristic, intermediate. By affording that all-important twist of originality, the precept for power and influence will be maintained.

4.27
This is a book cover image by American award-winning illustrator **Dave Palumbo**. A work of fiction, the book is a novella entitled *Binti*, written by Nnedi Okorafor and published by Tor.com in 2015. Effective communication will often utilize an immersive conceptual linguistic in order to engage an audience in a sensory manner. With reference to visual linguistics, the portrait is striking but far from intrusive. The story is about a young woman called Binti who belongs to the Himba people, an insular community dedicated to their land and rituals. She is the first of her people to be offered a place at Oomza University, the finest institution for higher learning in the galaxy. But to accept the offer will mean giving up her place in her family to travel between stars among strangers who do not share or respect her ways. ©Dave Palumbo

4.28
With regards to the effectiveness and function of illustration and its impact and significance, content and message need to be memorable and, where appropriate, controversial. The subject of HIV/AIDS has consistently reminded global societies about the need to practice safe sex. Certain cultures and religious communities find the subject taboo and display much discomfort talking about sex or any other 'immoral' practices associated with it. These attitudes clearly present demarcation lines regarding the irony of ignorance, preferring instead to banish and censure those images that are morally offensive rather than confront the seriousness of the topic. The illustration shown is part of a campaign for AIDES, the first French HIV/AIDS prevention non-profit-making organization. This campaign has not been afraid to tackle the issue of practicing safe sex 'head on', often using images and accompanying straplines many would find disturbing and shocking. One such example is two poster/billboard advertisements that explicitly show a naked man and woman independently having sex with a giant, human-sized spider and scorpion. The tagline reads, 'Having unprotected sex is like having a gigantic slavering arachnid perform cunnilingus on you, or mounting a spread eagled scorpion in the missionary position, its poison dripping tail wildly thrashing about in the throes of ecstasy. Without protection you are making love to AIDS'. It is doubtful if these posters would be put into the public domain in either the UK or the United States. The imagery shown here is entitled *Welcome to the World of Sex* and is by illustrator **Rod Hunt**. This would also be considered risqué *and* pornographic, in spite of the virtue, conviction and integrity underlying the message. The Sex Theme Park's tagline states, 'The Safer You Play, the Longer You Stay'. Devised by San Francisco–based agency Goodby, Silverstein and Partners, the campaign won silver for Print, Public Service Campaign, Clio Advertising Awards, 2011. ©Rod Hunt

4.27

4.28

4.29

4.30

4.31

4.29, 4.30, 4.31, 4.32, 4.33, 4.34, 4.35, 4.36, 4.37, 4.38, 4.39, 4.40, 4.41, 4.42 and 4.43

These images are from a campaign entitled No More Black Targets, commissioned by the New York Society for Ethical Culture; the agency is the **Fred and Farid** Group (New York, Paris, Shanghai, Beijing). Unconscious bias can be deadly and contributes to one of the biggest violence issues in the modern United States. No More Black Targets launched in January 2017 as an advocacy campaign to raise awareness of the dangers of unconscious bias and how it may be perpetuating gun violence against young black men. A disturbing statistic points to the fact that in the United States, young black men are three times more likely to be shot than their white peers. The data are clear: between 2015 and 2016, 69 per cent of these shootings were against victims who were non-violent and unarmed. There is an alarming correlation: the most popular static range target for US shooters to learn how to use their firearm is a *black* silhouette. European shooting ranges tend to use circular, archery-type targets.

An academic study published by the University of Illinois drew together findings from forty-two different studies of 'trigger bias' in order to assimilate whether race affects how likely a target is to be shot. 'In our study we found people were quicker to shoot black targets with a gun, relative to white targets – and people were more trigger happy when shooting black targets compared to white'. This campaign seeks to eliminate the use of these targets forever in shooting ranges and instruction environments – anywhere someone is learning to use a firearm. No More Black Targets is a collective of artists, diverse in backgrounds, ethnicities and nationalities, working in paint, digital media, pattern making and physical installation in order to bring new artwork to life. The collective stand for 'More Paint: Less Hate'. The campaign won a D&AD Award for Outdoor Advertising and Poster Advertising, 2017. The chief creative officers are Fred Raillard and Farid Mokart, creative director is Laurent Leccia, and special acknowledgement is given to Jessie Bowers (CYLPHA). ©Fred and Farid

4.32

4.33

4.34

4.35

4.36

4.37

4.38

4.39

4.40

4.41

4.42

4.43

The Illustrator as Polymath

A *polymath* is formally described as a person who excels and practices at the highest level in several fields at once, such as the arts and sciences combined. The term, derived from the Greek *polymathēs*, meaning 'having learned much', was first used to describe the great thinkers and practitioners of the Renaissance, the Enlightenment and the Industrial Revolution. Typical of these were Leonardo da Vinci, Galileo, Sir Christopher Wren, Johann Wolfgang Goethe and Charles Darwin. Collectively, their expertise represented subjects like astronomy, physics, engineering, invention, mathematics, architecture, philosophy, poetry, literature, anatomy, medicine and the biological sciences, and their superior knowledge and intellect were underpinned by research and intense observation. There was one discipline common to all: *illustration*. The great polymaths would externalize their ideas through superb draughtsmanship, exquisite drawings and paintings, figurative art and visual conceptualization.

THE POLYMATH PRINCIPLE

The notion of an illustrator having a professional status underpinned by a wide range of intellectual and knowledge-based pursuits – such as scientist, cultural historian, journalist or author of fiction – is not new. A typical example is in retail publishing, where there is an increase in the numbers of both fiction and non-fiction books, particularly for children, being authored and illustrated by the same individual. Why? What gives *illustrators* such upstart positions of importance and authority?

The status of the commercial art practitioner has increased in recent years, with seemingly more responsibility for project context and content. This has meant that illustrators and designers have a certain amount of ownership for the whole problem-solving process. Within the creative industries, there has always been a hierarchy of studio/agency-based competences, with the illustrator (and other image makers like photographers) coming in at the end of the process, often as freelance 'outsiders' and used solely as iconographers and 'finished artists'. This precept is fast becoming a thing of the past, in some ways attributed to renewals in recent art and design undergraduate education where there has been a reduction in emphasis on overt vocational practice. Subjects such as studio-based illustration are now fully integrated with contextual, liberal, historical and cultural studies, along with professional and business practice. This facilitates an educational experience that enables graduates to multitask, to be professionally independent and to be much more intellectually capable. The best art and design undergraduate education encourages the acquisition of appropriate transferrable skills. These are then developed into a broad range of high-level specifics that are technical, practical and innovative, but also – and most felicitously – *polymath-centrically* erudite, cerebral and knowledge based. Communication skills are also a prerequisite by having a distinguished command of written and oral language, presentation and research.

Professional and student illustrators undertaking research, whether through commission, by authorial self-generation or as an academic assignment, will often be required to engage with specialist subject matter. This can lead the illustrator to assume a position of authority and expertise in his or her thematic domain of operation. Continuous professional involvement with the topic, along with researching and illustrating books and other material at a national and international level, would soon qualify the illustrator as an expert, even without a formal

> **WE ARE BEGINNING TO SEE A RETURN OF THE POLYMATH PRINCIPLE, IN OTHER WORDS AN ILLUSTRATION PRACTICE THAT EXUDES AUTHORITY AND A BREADTH OF INTELLECTUAL SKILLS AND LEARNING. THE CONSEQUENCE IS THAT MANY ILLUSTRATORS WILL HAVE WIDE-RANGING AND IN-DEPTH KNOWLEDGE OF SUBJECT MATTER AND ACQUIRE AN ESTEEM DRIVEN OWNERSHIP FOR THEIR WORK.**

ALAN MALE *ILLUSTRATION: MEETING THE BRIEF* (BLOOMSBURY, 2014)

qualification in the subject. Opportunities to undertake focused postgraduate master's and research higher degrees can also facilitate and expand an illustrator's authorial status. As well as those illustrators who write fiction, there are a number who have trained specifically in subject matter such as archaeology, biology, zoology, palaeontology, astronomy, anthropology, cultural studies, history, philosophy and technology. These are just a few examples out of a myriad of subjects. The intrinsic link between words and image, as well as the increase in illustrators engaging directly with subject matter, suggest a firm establishment of a culture representative of and given for the non-fiction author-illustrator.

To conclude, the implication of the polymath principle will be insurmountable for some practitioners and students of visual communication as it clearly transcends the traditional concept of the commercial illustrator being chosen for his or her style in order to undertake a prescribed and heavily directed brief. Clients, audiences and media platforms will expect practitioners to have an individual, critical voice and the ability to be challenging and provocative; to be able to use their knowledge base to take ideas and move into new and exciting realms; and, where appropriate, to confront and contradict the wider communications world.

AUTHORSHIP AND INTERDISCIPLINARY PRACTICE

The parameters of illustration practice are changing constantly. Its realm of operation has become increasingly porous, with disciplines once thought of as professionally linked now overlapping and in some instances deeply intertwined. This has a significant bearing on the concept of professional practice for the illustrator, not only for the here and now but for the future. Broadly speaking, most illustration is commissioned by or generated for the creative, media and communications industry. This generic title represents a vast powerhouse whose reach and influence is prevalent throughout the world via the worldwide web, broadcasting, publishing, advertising and entertainment. There is now a rapidly changing, complex and accelerating media where the ability to communicate creatively, meaningfully and effectively for a global audience is key. The ever-changing

circumstances of modishness, customs and behaviour; the economy; and technological advancements have instigated the need in many audiences around the world for fresh and stimulating imagery, whatever its context. This alters perceptions held regarding established and 'discrete' disciplines – illustration, graphic design, photography, animation and film being a typical list – with practitioners often declaring ownership of and identification with just one of those disciplines. That is now considered a hackneyed perception. There are alternative, 'all-encompassing' roles being declared, such as 'creative' (working within the broad realm of media, design and communication), a supposition that is becoming the norm, and, with particular reference to the polymath principle, the role of 'author'. But what is meant by 'creative' and 'author' in this context, and what defines such roles?

A creative practitioner can be considered someone who has the intellectual, creative, managerial and technical skills to cut across a range of disciplines and perform largely unsupervised. It will command abilities for research; effective communication by having the personal confidence to engage in social and personal interaction, presentation and writing; innovation, problem solving and ideas generation; aesthetic discernment, having a complete objective appreciation and working knowledge of most visual languages and subjects; organizational and collaborative skills; and finally, media application and technical production. These attributes are essential for illustration practice as more and more talented communicators are identified within publishing houses, the media, advertising agencies, design groups and consultancies, television, film and online broadcasting, entertainment, game design, music and performance. Acquiring these specific skills and integrating other appropriate interests into one's portfolio can determine far-reaching opportunities.

Authorship defines the provenance of a concept, composition or creation; it also determines a clear marker for an author's artistic iconography and genre, subject speciality and recognition as an expert, documenter or commentator. In the context of the polymath, it also defines authority and ownership of a subject or range of subjects; it can engender favourable audience and media receptivity and respect – or notoriety – dependent on the thrust of one's thesis or artistic creation.

Authorship is also synonymous with the craft of writing. Illustration is writing: it is a language that fulfils the same function. Both writing and illustration are contextualized, communicate and deliver messages and codes. This is done by either using worded syntax, imagery or a combination of both. The illustrator who aspires to be a polymath can operate using all three of the aforementioned methods. Authorship also suggests 'having a voice' and being 'heard' throughout the public domain.

IN CONCLUSION

Illustration is a contextualized problematic surrounded by a string of narratives. The problematic is the assignment, and the narratives comprise the objectives needed for completion. The assignment will be the given brief: the advertising campaign, the children's book, the documentary, the editorial article. The narratives will be the subject research and critical appraisal of the job in hand, the conceptualization process, production and output.

Illustration educates, informs and bears knowledge. It is uncompromising and elicits propaganda and provocation. It persuades, advertises and promotes. It commentates, documents and bears witness. It is a raconteur and narrator of fiction. It enriches culture and dispenses identity. It serves society. There can be no doubt, as we progress into the future, the global community will continue to be touched and stimulated by the *power and influence of illustration*.

4.44, 4.45 and 4.46
Dispensing expertise and authority in subject matter across a range of communication and media platforms clearly designates a polymath-driven practice. **Victoria Fuller** is a Chicago-based natural science illustrator, sculptor, painter, singer, songwriter and musician. Her work is an exemplification of deep and meaningful insight into a particular subject, in this case the natural world. She stated, 'Nature's intricate workings and humankind's attempts to master them intrigue me. Humans originate from nature yet exploit it, trying to control it with dire consequences. Re-creating parts of nature lets me study their subject'. She continued,

'Education is part of the process: in learning to treat the planet with reverence and respect, we may – as a species – continue to survive'.

4.44
Global Garden Shovel is a bronze sculpture located at the Columbia City Train Stop in the Rainier Valley, Seattle, Washington State, USA. It is constructed by casting and fabricating live plants and trees from all over the world. Commissioned by Sound Transit, the sculpture represents the different ethnic groups that live in the Rainier Valley by the geographic location of the plants' origin. It stands at 35 feet (10.7 meters). ©Victoria Fuller

4.45
In My Back Yard is a combination of painting and sculpture and depicts humankind's exploitation of, manipulation *of* and interference *with* nature. The reproduction of a log, the hose and pipe attached to it, plus the beehive represents the encroachment of housing developments and the negative effect of insecticides. The message conveyed by this artwork helps to define how human activity disrupts the processes of nature by urban development, the destruction of plant and animal habitat, deforestation, wasteful water usage and the introduction of chemicals into the environment. ©Victoria Fuller

4.46
Factory Farm visually speaks for itself. It is a clear condemnation of questionable agricultural and livestock practices, complete with a genetically modified organism (GMO) here represented by the cornstalk. Figures 4.46 and 236 are part of a large and intensive collection of artworks, a solo exhibition at the Parker Schopf Gallery in Chicago, 2014. Its overall theme is facilitated by figurative representations of 'untouched' flora and fauna, juxtaposed with examples of ecological carelessness and abuse. Fuller is honoured with fellowships from the Colorado Council for the Arts and Humanities and the Illinois Arts Council. Her work is exhibited and published internationally. ©Victoria Fuller

4.44

4.45

4.46

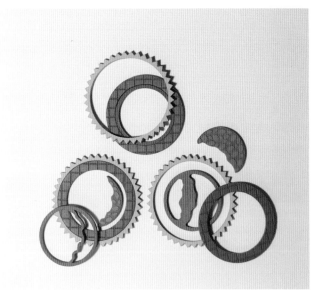

4.47

4.48

4.49

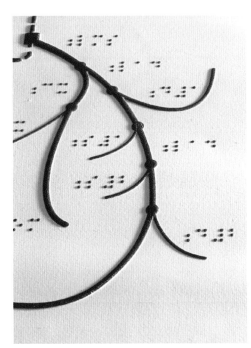

4.50

4.47, 4.48, 4.49, 4.50, 4.51 and 4.52
Tactile Illustration for the Visually Impaired, a project conceived, explored, designed and produced by **Sara Hougham-Slade**, is a body of work designed as an interactive patient education resource to enable doctors to describe prognoses regarding coronary artery disease to blind and partially sighted people. It is an original design concept, its development and production facilitated by considerable research and a methodology that displays substantive innovation for constructing knowledge-bearing imagery. Sighted people absorb information at a glance, whereas the visually impaired build up a piecemeal mental image based on haptic (sense of touch) feedback but also the other senses. Consequently, visual design and imagery are irrelevant, and a fresh, tactile set of rules must be followed. Figures 4.47, 4.48, and 4.49 represent anatomical cross sections of normal and diseased coronary arteries. Precise cuts and engravings, determined with a vector design programme, were made into plywood by a laser cutter to enable each part of the 3-D structure to fit

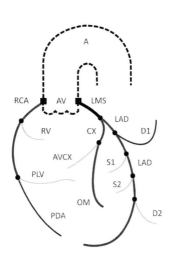

4.51

● The Coronary Arteries and Ascending Aorta

A	Aorta
AV	Aortic Valve
AVCX	Atrio Ventricular Circumflex
CX	Circumflex
D1	Diagonal 1
D2	Diagonal 2
LAD	Left Anterior Descending
LMS	Left Main Stem
OM	Obtuse Marginal
PDA	Posterior Descending Artery
PLV	Posterior Left Ventricular
RCA	Right Coronary Artery
RV	Right Ventricular
S1	Septal 1
S2	Septal 2
●	Intersection
■	Ostium

4.52

together in a precise manner. Medical concepts such as the progression of arterial disease can be difficult to understand, yet by exploring and comparing these models with medical guidance, a patient may be better informed. The floating disassembled sections in Figure 4.50 are a thoughtful response to loss of vision, the altered perception of light, dark, shadows, depth and focus. It is directed at the sighted. Figures 4.51 and 4.52 are schematic diagrams of coronary arteries that surround the heart. The design is not cluttered with irrelevant information, and each part is labelled with a key, in Braille, for reference. The illustration is printed onto 'swell paper', a material impregnated with microcapsules of ink that burst and swell when heat is directly applied in the form of a design and produces a palpable raised surface. The map-like anatomy can be traced with the fingers and allows the visually impaired patient to know the location of his or her abnormality. Figure 4.50 is a translation for the sighted. ©Sara Hougham-Slade

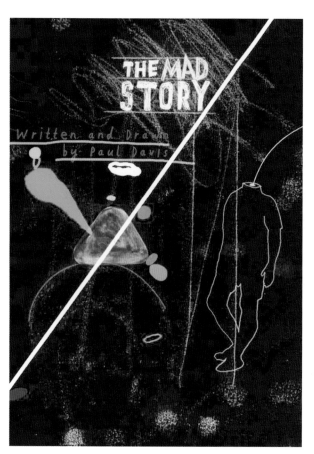

4.53

4.53, 4.54, 4.55 and 4.56
This is a book authored by **Paul Davis**. Known for his 'bleak humour' and unrelenting satire, Davis is a writer, artist and illustrator. A former Cartoonist of the Year, his work appears across the editorial domain and has exhibited all around the world, from London to Tokyo. He has said that his work 'describes the mad and beautiful state of the human species on this speck of dust called Earth'. This book is entitled *The Mad Story*. Figure 4.53 is the cover and Figures 4.54, 4.55, and 4.56 are selected spreads. Davis stated, 'It's a mad story about a mad man's madness that gets madder!' ©Paul Davis

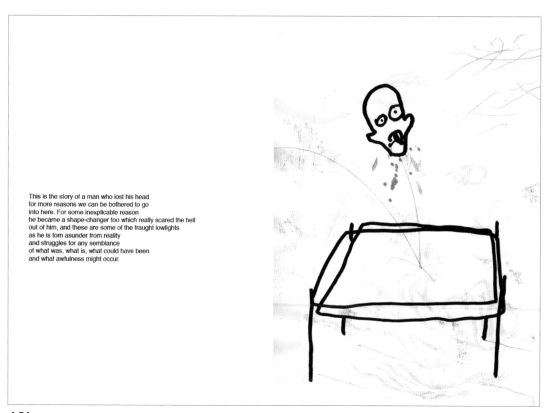

This is the story of a man who lost his head
for more reasons we can be bothered to go
into here. For some inexplicable reason
he became a shape-changer too which really scared the hell
out of him, and these are some of the fraught lowlights
as he is torn asunder from reality
and struggles for any semblance
of what was, what is, what could have been
and what awfulness might occur.

4.54

Considering he'd always
thought himself an atheist,
he was startled to meet God
and God spake unto him
with great anger and disgruntlement.

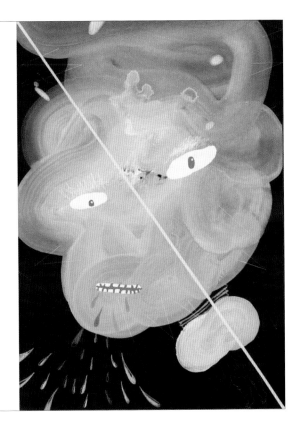

4.55

Now, after being picked up by a caring
member of the Great British Public and
medicated to the hilt by professional doctors,
he sits in his room wondering when true love
and some kind of peacefulness would enter his life.

And why the world can sometimes be a complete
and utter bastard.

I wish him well.

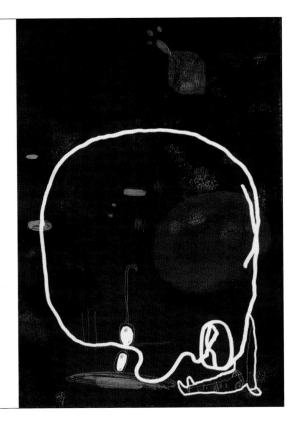

4.56

Glossary of Terms

Aesthetics
The application of beauty and recognition for artistic taste

Airbrushed
An image that is comprised of super-fine and hyper-gradated tones and colours, giving the illusion of precise yet exaggerated realism, particularly to mechanical subjects with shiny surfaces

Allegorical Images
Narrative illustration that describes a subject that is under the guise of another. Imagery in which meaning is symbolically represented

Ambient Imagery
Imagery that superficially surrounds or gives flavour without obvious or direct meaning

Animatronics
Three-dimensional models that usually represent living entities and digitally or physically appropriated realistic movement and action

Anthology
A defined selection of artworks or literature that is either thematic or originated by the same artist or author

Art Director
A creative or media employee (publishing or advertising, etc) who is senior in position and has responsibility for the design, production and quality of creative visual work. Normally assumes responsibility for the commissioning of illustration

Artistic Licence
The creative freedom to reinterpret or re-designate aspects of visual work that is being undertaken

Artwork
Material other than text only for reproduction

Autographic
Imagery that is rendered by traditional means using drawing, painting and other studio-based techniques

Avant-Garde
Pioneering and innovative illustration or art, particularly that which is contemporary in its context. Term often used to describe that which 'pushes the boundaries'

Branding
The corporate identity of an organization, company or individual: logotypes or trademarks

Bricolage
In illustration, art or literature, construction or creation from a diverse range of available sources such as media, techniques, ideas and theories

Cladogram
A type of diagram depicting evolutionary or generic relationships

Collage
A technique or visual stylization whereby an image is constructed either physically or digitally by mixing and gluing together various disparate elements such as photographs, drawings, abstract textures, etc

Copyright
The right of an artist, author, musician, etc to control the use of his or her original work; broadly controlled internationally, there are substantial differences between countries

Copywriter
An advertising or media creative who generates ideas for campaigns and prepares and writes words for publication or broadcast

Creative and Media Industries
The world of publishing, television, advertising, multimedia, design, etc

Decorative Imagery
That which uses elements of pattern, visual ornamentation or adornment and usually without any form of representation

Digital Revolution
The emergence and impact of the computer regarding the generation of visual imagery and the subsequent changes and attitudes it has imposed onto working practice

Diorama
A large, scenic image which is often used as a museum backdrop and having accompanying three-dimensional elements; also used for film set purposes

Dummy
A sample for a job made up with the actual materials and to the correct size to show bulk, style of binding, etc. A complete mock-up of a job, such as a book, showing position of type matter and illustrations, margins and other details

Fantastical Imagery
Extravagant and often wildly fanciful images, usually applied to narrative fiction; fantasy illustration and science fiction are examples

Fine Art
Paintings, sculptures, films or other visual entities, cultivated subjectively and often produced to express opinions or experiences of the artist. Normally accessed in its intended and original form, traditionally in galleries but could be in any other prescribed venue or situation

Frescos
Original images painted directly onto the surface of a wall or ceiling. Traditionally rendered in watercolour before the plaster is dry

Genre
In art generally, a specific style, kind or class. Within the discipline of illustration, describes a particular visual language

Geometry
The drawing and visual representation of the properties and relations of magnitudes such as lines, surfaces and solids in space

Gouache
Opaque watercolour paint prepared with gum

Graph
A type of diagram that depicts the relation between two variable quantities

Graphic Design
A generic term for an applied, creative, visual practice that incorporates the management and generation of concepts, ideas and finished design solutions for a number of media concerns and outlets such as print, publishing and multimedia. Contextually broad, with practitioners often specializing: packaging, corporate identity, advertising and promotion, typography and webpage design

Hermeneutics
The principles of interpretation for all forms of communication

House Style
A thematic and graphic representation for a series of books (e.g. by the same author) or packaging for an associated range of products

Iconic
Of an image; its nature or essence

Iconography
The essence of pictures or images; personal style or visual language

Impressionism
Theory or method of suggesting an effect or impression without elaboration of the details

Juxtaposition
The placement of individual visual elements, either side by side or designed specifically to 'free float' within a graphic layout and not held by 'real space' or illusion of three-dimensionality

Layout
Indication for the organization of text and images with instructions about sizing for repwroduction or printing

Metaphorical Imagery
That which is imaginative but not literally applicable. Visual depiction of ideas or theories with accent on the conceptual as opposed to pictorial realism

Moving Images
Generic term for animation (traditional and digital) and live-action filming

Mural
A painting or image applied to a wall surface

Opacity
The application of an opaque medium rendered in a solid consistency such as oil paint or gouache. The opposite of transparency

Paradigm
A model, structure or pattern: an archetype or clear example

Pastiche
An image produced in the style of another, usually of a well-known illustrator or artist

Pictorial Representation
An image that represents 'real space'; an accurate depiction of a scene, usually literal in nature and not conceptual

Polymath Principle
A sphere of professional operation, such as illustration, that exudes authority and a breadth of knowledge specialisms, intellectual skills and creative practices: high-level multi-tasking and interdisciplinarity

Polysemy
The capacity for an illustration, symbol, word or phrase to have multiple meanings

Recto
Right-hand page

Semiotics
Theory of the functions of signs and symbols

'Spot' Illustrations
Small free-standing images, vignette in nature and used mainly in an editorial context. Often surrounded by a typographic layout

Stock Art
The assignation of secondary rights to images with potential mass use and exposure

Storyboard
A sequence of images that depict ideas or concepts for films, children's books, etc; usually produced as drawings and often act as instructional guidelines for moving image directors or as a publication overview

Surface Pattern
Imagery that is often repetitive and decorative in nature and used in textiles, fashion and interiors. Does not communicate contextually and not to be associated with illustration

Surrealism
Fantastical imagery with incongruous juxtapositions; original twentieth-century art movement with the remit to represent unconscious thoughts and dreams

Symbolism
The use of signs and other visual, graphic characters to represent subjects; to visually express by suggestion

Synopsis
A summary, proposal or outline

Taxonomy
A system of classification that depicts inherent hierarchies

Theorist-Practitioner
An individual who combines theory, research, and/or subject expertise with creative, design or craft-based practice

Transferable Skill
A skill, either intellectual or practical, acquired through a specific course of study that can be utilized by employment within a different discipline, professional practice or sphere of operation

Typographic
The use of type; printed/reproduced letterforms within graphic layout or concept

Verso
Left-hand page

Vignette
Effect applied to halftones that, instead of being squared up or cut out, have the tone etched gently away at the edges

Vista
A view of a scene; landscape imagery

Visual Communication
The transfer of contextualized messages to prescribed audiences

Visual Language
A style of illustration, either generic or associated with an individual illustrator

Visual Syntax
The ability to construct and depict the appropriate connections and relationships with elements within illustration and design; visual literacy

Volumatic Representation
A two-dimensionally rendered image that depicts three-dimensionality

General Index

Illustrator Index

Bibliography

SELECTED READING

Steve Heller & Marshall Arisman
The Education of an Illustrator
Allworth Press/School of Visual Arts, 2000

Dale M. Willows
The Psychology of Illustration
Springer-Verlag New York, 1987

Evelyn Goldsmith
Research into Illustration: An Approach and a Review
Cambridge University Press, 1984

Graham Vickers
Illuminations: Solving Design Problems Through Illustration
Elfande Publishing, 1993

Tamsin Blanchard
Fashion and Graphics
Laurence King Publishing, 2004

Mario Pricken
Creative Advertising
Thames & Hudson, 2002

Leo Duff & Jo Davis
Drawing: The Process
Intellect Books, 2005

Howard J. Smagula
Creative Drawing
Laurence King Publishing

Mick Maslen and Jack Southern
Drawing Projects
Black Dog Publishing, 2011

J. G. Heck
The Complete Encyclopaedia of Illustration
Merehurst Press, 1988

Elaine R. S. Hodges (Ed.)
The Guild Handbook of Scientific Illustration
Van Nostraad Reinhold, 1989

Stephen J. Gould, Chris Sloane & Alice Carter
The Art of National Geographic
National Geographic, 1999

Roanne Bell & Mark Sinclair
Pictures and Words: New Comic Art and Narrative Illustration
Laurence King Publishing, 2005

Sylvia S. Marantz
The Art of Children's Picture Books
Garland Publishing, 1995

Berthe Amoss & Eric Suben
Writing and Illustrating Children's Books for Publication
Writer's Digest Books, 1995

Martin Salisbury & Morag Styles
Children's Picture Books: The Art of Visual Storytelling
Laurence King Publishing, 2012

Ian Noble & Russell Bestley
Visual Research
AVA Publishing (2nd ed), 2011

John Vernon Lord
Drawn to Drawing
Nobrow Press, 2014

Fig Taylor
How to Create a Portfolio and Get Hired
Laurence King Publishing, 2010

Kevin S. Hile
Something About the Author: Facts and Pictures About Authors and Illustrators of Books for Young People
Gale Group, 1994

Stuart Medley
The Picture in Design
Common Ground Publishing, 2012

Andrew Loomis
Creative Illustration
The Viking Press, 1947

Alan Male
Illustration: A Theoretical and Contextual Perspective (2nd ed)
Bloomsbury, 2017

Alan Male
Illustration: Meeting the Brief
Bloomsbury, 2014

Mirko Ilić & Steven Heller
Head to Toe: The Nude in Graphic Design
Rizzoli, 2018

E. H. Gombrich
Art and Illusion: A Study of Pictorial Representation in Pictorial Representation
Princeton and Oxford University Press, 2000

Klanten and Hellige
Illustrators Unlimited: The Essence of Contemporary Illustration
Gestalten, Berlin, 2011

Derek Brazell and Jo Davies
Understanding Illustration
Bloomsbury, 2014

Christopher Frayling
Research in Art and Design
Royal College of Art Research Papers, 1993

Kyna Leski
The Storm of Creativity
MIT Press, 2015

Guy T. Buswell
How People Look at Pictures: A Study of the Psychology of Perception in Art
University of Chicago Press, 1935

Perry Nodelman
Words About Pictures: The Narrative Art of Children's Picture Books
University of Georgia Trust, 1988

Karenanne Knight
The Picture Book Maker: The Art of the Picture Book Writer and Illustrator
Institute of Education Press, 2014

Roland Barthes
Rhetoric of the Image
Fontana Press, 1964

Gary Embury and Mario Minichiello
Reportage Illustration: Visual Journalism
Bloomsbury, 2017

ORGANIZATIONS

D& AD
Communication Arts
Society of Illustrators (New York)

Guild of Natural Science Illustrators
Society of Children's Book Writers and Illustrators
Association of Illustrators

Acknowledgements

I owe a great debt to the many who have donated imagery and would like to thank the following for their generous and invaluable contribution to this book.

In order of appearance:

Mr Alan Clarke; Simon Pemberton; Billelis; Paul Slater; Olivier Kugler; Valentina Brosdean; Benedetto Cristofani; Scott Balmer; Dexter Maurer; Piotr Naszarkowski; Lola Dupre; Chiara Chigliazza; Richard Borge; I Gede Widtantara; Maria Svarbova; Briony May Smith; David Plunkert; Ori Tor; Matais Santa Maria; Anna and Elena Balbusso; Chiara Dattola; Paul Davis; Simon Dubuc; Slava Shults; Suen Jie; Jaime Anderson; Vladimir Zimakov; Rebecca Hendin; Patrick George; Hannah Barcyzk; Paul Garland; Blaz Porenta; Julinu; Haydn Symons; Julia Allum; Caroline Macey; Sam Weber; Davide Bonazzi; Anita Kunz; Jake Abrams; Cyriak; Ian Pollock; Mario Minichiello; Andrew M. Kish III; Spooky Pooka; Rod Hunt; Coque Azcona; Victoria Fuller; Melanie Reim; Saatchi and Saatchi, Singapore; Tom Gauld; Ashraf Foda; Emily Johns; Hew Morrison; LouLou & Tummie; Andrew Selby; Juliet Percival; Nancy Liang; Emma Lewis; Lin Fritz; Private Eye Magazine; Sue Clarke; Dave Palumbo; Neil Webb; Su Blackwell; Katie Ponder; Orly Orbach; McCann Worldgroup India; Stéphane Casier; Grabartz & Partner; Sam Pierpoint; Manual Rios; Cécile and Roger; Stephen Fuller; Zaria Forman; Fang Qi; Fred and Farid Group; Sara Hougham-Slade

I wish to give a special thank you to Anna and Elena Balbusso for permission to use their stunning illustration for the front cover.

ABOUT THE AUTHOR

Professor Alan Male is an academic, author, editor and illustrator. He directed the Illustration Programme at Falmouth University, leading it to gain an international reputation for excellence. He is now Emeritus Professor of Illustration and a keynote speaker on the international stage; he has also lectured throughout the United States. An authority on communication and cultural studies, professional practice, science and knowledge-bearing imagery, he contributes widely to debates across a range of journals, conferences, magazines and learned papers.

Male is the author of *Illustration: A Theoretical and Contextual Perspective*, (Bloomsbury, 2007 and 2017) and *Illustration: Meeting the Brief* (Bloomsbury, 2014) and editor to *The Companion to Illustration* (Wiley Blackwell, 2019). He has worked across the advertising, creative and communication industries and illustrated more than 170 books. He has won numerous awards, among them gold from the Society of Illustrators Los Angeles and a Texas 'Bluebonnet' for children's books, and has exhibited internationally, including in New York State Museum's permanent collection, where he has won the critically acclaimed Focus on Nature Jury Award three times.